80 001 983 017

BLOODFEUD

1175

Northamptonshire County Council
Libraries and Information Service

ST JAMES

Abington

B115

27 FEB 2008

08 DEC 04

T.N.A

14 MAR 2008

14. FEB 07

7/10/11

28 FEB

2/2/13

21 MAR 2007

20/2/13

23. APR

14 may

942.018
FLETCHER, R.A.
Bloodfeud: murder and
revenge in Anglo-Saxon
England

Please return or renew this item by the last date shown.
You may renew items (unless they have been requested
by another customer) by telephone
in at any library.   100% recycled

D1420181

NJ   M

ABOUT THE AUTHOR

Richard Fletcher is the author of *St James's Catapult*, *Moorish Spain*, *The Quest for El Cid*, which won both the Wolfson Literary Award for History and the *Los Angeles Times* History Prize, and *The Conversion of Europe*. He recently retired from the post of Professor of History at the University of York.

RICHARD FLETCHER

Bloodfeud

MURDER AND REVENGE
IN ANGLO-SAXON ENGLAND

PENGUIN BOOKS

PENGUIN BOOKS

Published by the Penguin Group
Penguin Books Ltd, 80 Strand, London WC2R ORL, England
Penguin Putnam Inc., 375 Hudson Street, New York, New York 10014, USA
Penguin Books Australia Ltd, 250 Camberwell Road, Camberwell, Victoria 3124, Australia
Penguin Books Canada Ltd, 10 Alcorn Avenue, Toronto, Ontario, Canada M4V 3B2
Penguin Books India (P) Ltd, 11, Community Centre, Panchsheel Park, New Delhi – 110 017, India
Penguin Books (NZ) Ltd, Cnr Rosedale and Airborne Roads, Albany, Auckland, New Zealand
Penguin Books (South Africa) (Pty) Ltd, 24 Sturdee Avenue, Rosebank 2196, South Africa

Penguin Books Ltd, Registered Offices: 80 Strand, London WC2R ORL, England

www.penguin.com

First published by Allen Lane The Penguin Press 2002
Published in Penguin Books 2003
4

Copyright © Richard Fletcher, 2002
All rights reserved

The moral right of the author has been asserted

Printed in England by Clays Ltd, St Ives plc

Except in the United States of America, this book is sold subject
to the condition that it shall not, by way of trade or otherwise, be lent,
re-sold, hired out, or otherwise circulated without the publisher's
prior consent in any form of binding or cover other than that in
which it is published and without a similar condition including this
condition being imposed on the subsequent purchaser

NORTHAMPTONSHIRE LIBRARIES	
801983017	
Cypher	20.02.04
942.018	£7.99
NS	

To my sisters
CAROLINE and LUCINDA
who on a well-remembered occasion
more than forty years ago
heroically and almost uncomplainingly
endured their brother's obsession with eleventh-century history

Contents

List of Maps

List of Genealogical Tables

List of Plates

What you look hard at seems to look hard at you.

GERARD MANLEY HOPKINS

Preface

I first came across the story in this book at the age of fourteen in 1958, when it immediately acquired a special interest for me by virtue of the fact that I read it at my family home in Wighill, the village near York where I was brought up, which has some claim to have been the site of the first murder in the series of killings examined here. The tale has intrigued me ever since then. The series of bloody events which lies at the heart of it has long been known to historians of Anglo-Saxon England. It is not, however, widely known to readers outside this restricted circle, and it is for this larger non-specialist readership that my book is intended.

I might not have brought myself to attempt a re-telling in quite the manner employed here without the encouragement of Stuart Proffitt; certainly the book would have lacked such finish as it might be judged to possess without the guidance of his unerring editorial hand: I am extremely grateful to him. I also extend my sincere thanks to Stuart Carroll for guidance on the literature concerning feud; to Paul Hyams and Charles Insley for generously allowing me to consult their work in advance of publication; and to Sir Richard Storey for permitting me to wander over his land at Settrington when I was trying to work out the likely mechanics of the massacre that took place there over nine centuries ago.

The commencement of this book, in September 1999, coincided with the beginning of serious structural work of a remedial kind upon my house, operations which in themselves and their aftermath continued intermittently for the next fourteen months. It was a period of considerable domestic upheaval during which sustained literary work was often difficult; additionally lowering, therefore, to the spirits. During this period I realized, not for the first time, how much I owe to the unfailingly cheerful spirits and good-humoured resilience of my wife Rachel: I cannot imagine what I have done to deserve her.

Nunnington, York
June 2001

A Note on Bibliography and References

A full and formal bibliography would be inappropriate to a work of this character. Each chapter has been provided with a short list of further reading which should be adequate to direct enquirers to the principal sources and secondary authorities. The endnotes, which have been kept to a minimum, have been used simply to identify the more important quotations in the text from original or modern authorities. The following abbreviations have been used: *ASC* – *Anglo-Saxon Chronicle*; *DB* – *Domesday Book*; *EHD* I – *English Historical Documents* volume I, edited by Dorothy Whitelock (2nd edition, London, 1979); S – P. H. Sawyer, *Anglo-Saxon Charters. An Annotated List and Bibliography* (Royal Historical Society: London, 1968), cited by number.

I

Wiheal

Everybody knows what happened in England in 1066. Duke William of Normandy mounted an invasion, defeated the last Anglo-Saxon king, Harold II, at the battle of Hastings, and acquired thereby the kingdom of England; gaining also the title by which he has ever since been known, 'the Conqueror'. Fewer people, outside the ranks of professional historians, are aware that the Norman Conquest was the second conquest of the kingdom of England in the eleventh century. The first had occurred fifty years earlier, and the conquerors were Danes led by their king Sweyn (or Swegen) and subsequently, after his death in the moment of victory, by his son Canute (or Cnut), who reigned as king of England from 1016 to 1035.

The Danish conquest, unlike the Norman, was a long-drawn-out affair. It culminated in a year which was crowded with campaigning. In the course of the year 1016 there were five battles between English and Danes, a long Danish blockade of London, and much laying waste of territory. In the early spring Canute had led his army north to attempt the subjugation of Northumbria, the northernmost English province, which stretched from the Humber up to the Anglo-Scottish border. Northumbria was governed, under the king, Ethelred II, by an earl named Uhtred. He belonged to one of the great magnate families of northern England, had held his office of earl for at least ten years, was famed for his military prowess, and was the lord of extensive acres and many retainers. What is more, he was connected by marriage to the royal family: his third and current wife, in 1016, was a daughter of King Ethelred II. Earl Uhtred was, thus, a figure of immense wealth, power and prestige; quite simply, the most important man in the north of England. It was essential for Canute to secure his submission and gain his loyalty.

In the early part of the year Earl Uhtred had been campaigning in Staffordshire, Shropshire and Cheshire, devastating the land there because it was the power base of his enemy Earl Eadric of Mercia – midland England – who had gone over to Canute. Canute, making his way north through Lincolnshire and the northern tip of Nottinghamshire into Yorkshire, contrived to slip past Uhtred and head towards York, the leading city of Northumbria. Uhtred must have judged that Canute's position was too strong for him and decided to submit. We must imagine negotiators going to and fro. According to eleventh-century convention Uhtred gave hostages as guarantee of his good faith, and arrangements were made, including a promise of safe-conduct, for his formal submission to Canute.

The place decided upon for this important and public ceremony is named in one of our sources as *Wiheal*. We cannot identify it with absolute certainty. The village of Wighill has been suggested, and it is close to what would almost certainly have been Canute's itinerary, being near Tadcaster which is on the Roman road, now the A64, to York. The difficulty with this identification is that the earliest written version of Wighill, from the record of Domesday Book in 1086, is *Wichele*, and place-name scholars tell us that there is no equivalence between *Wiheal* and *Wichele*. Another possibility is Worrall, just to the north-west of modern Sheffield, rendered plausibly as *Wihala* and *Wihale* in 1086. Worrall makes sense in terms of Uhtred's journey from Cheshire: on the other hand, it would have involved Canute in an improbably long detour into hilly and perhaps hostile country well to the west of his line of march. The true identity of *Wiheal* remains a mystery. Wighill seems the more likely of the two.

Wherever *Wiheal* was, it was decided upon as the place for the encounter between Uhtred and Canute. The meeting was to take place indoors, as is appropriate given the sort of weather one can expect in Yorkshire in March, in the most imposing secular building in the village, the hall of the lord of the manor. The characteristic Anglo-Saxon hall was a big, barn-like structure, timber-framed with plank or cob walls, its high-pitched roof covered with thatch or wooden shingles. A hall was entered by doors usually set in its long (or side)

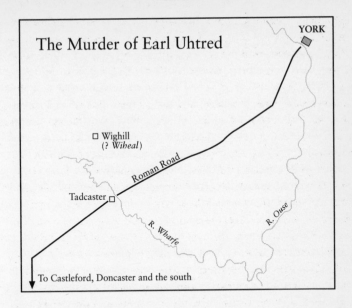

The Murder of Earl Uhtred

YORK

Wighill
(? *Wiheal*)

Roman Road

Tadcaster

R. Wharfe

R. Ouse

To Castleford, Doncaster and the south

walls, was probably windowless (though we can't be certain about this, since archaeologists can reveal only foundations), and was inefficiently warmed by a fire in a centrally placed hearth, whose smoke was meant to escape through an aperture in the roof. Within, therefore, a hall was ill-lit, draughty and smoky. The murk and the chill could to some degree be offset by the hanging of textiles, sometimes colourfully decorated, along the walls, or curtained across the open space in such a fashion as to create subsidiary 'rooms' inside the hall. On gusty days in spring these hangings would flap and rustle; background movement and noise that people would expect and take for granted.

Earl Uhtred came to the meeting accompanied, as a great nobleman should be in a display of status, by an escort of military retainers – forty of them, we are told, and though the figure be both round and biblical we are not required to disbelieve it. As befitted a ritual exchange of peace, and given the guarantee of safe-conduct, weapons and body-armour would have been left with the horses outside, in the care of grooms and servants. Uhtred and his men entered the hall and stood in a body before Canute. If it were one of those brightly sunny days that you sometimes get in northern England in early spring they would have needed time for their eyes to accustom themselves to the gloomy interior.

Treachery was afoot. Another northern magnate, an old enemy of Uhtred's named Thurbrand, had prepared an ambush with Canute's connivance. Suddenly, armed and mailed men sprang out from concealment behind the hangings and slaughtered Uhtred and his men, every one. After a desperate and bloody mêlée which lasted perhaps only a few minutes, forty-one corpses lay among the rushes on the floor.[1]

This act of treachery and slaughter set in motion the chain reaction of counter-violence and yet further violence, a bloodfeud that lasted for three generations and almost sixty years, which is the subject of this book.

The eleventh century is a long way away from us: a foreign country. We should expect to find its concerns and its values, its assumptions and its aspirations, its hopes and its fears, almost unreachably different from ours.

In large part this is owing to the extreme paucity of the sources that have come down to us from that distant epoch. Everything that we know about Earl Uhtred of Northumbria could be written on a postcard. His death was reported in a single sentence by one strictly contemporary witness, the anonymous annalist who compiled, possibly at York, what is known as manuscript D of the year-by-year account of public events which historians call the *Anglo-Saxon Chronicle*. Our knowledge of the cycle of violence which was precipitated by his death is furnished only by a single later writer.

This later writer, also anonymous, composed his work at least sixty years, even perhaps as much as a hundred years, after Uhtred's murder.[2] He wasn't primarily interested in the bloody consequences of the slaying. What he was concerned about was the landed endowment of the bishopric of Durham, and in particular the descent of six estates in lower Teesdale. These estates had passed out of the possession of the cathedral community, which wished to reclaim them. Our anonymous author, presumed to have been a cleric, possibly a monk, of Durham, chose or was commissioned to write a short pamphlet tracing the history of these estates, perhaps by way of preparation for a lawsuit to decide their ownership.

Uhtred and his descendants were involved in all sorts of complicated ways with the possession of the lands in question. So our author had to write a little about the family. But he regarded this as a digression: after telling his tale he observed crisply, *Sed ut ad superiora redeat stilus* ('But let the pen return to more important matters') and went back to the story of the Teesdale estates. If he had not indulged in that digression, the tale that follows could not have been told.

The anonymous pamphlet survives under a misleading title on two leaves of a manuscript copied at Durham in the second half of the twelfth century. At a later date this manuscript passed into the possession of the Cistercian monastery of Sawley in the West Riding of Yorkshire. After the dissolution of the monasteries in the reign of Henry VIII it came into the possession of Matthew Parker, archbishop of Canterbury from 1559 to 1575. Parker bequeathed it to Corpus Christi College, Cambridge, in whose library it remains to this day. Had it not survived the various hazards of travel, damp, neglect, fire, mice, worm and old age, and come safe into the hands of skilled and loving curators – again we may say it, the tale that follows could not have been told.

But we do have it, this digression, this laconic parenthesis, however slender the thread by which it hangs before us, surviving the centuries in a single copy on a couple of sheets of vellum. It opens perspectives on the history of Anglo-Saxon England of which its author could never have dreamed.

In outline, the story that the Durham anonymous had to tell was straightforward. Earl Uhtred's son, by name Ealdred, avenged his father's murder by slaying the killer, Thurbrand. Thurbrand's son Carl in turn avenged *his* father's death by killing Ealdred. In due course Ealdred's grandson Waltheof contrived to avenge that murder by cornering all Carl's sons and grandsons when they were feasting together at a family estate not far from York and killing nearly all of them. This massacre, the last recorded bloodshed in this family feud, occurred probably in the winter of 1073–4.

Common sense is prone to assert that 'the facts speak for themselves'. Historians know that this is just what they don't do. Facts have to be coaxed and entreated into utterance. And if they are to speak, however hesitantly, however indistinctly, however obscurely, they have to be scrutinized against a background, a setting, in a context. Consider two examples of other acts of violence, at other times and in other places.

In the year 1165 violent scenes occurred in the town of Medina del Campo in central Spain. In the course of riots three hundred people sought refuge in the church of St Nicholas where they were then besieged by their fellow-citizens. After three days the patience of the besiegers ran out. They set fire to the church and all three hundred refugees were burned to death.

On 14 March 1912, at the courthouse of Hillsville in Carroll County, Virginia, at the foot of the Blue Ridge Mountains, Floyd Allen refused to go to jail when convicted and sentenced. Allen, a local farmer, storekeeper and illegal distiller, was notoriously the hardest man in a society of hard men, proud, quick-tempered, ready with a gun, who had had repeated brushes with the law. On this occasion he stood arraigned with obstructing the course of justice by forcing Deputy Sheriff Samuels to release from custody Allen's nephews Sidna and Wesley Edwards, assaulting and wounding Samuels in the process. Convicted and sentenced, Floyd Allen uttered the words, 'Gentlemen, I ain't a-going' and with them precipitated a gun battle in which Judge Massie and five other persons in the courtroom were shot dead. The story was a sensation in the press of the English-speaking world until displaced by the sinking of the *Titanic* a month later.

We know of the first of these incidents solely because of the survival of a papal letter instructing the bishop of Salamanca to investigate the inferno of Medina and punish the guilty.[3] We have absolutely no context whatsoever in which to place the tragedy. The second of these incidents is amply documented in press reports, judicial records, printed memoirs and oral recollections. Researchers have been able to build up a vivid and compelling picture of the smouldering rivalries and resentments of family and neighbourhood in a remote rural part of the United States which flared up in the violence at Hillsville courthouse nearly a century ago.[4] I have no doubt that a background quite as complex as the Virginian one lay behind the twelfth-century massacre at

Medina del Campo. Had Bishop Pedro Suárez of Salamanca written his memoirs – and had they come down to us – we might have learned a little more about it. But twelfth-century bishops didn't write memoirs, at any rate not as we understand the term today. We cannot interrogate witnesses who have been dead for over eight centuries. We cannot consult newspapers because they didn't exist in twelfth-century Spain. In short, we'll never know what went into the violence at Medina.

The context of the violent events which were unleashed by Thurbrand's murder of Uhtred falls somewhere between those extremes of ignorance and information. We can find out quite a lot about eleventh-century England. If it's not as much as we'd like to know, no useful purpose is served by lamenting that we haven't got more. If we can reconstruct that English context, and especially that northern English context, patiently and honestly, we might hope that the facts of this gruesome story will begin to whisper to us across those hundreds and hundreds of intervening years. If we listen humbly and attentively we might begin to understand some of those concerns and values, assumptions and aspirations, hopes and fears. We might hope to edge a little closer to what a great medievalist, F. W. Maitland, called 'the thoughts of our forefathers, their common thoughts about common things'. At any rate, it's worth a try.

'*Revenge* is a kinde of Wilde Justice.' So wrote Francis Bacon in his *Essays*, first published in 1597. How right he was. You hit me, I'll hit you back: the primal, instinctive satisfaction of such a remedy dates from long before *Homo* became remotely *sapiens*. It is from this primordial response that what we call the bloodfeud has developed. '*The* bloodfeud': that use of the definite article alerts us to the hovering presence of an interpreter, the social anthropologist. The bloodfeud, like other social institutions such as property, marriage or gift-exchange, has indeed been very fruitfully studied by social anthropologists. We now know, or think we know, a great deal about the nature and process of feuding in those human societies which lack most of the apparatus for maintaining order which we associate with the modern state.

Ever since the emergence of anthropology as a scientific discipline in the nineteenth century, medieval historians have been aware that it might be of assistance to them. The early middle ages, so ran the argument, were a time of social simplicity relative to the complexities of our own day. They are also ill-documented. Might it not be the case that anthropological study of chronologically modern yet culturally traditional societies – it is no longer fashionable to refer to them as 'primitive' – could shed suggestive light into the obscurities of the European medieval past? Experiment encouraged an affirmative answer to this question. For over a century, at an ever-accelerating rate, medievalists have been applying anthropological methods and insights to the study of their subject. The gain to understanding of such matters as kingship, ritual, law, family, religious observance and so forth has been incalculable. Violence in its various forms – war, pillage, mutilation, judicial combat, bloodfeud, to name but a few of them – has not been immune from the anthropological approach, and here, too, sympathetic understanding has been enhanced.

Some of the assumptions on which 'anthropological history' used to rest so confidently now look a little unsteady. Evolutionary optimism is one such. The more we have learned about the society of Anglo-Saxon England, the less traditional or simple does it appear. The trend of much recent investigation has been very strongly to suggest, sometimes indeed to be able to demonstrate, that eleventh-century England was a good deal more 'developed' than many parts of the 'developing' world today. Uncritical deployment of what we know about the Nuer or the Trobriand Islanders as an aid to understanding the England of Uhtred and Thurbrand may not necessarily enlighten. Far worse, it is also prone to encourage the most terrible of all the sins that an historian can commit, that of patronizing the past by claiming that it is easy to understand or interpret. Anthropological insights, in short, need to be employed cautiously and sparingly. To quote Maitland once more: 'The traveller who has studied the uncorrupted savage can often tell the historian of medieval Europe what to look for, never what to find.'

What the anthropologists have to tell us about feud may be summarized as follows. Feud is not simply revenge, though the instinct of revenge underlies it. Revenge is a matter, essentially, for individuals and acts of revenge tend to take place in hot blood. It is of the essence of feud that it is a matter for groups and that its prosecution is governed by accepted social conventions. The groups concerned are most usually groups of kinsfolk, though they may be groups of retainers, neighbours or clients. Often these categories overlap, in such a manner that retainers, neighbours and clients may also be kin to some near or distant degree. A state of feud means hostile relations between these groups of people. Hostility is usually sparked by a public affront to honour. Feuding cultures tend to be those which set a high value upon the maintenance of group, especially family, honour; in which, as a corollary, there is marked awareness of insult to honour and social shame. Affronts can come in all manner of guises – verbal mockery, insult to precedence or status, abduction or rape of women, maltreatment of dependants or animals, theft, arson, blows, murder. Convention enters the equation in that the state of hostility between the groups concerned is recognized by outsiders as a regular form of relationship. 'Regular', in that accepted norms exist for the conduct of hostility within the feuding relationship: norms relating to the extent of collective liability, the acceptable degree of violence and bloodshed, the notion of approximate parity in the rhythmic alternation of hostile encounters, the condemnation of what is judged unacceptable. Convention features also in the common acceptance of an apparatus for negotiating between the hostile parties, for satisfying grievances in a mutually acceptable manner and for making, being seen to make, peace on terms that are satisfactory to the sense of honour of all concerned. Such negotiation is often a matter for impartial go-betweens whose authority to mediate is widely recognized: friends, elders, holy or numinous persons, even perhaps kings. The places where negotiation and reconciliation are conducted may matter too, as may also the tangible symbols and rituals – gifts, gestures, clothing, accoutrements, food and drink – associated with peacemaking. Negotiation and settlement may or may not be permanent. There is a sense in which a feud can never be terminated. 'Feuds are like volcanoes,' as a distinguished medievalist, Michael Wallace-Hadrill, has acutely commented: 'a few are in eruption, others are extinct, but most are content to rumble now and again and leave us guessing.'[5] They may lie dormant for long periods of time, but hostility can be reactivated, sometimes by further overt incidents of affront but frequently by simple recollection of unfinished business. The means by which, the occasions at which, such recollection can be flicked into life are also an important part of the apparatus of feuding.

The fundamental point, alien to us, is that feud was a permanent feature of the assumptions of early medieval Europeans about their world. It was not 'a relic of the past due to be superseded' as some historians have erroneously supposed. 'Feud and vengeance,' a noted Austrian historian, Otto Brunner, has observed, 'were inseparable from concepts of Right' – or justice, or order, or equity, or stability, depending on how you choose to render the many-faceted German word *Recht*.[6] Peace was not the natural order of society in the age of Uhtred and Thurbrand. It was a social condition that had to be brought about, had to be made, and, like all human constructs, peace was frail. Regrettable though this might have been to high-minded churchmen, it was a fact of life that violence and conflict were as much a part of the social order as was peace. It follows that feud and conflict were not – as they tend to present themselves to a modern understanding – 'disruptive, dissociating and dysfunctional'. On the contrary, 'peace and conflict together create an unending rhythmic alternation through time'.[7] The words are quoted from a modern study of feud in contemporary Mediterranean and Middle Eastern societies, but they seem accurately to describe the situation in eleventh-century England.

'What is left of the vernacular literature of Germanic aristocracies pulsates to the rhythm of feud.'[8] The Anglo-Saxons are no exception. By way of illustration of the point we may turn to the only complete surviving epic poem in Old English, *Beowulf*. The work has come down to us in a single manuscript copy datable to round about the year 1000. The approximate date of this manuscript survival is evidence enough to indicate that regardless of the question, the very difficult and vexed question, of when *Beowulf* was actually first composed, the tale appealed to the taste of the age of Uhtred and Thurbrand. The poet referred to episodes of feud, Old English *fæhð*, cognate with German *Fehde*, on no fewer than thirteen occasions in the course of the epic. For example, in the first such reference, God is said to have pursued a feud with Cain and his kindred for the slaying of Abel (lines 106–10). This is a tangential reference, though it has significance as showing how the poet conceived it most appropriate to present an Old Testament story to the sympathetic understanding of his audience. Absolutely central, however, to the plot of *Beowulf* is the feud between the monster Grendel (and his kin) and King Hrothgar

and his subjects. Here are lines 152–8 in Seamus Heaney's fine translation published in 1999:

> . . . the vicious raids and ravages of Grendel,
> his long and unrelenting feud,
> nothing but war; how he would never
> parley or make peace with any Dane
> nor stop his death-dealing nor pay the death-price.
> No counsellor could ever expect
> fair reparation from those rabid hands.

The point here is that Grendel's refusal to negotiate put him, morally
and socially speaking, beyond the pale. He did not play by the rules.
The poet's audience did not need to be told this. They lived in a feuding
culture; they were familiar with the conventions.

Or again, consider the poignant poem known as *The Husband's
Message*, in which the 'speaker' is a wooden token sent by the absent
husband to his wife, here quoted in the translation by Michael
Alexander:

> The carver of this token entreats a lady
> clad in clear stones [i.e. jewellery] to call to mind
> and hold in her wit words pledged
> often between the two in earlier days:
> then he would hand you through hall and yard
> lord of his lands, and you might live together,
> forge your love. A feud drove him
> from this war-proud people.

The poet felt no need to dwell on the cause of this sundering of husband
from wife. Feuds which could lead to exile were a feature of the cultural
landscape inhabited by the poet and his audience. The poem has come
down to us in a manuscript of about the same age as the *Beowulf*
codex, the famous Exeter Book, copied possibly towards the end of
the tenth century and bequeathed to the cathedral library of Exeter –
where it still remains – by Bishop Leofric in 1072.

Yet another example may be drawn from the poem called the *Battle of Maldon*, probably composed within a generation of the combat it immortalizes, which was fought in the year 991. When the English leader Earl Byrhtnoth lay dead upon the field his followers refused to desert him but fought on against the Danes until they were all slaughtered. 'He was both my kinsman and my lord', the poet makes one of them exclaim. And then, continues the poet, 'mindful of his feud' he fell upon the enemy. Byrhtnoth's death at the hands of the Danes had laid an obligation upon his retainers to pursue a bloodfeud. It was simply something one did; no call for argument or explanation.

The great French medievalist Marc Bloch once observed that 'in every literature a society contemplates its own image'.[9] Uhtred, or Thurbrand, or Ealdred, or Carl, or Waltheof could have been familiar with recitations of *Beowulf* or *The Husband's Message* or the *Battle of Maldon* delivered to the company assembled to eat and drink in those draughty halls during the winter months. Stories of honour and treachery, of courage and endurance, of cunning and feud, both shaped their moral world and were shaped by it. But so did other habits and pressures. These men, their women and children and their wider kin lived in a kingdom of England, and in a province of that kingdom called Northumbria. What might this have meant?

2

England

At the time of Uhtred's murder the kingdom of England extended over, roughly speaking, the area which it still occupies ten centuries later. It had not been so for long; only a couple of generations.

After the end of Roman rule in Britain in the early years of the fifth century the island was invaded by Germanic peoples from across the North Sea conventionally referred to as the Angles, the Saxons and the Jutes (though there were certainly others besides). During a period of deep obscurity in the fifth and sixth centuries these newcomers established themselves as overlords of the indigenous Romano-British Celtic-speaking population. By the time a fitful light begins to dawn in the seventh century, lowland Britain or, as we may now begin to call it, Anglo-Saxon England was a patchwork of modest principalities governed by an élite of warrior-noblemen headed by kings. Warfare was the principal occupation of these people. In the course of the endemic strife that occupied the seventh and eighth centuries their petty kingdoms rose and fell, were absorbed by others, were split up and reunited, disappeared and reappeared, in bewildering kaleidoscopic movement.

By about the year 800 four leading and reasonably stable kingdoms had emerged from this turmoil. From south to north these were Wessex, the kingdom named after the West Saxons, which occupied the regions south of the Thames from Kent to Cornwall; Mercia, which embraced the midlands between the Thames and the Humber; East Anglia, the realm of the eastern Angles; and Northumbria, the kingdom to the north of the Humber river system, which then extended far into what is now lowland Scotland.

In the past, historians have claimed to discern the faint lineaments of a united kingdom of England in the meagre records which have come down to us from the eighth and ninth centuries. Modern investigators are more cautious. There were, however, significant elements of a shared culture uniting the peoples who dwelt between the Isle of Wight and the Firth of Forth. The most fundamental of these was language. The principal language of the inhabitants of Wessex, Mercia, East Anglia and Northumbria was the Germanic tongue known as Anglo-Saxon or Old English, although there were regions where Celtic was and would long continue to be spoken, such as Cornwall and Cumbria. Of course, there were marked differences of dialect, as there still are, but it seems likely that a ninth-century inhabitant of the valley of the Tweed could have made himself intelligible to a dweller in the valley of the Torridge – though possibly not the Tamar – without a great deal more difficulty than he might experience today.

A shared Christian faith was scarcely less important than a shared language among the elements of a common culture. Christianity had reached the Anglo-Saxons from diverse quarters and through various agencies. It had come in the guise of missions sent from Rome or from Christian Ireland. It had accompanied brides from the Christian kingdoms of Francia, the ancestor of France, who were married across the Channel to cement political alliances. It had seeped up from the conquered Britons. It had been diffused by solitary hermits and wandering pilgrims who sought in self-imposed exile a faith untrammelled by the ties of home and kin. By the eighth century the Church was solidly established, with its two archbishoprics at Canterbury and York and their sixteen subordinate bishoprics, its scores of monasteries and its ever-denser network of lesser churches to conduct a pastoral ministry. Its early growth had been skilfully chronicled by Bede (d. 735), monk of Jarrow in Northumbria and author of (among much else) the *Historia Ecclesiastica Gentis Anglorum* ('Ecclesiastical History of the People of the English'), one of the great masterpieces of European historical writing. Bede was, arguably, the single most important agent in furnishing a sense of identity as 'the English' for the diverse peoples who made up the population of Anglo-Saxon England. He also gave them, closely allied, a sense of pride in their Christian past. They could be proud of their godly kings such as Edwin (d. 633), the first Christian king of Northumbria; of their devout bishops such as Aidan (d. 651), missionary from Iona to Northumbria; and of their saints such as Cuthbert (d. 687), monk at Melrose and Lindisfarne (or Holy Island), hermit of Farne Island, and for the last two years of his life a reluctant bishop.

Institutions, societies and customs were broadly similar among the Anglo-Saxon peoples. Social structure was hierarchical. In every kingdom the men and women of the small ruling élite were supported by the labours of the many, who ranged from prosperous freeholding farmers down to an underclass of slaves. Although the tenor of life was violent, kings took seriously their duties to maintain peace and to administer good justice. Systems existed for the extraction of tribute or tax, with liability graded in accordance with landed wealth. Stable authority is implied by the good-quality silver coinage issued by eighth-century kings. Major monuments of engineering such as Offa's Dyke, the massive bank-and-ditch defining the frontier between English and Welsh attributed to King Offa of Mercia (d. 796), presuppose formidable organizational and directive capacity.

Anglo-Saxon England was prosperous by the standards of the early middle ages. Archaeologists and historians of landscape have demonstrated that arable, woodland, rivers, quarries and mines were effectively exploited. Towns and trading-places were growing. Coin circulated in abundance. English merchants trafficked with Frisia, the Low Countries, the Rhineland, northern Gaul and perhaps further afield. Only a wealthy society could have supported the superstructure of aristocracy and Church. Only a wealthy Church could have produced such wondrous achievements of Christian art as the Lindisfarne Gospels or the Bewcastle Cross.

Wealth attracts predators. In these three words we have the simplest and the most cogent explanation for the Viking assault upon Anglo-Saxon England in the ninth century. The word *viking* means a pirate or raider by sea, and though the English were no mean seafarers they were far outclassed by the peoples of early medieval Scandinavia. Advances in shipbuilding and seamanship enabled the Danes – most of the Vikings who attacked England were from Denmark – to cross the North Sea and swoop on their prey unawares. They chose 'soft' targets whenever they could, especially the monasteries, which were static, undefended and rich. Lindisfarne and Jarrow were among the first to be ransacked, in 793 and 794 respectively. As the ninth century advanced, the Viking assaults on England – and Francia, and Ireland – changed in degree. The fleets grew larger, the armies of freebooters they carried grew correspondingly bigger, they came with better weaponry and more experienced leaders, and they were prepared to overwinter and campaign for several seasons at a stretch. They also changed in kind. Plundering was superseded by conquest, and conquest followed up by settlement. In the 860s two of England's four kingdoms, East Anglia and Northumbria, were taken over by the Danes and a third, Mercia, was reduced to client status. The line of the Roman road known as Watling Street, which ran from London to Chester, now formed the approximate boundary between 'English' England and the zone under Danish rule. The regions to the east and north of Watling Street came to be known as the Danelaw in recognition of this fact.

The elimination of Northumbria and East Anglia, and the collapse of Mercia, left only Wessex to face the Danes. The defence of Wessex against them is indissolubly connected with the name of King Alfred (871–99). It is not easy to grasp the historical reality of Alfred as man and king. This is not because of a lack of sources: far from it; we know more about Alfred than we know about any previous Anglo-Saxon ruler. The difficulty is that our two principal narrative sources emanate from circles very close to him. The full and informative set of annals known as the *Anglo-Saxon Chronicle* is no longer attributed to the king himself, but there is general (if not universal) agreement that the work was edited in a milieu enjoying close contacts with the royal court. A remarkable biography of the king was composed during his lifetime, in 893, by his friend, confidant and courtier, the notably loyal and discreet Welsh cleric Asser. It is impossible to believe that Alfred had no hand at all in shaping the manner in which his propagandists presented an image of him to contemporaries and to posterity.

Professional historians are prone to make heavy weather of the resultant difficulties of interpretation. There is no occasion to linger on them here. What is clear beyond doubt is that Alfred was a courageous and gifted ruler who guided Wessex to survival. In the years 871–8 he fought the Danes to a standstill and cleared them out of Wessex. In the succeeding fourteen years, generally peaceful, he put measures in place for the future defence of his kingdom. A network of

GENEALOGICAL TABLE I
THE ROYAL HOUSE OF WESSEX

This family tree, much simplified (and almost exclusively masculine), is intended as no more than the most basic guide to the structure of England's royal family in the tenth and eleventh centuries.

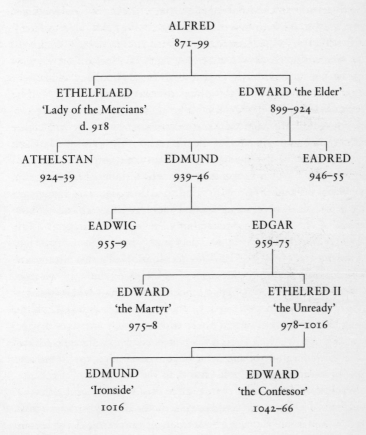

ALFRED
871–99

ETHELFLAED
'Lady of the Mercians'
d. 918

EDWARD 'the Elder'
899–924

ATHELSTAN
924–39

EDMUND
939–46

EADRED
946–55

EADWIG
955–9

EDGAR
959–75

EDWARD
'the Martyr'
975–8

ETHELRED II
'the Unready'
978–1016

EDMUND
'Ironside'
1016

EDWARD
'the Confessor'
1042–66

fortresses to defend the frontiers of Wessex was planned and their construction set in train. Military reforms were effected, their precise nature not wholly clear in detail, but plausibly interpreted as designed to yield a more efficient army – better equipped, better mounted, better trained – which would be able to complement the static defences as a mobile field force. Ships were built to counter the Vikings at sea. These defensive measures were tested during the next serious Danish attack in the years 892–6 and proved triumphant. The enemy could not get into Wessex and was more easily defeated in the field. Under Alfred's leadership Wessex had survived.

Alfred was much more than a talented general. He had been brought up with convictions about the duties and responsibilities of a Christian king, notions which owed something to earlier English writers such as Bede, something to the remarkable group of churchmen gathered at the court of Charlemagne and his successors across the Channel in the Frankish kingdom. Pondering the melancholy history of the English in his lifetime, he saw the hand of God at work, using the Danes to punish them for their backslidings. Only by turning again to a godly life would the English be able to stand up to their enemies. That meant, in the first place, observing good and godly law. Alfred's code of law was more comprehensive and ambitious than the laws issued by any previous Anglo-Saxon king, and deliberately set him in the tradition of holy lawmakers stretching back to Moses. Godly rule also meant the encouragement of righteousness and wisdom among those who governed. To that end Alfred, a scholarly man who could read Latin as well as his own tongue, commissioned translations into Old English of, in his own words, 'certain books which are the most necessary for all men to know', works which were intended to form the basis for the Christian education of the West Saxon governing class. It meant, finally, restoring the English Church to the standards of excellence which Bede had chronicled two centuries earlier. Alfred wanted devout and learned bishops who could provide moral leadership and spiritual discipline in troubled times; he wanted to restore the 'regular' religious life of communities vowed to live according to a *regula* (monastic rule) in monasteries such as those which had once existed in England but had been sacked by the Vikings or had fallen into decay. These monastic initiatives did not bear fruit in his own lifetime. But in his far-reaching plans for the Christian regeneration of his people Alfred laid down the programme which succeeding kings and churchmen would follow as the tenth century developed.

Alfred's son Edward 'the Elder' (899–924) is less well served by the surviving sources and consequently less distinct to us than his father, but the outlines of a ruler of talent almost equal to Alfred's are reasonably clear. In a series of striking military campaigns Edward shattered the power of the Danish rulers of East Anglia and the eastern midlands. In this he was ably assisted by his sister Ethelflaed, the 'Lady of the Mercians', who governed the western parts of 'English' Mercia until her death in 918. Victories in the field were consolidated by the building of further fortresses. Their jointly co-ordinated conquests advanced West Saxon authority in the course of Edward's reign from the Thames to the line of the Mersey and Humber estuaries. Edward even received, in 920, the submission of those princes who ruled beyond that line – the Viking king of York, the British king of Strathclyde and the king of Scots – though what such a submission meant in terms of authority effective in practice cannot be known.

By the time of Edward's death in 924 the area of territory under his direct rule was more than double what he had inherited from his father. A 'greater Wessex' had come into being as the ruling dynasty laid hold of East Anglia and Mercia. Military operations, however successful, had to be supplemented by more permanent means of control. In the original Wessex south of the Thames, administrative districts known as 'shires' can be traced from the eighth century onwards. Typically, the shire was administered by an official nominated by the king as his deputy, known as an *ealdorman* (whence our modern 'alderman'). Shires tended to take their names from the prominent royal estate at which the ealdorman was based for the purposes of receiving renders and services due to the king and of presiding over courts of law. Thus, for example, Wiltshire was the shire administered from the royal estate at Wilton, and Hampshire the shire administered from *Hamtun*, the ancestor of Southampton. This West Saxon administrative framework was imposed where deemed appropriate upon the territories conquered by Edward in the early tenth century. The results may be seen most vividly in the west midlands, where several shires – for instance Shropshire, Staffordshire,

Warwickshire and Worcestershire – appear to be artificial creations dating from this period which overrode earlier administrative divisions in disregard of local habits and ingrained loyalties. The creation of these new shires is a measure of the power, determination and ruthlessness which distinguished the West Saxon rulers of the tenth century.

The northward expansion of Wessex continued during the reigns of Edward's three sons, Athelstan (924–39), Edmund (939–46) and Eadred (946–55), but it proceeded less smoothly. There were setbacks. This was not owing to any lack of ability on the part of these three brothers. Athelstan was a ruler of the stature of his father and grandfather; and though we know less of his short-lived siblings we can sense that they were formidable kings also. The trouble was that they came up against more determined opponents, and at a greater distance from their base in Wessex.

The full complexity of northern affairs will confront us in the next chapter. Suffice to say for the present that the Anglo-Scandinavian kingdom of York, which extended, roughly, over modern Yorkshire and Lancashire, proved formidably difficult to subdue. Athelstan married one of his sisters to its king, Sihtric, in 926 and upon Sihtric's death in the following year he moved swiftly to annex it. Hastening immediately onwards to the north-west, he received in July 927, at the bridge over the river Eamont near Penrith, the submissions of the kings of Strathclyde and of Scotland, and of the English ruler of Bamburgh (the northern rump of the earlier kingdom of Northumbria). These submissions may have been as ephemeral as those of 920, but what followed them was not. Athelstan returned to York and held court there, handing out treasures to his followers and destroying the fortifications built by the Viking kings. These were important public symbolic gestures. Athelstan was proclaiming that the kingdom of York had come under the direct authority of the crown of Wessex. His northern frontier had been advanced from the Humber–Mersey line to the valleys of the Tees and the Duddon, northern boundaries of Yorkshire and Lancashire respectively.

There it remained for the rest of his reign; not, however, without challenge. In 934, presumably in answer to some provocation of which we know nothing, Athelstan attacked the Scots by land and sea. At the head of a land force the king ravaged beyond the Firth of Forth as far north as Kincardine, while his fleet selectively harried the coastline even further to the north, as far as Caithness. The counterstroke came three years later. Constantine, king of Scots, Olaf, the Norse king of Dublin and claimant to the kingdom of York, and Owen, king of Strathclyde, came together in an alliance directed against Athelstan. Invading England, they were confronted at *Brunanburh* – never convincingly identified, but probably somewhere in the east midlands – and defeated in a hard-fought battle.

With hindsight, the battle of *Brunanburh* may be appreciated as one of those decisive military turning-points in the making of an English kingdom. Contemporaries did indeed judge it a memorable fight, worthy of celebration in verse, but for them it was just an episode, albeit a glorious one, in a struggle that was not yet over. As soon as King Athelstan was in his grave, Olaf of Dublin was back. Occupying York, he went on to raid deep into the Mercian midlands south of the Humber. Athelstan's successor, Edmund, recognized this *fait accompli*, granting away the shires of Derby, Nottingham, Lincoln and Leicester to the invaders, so that Olaf found himself briefly the ruler of a Hiberno-Anglo-Scandinavian principality that stretched in a crescent from Dublin to Stamford by way of Lancashire, Yorkshire and the east midlands. Briefly, because Olaf died the following year (941) and Edmund succeeded in reimposing West Saxon authority over the areas where it had lapsed.

But this fragile southern overlordship was challenged again. Another Olaf, son of the Sihtric who had ruled in York in the 920s, established himself as king there and ruled from 947 until 950. He was displaced by the most famous Viking adventurer of the day, Eric Bloodaxe, in exile from his native Norway, who seems to have ruled at York between 950 and 952. (There are difficult chronological problems about this mid-century period which we need not enter into here.) Eric's reign ended when he was expelled from the kingdom of York in circumstances which remain obscure and met his death through treachery high in the Pennines a little later. King Eadred of Wessex resumed his authority over Northumbria. Thereafter it remained a part of the kingdom of England – though, as with the battle of *Brunanburh*, we must remember that it is easier for us than it was for contemporaries to appreciate the finality of the reign of the last Scandinavian king at

York. There were to be several occasions over the course of the following century when 'England' might have fallen permanently apart.

Such in briefest outline was the process by which a kingdom of Wessex transformed itself by conquest into a kingdom of England. The most obvious beneficiaries of the transformation were the kings themselves. They 'won undying glory by the sword's edge', as the poet who commemorated *Brunanburh* put it. Indeed they did, and they also won land, livestock and slaves, much treasure and the spoils of war in weapons, equipment and horses, access to new sources of patronage in Church and lay society – in a word, vastly more power. But it was not kings alone who benefited from this phase of imperial expansion. The warrior-noblemen who served them loyally, if they survived the hazards of battle, could also expect rewards in the form of land, treasure, slaves, offices. Take for example the West Saxon nobleman also called Athelstan. Through loyal service to two generations of kings he acquired extensive estates, not just in the newly conquered lands but also in Somerset and Devon, the heartlands of Wessex. He served as ealdorman of East Anglia for nearly a quarter of a century, and though this was his title it is fairly clear that the area of his jurisdiction extended well beyond the bounds of East Anglia proper to embrace large parts of the eastern midlands. One of his brothers was ealdorman of the south-eastern counties of Kent, Surrey and Sussex; another became ealdorman of Wessex. At the height of their influence around the mid-century they were the most powerful secular noblemen in the English kingdom. Athelstan's wealth and power were so extensive, indeed, that he was nicknamed 'Half-king'. He was the foster-father of the young prince Edgar, son of King Edmund. He was a generous benefactor of the abbey of Glastonbury, to which he retired to end his days as a monk after leaving public life in 956. His two sons succeeded him as ealdormen of East Anglia one after the other, between 956 and 992: by the latter date the family had been running East Anglia, under the king, for at least sixty years.

The Church was another agent of consolidation, another beneficiary of royal expansion. Its higher-ranking ecclesiastics, the bishops and abbots, were usually nominated by the crown and were almost

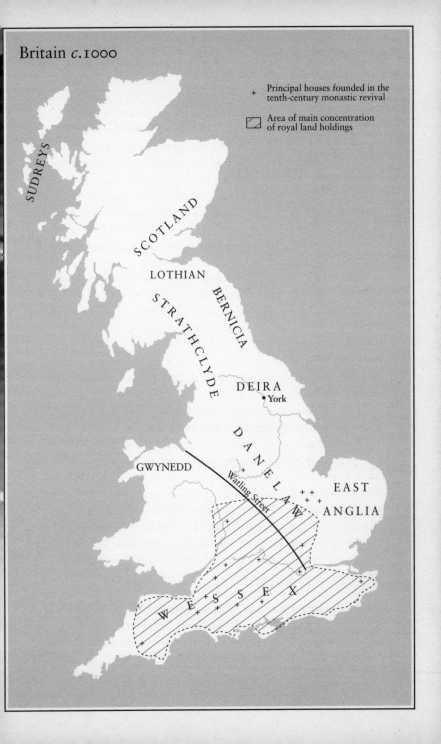

Britain *c.* 1000

+ Principal houses founded in the
  tenth-century monastic revival

▨ Area of main concentration
  of royal land holdings

SUDREYS

SCOTLAND

LOTHIAN

BERNICIA

STRATHCLYDE

DEIRA
• York

DANELAW

GWYNEDD

Watling Street

EAST
ANGLIA

WESSEX

invariably drawn from the ranks of the aristocracy. The clerical establishment, therefore, constituted the ecclesiastical arm of royal power, counterpart to the secular arm formed by the lay aristocracy. The archiepiscopal see of Canterbury was rewarded with estates in the conquered Danelaw territories, just as were Athelstan Half-king and others. It acquired relics from churches in the Danelaw to swell its collection of the holy – and therefore powerful – dead. Archbishop Oda of Canterbury (d. 958) received an enormous bequest in gold under the will of King Eadred; had other tenth-century royal wills survived, it would not be surprising to find that other archbishops benefited similarly.

West Saxon royal power reached its tenth-century apex during the reign of King Edgar (959–75), the prince who had been fostered in the household of Athelstan Half-king, whose widowed daughter-in-law he would subsequently marry. This was how the homilist Ælfric of Cerne Abbas in Dorset would remember him, looking back from the darker days that ensued:

Edgar, the noble and resolute king, exalted the praise of God everywhere among his people, the strongest of all kings over the English nation: and God subdued for him his adversaries, kings and earls, so that they came to him without any fighting, desiring peace, subjected to him for whatever he wished, and he was honoured widely throughout the land.

Compared to the unceasing warfare of the previous hundred years, Edgar's reign was indeed peaceful. 'Nor was there fleet so proud nor host so strong that it got itself prey in England as long as the noble king held the throne,' as the compiler of the *Anglo-Saxon Chronicle* boasted. This *pax Anglicana* rested on military readiness and the caution it instilled into potential aggressors: it was said that Edgar regularly circumnavigated Britain with his fleet in a display of preparedness for combat.

Three notable developments of Edgar's reign evoke in different ways the quality of his kingship. One was the large-scale foundation of Benedictine monasteries under lavish royal patronage. At the beginning of the reign Glastonbury, chosen retirement home of the elderly Half-king, was the only properly constituted monastic house in

England; by its end there were at least twenty-two (precise dates of foundation can be hard to pin down). A good instance is furnished by the monastery of Ely. The house was re-founded in 970 on the site of a celebrated early Anglo-Saxon monastery which had faded away during the period of Viking disruption. Its tenth-century reactivator was Ethelwold, West Saxon aristocrat, leading royal counsellor and bishop of Winchester, the town which was the closest thing to a capital city in tenth-century England. Ethelwold was therefore intimately associated with the West Saxon monarchy, and he was backed to the hilt by the kings he served, who were cannily aware of the value of having a distinguished monastic community under their patronage in an area which had only recently been incorporated into their expanding kingdom. A skilful – and none too scrupulous – man of business and a fund-raiser of genius, Ethelwold ensured that his Ely rapidly acquired great wealth. By 1066 it was the second richest monastic house in England, surpassed only by Glastonbury, its abbot the lord of a colossal acreage of fen and flat inhabited by thousands of tenant farmers and fishermen – a jewel in the crown as well as in the Church. The impulse to establish reformed monastic houses was as much about royal power as it was about royal piety; the two were inseparable.

The second notable development was the ambitious reform of the English monetary system put into effect in 973, whose chief feature was regular periodic recoinages. At given intervals, initially of six years, every coin-owning person in the kingdom had to take his stock of silver pennies – the only unit of currency in Anglo-Saxon England – to the local mint-town where moneyers operating under licence from the crown would melt them down and reissue them, for a fee, struck afresh with new dies. The king retained overall control by a monopoly on the production and distribution of dies, and made a handsome profit by charging the moneyers heavy fees for their licences (who could recoup this from their clients, the public). The incontrovertible evidence of the surviving coins themselves has enabled modern numismatists to pronounce with confidence that the system instituted in 973 worked triumphantly well until the end of the Anglo-Saxon period and indeed beyond. No other kingdom in western Christendom in the tenth or eleventh century managed its coinage in a fashion which even approached the efficiency and sophistication of the English kingdom.

The monetary system of the later Anglo-Saxon kings is perhaps the most formidable evidence of their power.

And thirdly, it was also in 973 that rituals were performed which were evidently intended to make assertions about Edgar's kingship; assertions which were perhaps more intelligible to contemporaries than they are to us. On 11 May he was crowned and anointed at Bath and, processing at once thereafter to Chester, he was rowed on the river Dee by a number of lesser kings from different parts of the British Isles, himself acting as steersman. The ceremony at Bath, a place heavy with Roman and therefore imperial associations, looks as though it might have been a ritual designed to inaugurate the king into some sort of 'Empire of Britain'. Not all the rulers alleged to have rowed Edgar on the Dee can be identified, but those who can included the kings of Scotland, Strathclyde (or Cumbria), the Sudreys (the Norse kingdom of the Western Isles) and Gwynedd (north Wales). The point of the operation, surely, was the public display of Edgar as a super-king who lorded it over subordinate kings; an emperor, indeed.

What was involved in being a king in the tenth century? What did kings do? What was government about? In considering such questions as these we need to shed all sorts of modern conceptions about the responsibilities of government. We need to project ourselves into an era long before the state began to arrogate to itself the multifarious duties it assumes today. The oath sworn by English rulers at their coronations in the tenth and eleventh centuries will give us an idea of what was expected of them. Kings swore to maintain peace, to protect the Church, to prohibit wrongful acts and to give good justice: that was it; a limited view (according to modern expectations) of what kingship was about. No more and no less was expected of any contemporary ruler in the other kingdoms of western Europe. (Rulership was a somewhat different affair in the East Roman or Byzantine empire, and in the Islamic world.) We also need to bear in mind that the conditions under which kings operated were wholly different from those of today. In particular – obvious points, but they bear repetition – movement of people or commodities from place to place was slow, technology was simple and literacy was restricted. Communication is central to the exercise of power. How did kings communicate with their subjects? The short answer is that they moved about and talked to them. Historians today call it government by itineration, which is just a fancy way of saying that the most constant royal activity was travel. The fundamental reason why kings travelled was to consume. Their scattered estates all over the kingdom were geared to the production of food and drink for the king and his household. Because transport was so slow and costly, and because known techniques of food preservation (e.g. steeping sides of beef in huge vats of brine) did not lend themselves to mobility, it made sense for the king to go to his food, not to wait for it to come to him. This kings had done since immemorial antiquity.

The logistics of royal itineration, of which we know regrettably little, must have been fairly complex. They would have demanded high powers of forethought and organization, as well as a talent for last-minute improvisation on the part of those to whom the kings delegated the management of the royal household. This household already comprised at any one time a substantial number of persons. At its heart lay the royal family itself with the domestic servants attendant on king and queen. There would have been a troop of picked military retainers to act as the royal bodyguard. At any moment there would have been a number of senior advisers – ealdormen, bishops, abbots – in attendance, and each of these very great persons would have had his own smaller household. There would have been a small army of specialist servants – clerks, grooms, carpenters, smiths, falconers, dog-handlers, cooks, washerwomen and entertainers. We must make allowance for all sorts of floating extras too: aristocratic youths who were being fostered by the kings, hostages, visiting Welsh princes and their entourages, the occasional ambassador from Germany or Francia. There would also have been an enormous number of animals: the king's own stables; the mounts (and the spare mounts) of all his grander attendants; hawks and dogs in abundance (for the West Saxon kings of this era were passionately keen sportsmen); draught animals and pack animals; and very likely, just to be on the safe side in case the supply system broke down, a walking larder of sheep and a cartload or two of chickens.

Basic needs such as the collection and consumption of food can have far-reaching constitutional implications. The royal presence at any given centre fostered royal power in that area. Temporary residence at a royal estate created for the few days that the king was there a static court. There he could display himself to his subjects in a pageant of ritual magnificence. There business could be transacted. Local notables would attend; and if they failed to the king would want to know why. The presence of these local gentry and clergy enabled the king to acquaint himself with what was going on in the area. He could check up on the conduct of his officials, from the ealdorman of the shire down to his estate bailiffs. He could hear and judge local lawsuits, help to arbitrate in local quarrels, collect the fines of malefactors, dispose to the deserving of property forfeited by criminals. Personal relations at this local level were of critical importance in the maintenance of royal authority. The king's frowns and smiles, the gifts he gave and received, the pleasure he took in the hunting he was offered, the devotion he showed for the shrine of the local saint, the quality of the entertainment he provided or was provided with – these were not the trivial matters they might seem to us. They were absolutely of the essence of Anglo-Saxon royal government. Alas, they leave precious little trace for the historian.

Apart from the fatigue and discomfort of court life, it all sounds rather homely and cosy. But royal courts are rarely harmonious places. Dissensions within the ruling élite of counsellors over issues of policy, lines of tension within the royal family itself, questions of access to the king, who was in favour and who was not, who was in whose faction and how they might do down their rivals – such human foibles as these were always liable to be causes of friction. And friction, in this delicate network of human relationships which was 'government' in the tenth century, had potentially damaging 'political' consequences. It could turn into violence.

The peace that kings swore to maintain was something that had to be striven for. It didn't just happen. Everything that we know about early medieval society, in England or elsewhere in Europe, suggests that this was an extremely violent world. Peace was something that had to be imposed by authority in a blunt and hard-nosed fashion. When merchants from York were imprisoned and robbed on the Isle of Thanet in east Kent in about 970 the perpetrators of this breach of the peace were deprived of their property, and some among them of their lives, on King Edgar's order. A contemporary writer attributed to the same king a 'very severe' law under which convicted felons were to be blinded, mutilated and scalped, after which what was left of their bodies was not to be given Christian burial but to be devoured by beasts and birds. In these savage measures one can see kings responding to violence with violence in an attempt to impose the king's peace. How effectively it worked one may legitimately wonder. After all, kings themselves were not above the arena of violence. Edgar's father King Edmund had perished by violence, killed by a robber at his royal estate of Pucklechurch in 946. His own son King Edward 'the Martyr' was to be murdered in treacherous circumstances in 978. Their royal anointing may have set them apart from other men; it did not render them immune from the assassin's dagger.

How far – in the most literal sense, of the actual distance on the ground – did the king's authority reach? This was a critical question in the tenth century. We can look for approaches to an answer in the geographical distribution of the royal estates, the pattern of royal itineration, the names of persons attending (or not attending) the royal court, the web of mints and monasteries under royal control, the choice of marriage partners for kings, the sites chosen for major ritual displays of royalty, and the churches in which monarchs opted to be buried and remembered. On most of these matters we are under-informed. But enough evidence has survived to give a fairly clear general impression. By whatever criterion we judge the matter, the tenth-century English kings were first and last kings of Wessex.

Royal association with one primary region was not peculiar to England. It was characteristic of the era. Consider the contemporary rulers of Germany, known as the Ottonians after their most formidable representative Otto I who reigned from 936 to 973. The Ottonians originated in Saxony, and had the bulk of their family estates there. We can know their royal itinerary in more detail than we can that of English kings, and what it tells us is that Saxony remained their favourite region of residence. It was in Saxony that they were most confident about their support network, in Saxony that they founded monastic communities, in Saxony that they were most warmly regarded and remembered. When an Ottonian king went – which he rarely did – to a distant part of his huge kingdom, such as Swabia in south-eastern Germany, he went as a foreigner, with precaution tempered by bluster, he was not made particularly welcome there, and he didn't stay long. In Saxony he was safe. Away from home territory, little could be taken for granted. The Swabia of the West Saxon kings was Northumbria.

3

Northumbria

When kings of England visited Northumbria, wrote William of Malmesbury, they did so only if accompanied by a great number of extra troops over and above their normal military retinue. William was a monk, an acute observer of people and affairs, and a gifted historian, writing in the first quarter of the twelfth century. We may be confident that what he had to say about his own era was also true of the pre-Conquest period. In southern eyes, Northumbria was a dangerous place, not to be visited without prudent military precaution.

In addition, Northumbria was difficult to get to. Although in emergencies a royal entourage might travel at great speed – in 1066 King Harold II managed York to London in perhaps as little as four days – in normal circumstances so diverse and cumbersome a gathering as a royal household travelled at the pace of its slowest vehicles, the carts which carried its tents and bedding. Ten to fifteen miles each day is probably a reliable estimate. To put it in a slightly different way, this meant that at the beginning of any day's march the area where you would be likely to spend the following night would be within your range of vision (English weather permitting). A journey from Winchester to York, of some 215 miles as the crow flies, would usually have taken between two and three weeks; more, if you add in the likelihood of broken axles, rest days and other delaying business en route.

And then of course humans are not crows, though kings and their companions must often have wished they were, as they struggled with the obstacles which nature placed in the way of access to northern England. Water was the most pervasive among them. The broad estuary of the Humber, that 'level drifting breadth / where sky and

31

Lincolnshire and water meet', could be crossed by ferry from Barton-on-Humber to Brough. This ferry had existed since the Roman era, if not before, at the point where Ermine Street, the road running due north from Lincoln, meets the river. Substantial remains of two Anglo-Saxon churches at Barton witness to the continuing importance of this crossing-point in the late Old English period. After landfall on the northern bank at Brough, the Roman *Petuaria*, the Roman road swung north-westwards, hugging the dry ground at the foot of the Yorkshire Wolds, towards York. Flat, marshy land lay to the west of the road, where the Derwent and the Ouse wind their sinuous way towards the Humber; land that is still called in Yorkshire *ings*, a term derived from an Old Norse word for swampy land liable to flooding.

If entry to Northumbria by land were desired, the traveller would have to make use of the other north-going Roman road which still remained in use in the Anglo-Saxon period. From Doncaster (the Roman *Danum*), where the roads from Lincoln and Leicester joined, it swung in a loop to the west through Castleford (*Lagentium*) and Tadcaster (*Calcaria*) to York. This is the route, it was suggested in chapter 1, taken by King Canute in the early weeks of 1016. The area between the Ermine Street crossing of the Humber and the Doncaster–York loop is where all the rivers that flow into the Humber system converge: Trent and Don, Aire and Wharfe, Ouse and Derwent, pouring their waters into the North Sea through the funnel of the Humber. Still today notoriously liable to flooding, even after a millennium of dyking and banking – as we saw in the exceptionally wet autumn of the year 2000 – in the eleventh century it was a region of sparsely settled marshland across which only the rheumaticky locals might be induced to act as guides, of myriads of waterfowl, of sluggish eel-infested channels, of spirit-haunted meres.

West of the Roman road, you were quickly in the foothills of the Pennines where south-to-north communication became steadily more difficult, and finally impossible, as you moved westwards. Over on the far side, the coastal plain of Lancashire appeared to offer an easy route north, and here too there were Roman roads running north from Chester to help the traveller. But soon there would loom on the horizon the really formidable barrier of the mountains of the Lake District to thwart your progress and drive you back up Ribblesdale and down Wharfedale, again following a Roman road, to the plain of York.

Distant, dangerous, difficult of access, poor of soil and inclement of weather, Northumbria was not visited often – it's another of William of Malmesbury's observations – by English rulers whose homeland lay to the south of the Thames. Given the relationship between presence and power, it follows that the royal grip upon Northumbria was significantly shakier than it was upon Mercia or East Anglia, let alone Wessex.

This point can be illustrated in a variety of ways. In an age in which the possession of land was what gave wealth and influence, English kings owned few landed estates north of the Humber. Ancient administrative divisions were not broken up and redrafted as they had been in the west midlands; the colossal county of Yorkshire survived intact. About seventy royal mints were striking the king's coin in England south of the Humber at the time of Earl Uhtred's murder; north of the river only a single one was operative, at York. Not a single monastic house was founded under royal patronage in Northumbria in the course of the tenth-century monastic revival. Kings could make themselves felt, and very impressively and alarmingly, as Athelstan, for instance, had done in 927. But such occasions were rare. In Northumbria royal power did not bear down upon the subject, did not shape and mould institutions, was not a constant looming presence, as it did or was in Berkshire, let us say, or Northamptonshire or Dorset or Sussex.

The person who mattered most in northern England in the later Anglo-Saxon period was not a living king but a dead saint. Cuthbert was the most tremendous presence in the north, hovering with a special protective intensity over the area between the Tees and the Tyne known as St Cuthbert's Land. Very rapidly after his death in 687 Cuthbert was venerated as a saint. His body, transferred to a new tomb by the bishop and monks of Lindisfarne in 698, was found to be incorrupt, always considered a sign of sanctity. Two lives of Cuthbert, one by an unknown monk of Lindisfarne and the other by Bede, were written to commemorate him and to record the miracles of healing which he had worked during his lifetime and which had occurred at his tomb after his death. His relics were carefully preserved by the community inside

Northumbria and southern Scotland

The disputed Teesdale estates
Principal (Roman) roads

NORTH

SEA

LOTHIAN

St Andrews

Carham
✕ 1018

R. Tweed

BERNICI

Lindisfarne or Holy Island
Bamburgh

Tynemouth

Newburn
Chester-Le-Street
Durham

R. Tyne

Hexham

STRATH CI

R. Clyde

Carlisle

GALLOWAY

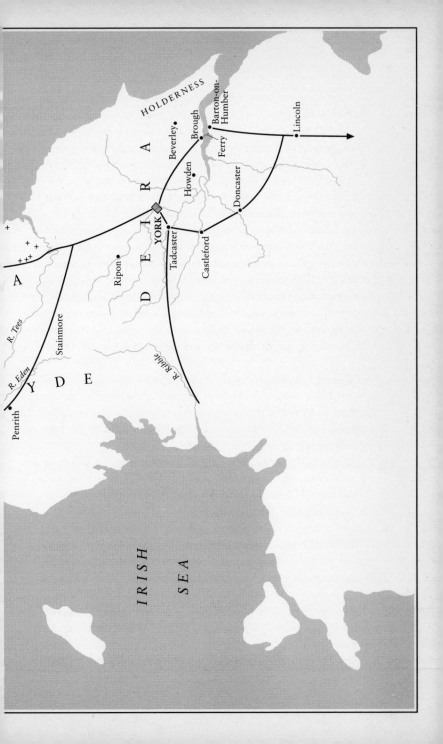

the carved wooden coffin still to be seen in Durham cathedral: not just the miracle-working corporeally intact body, but the Byzantine silk in which it was wrapped, his pectoral cross of gold set with garnets, his portable altar encased in silver, his paten, his chalice, his ivory liturgical comb and his copy of St John's Gospel. (Cross, altar and comb are also to be seen at Durham; the gospel book is in the possession of Stonyhurst College but on loan to the British Library.) The Northumbrian king to whom Bede dedicated his *Ecclesiastical History*, Ceolwulf (729–37), abdicated to become a monk of Lindisfarne. Prominent Northumbrian noblemen followed his example. In the course of the eighth century Cuthbert became something like the patron saint of Northumbria. The Viking attack on his monastery in 793 provoked widespread shock and consternation: from hundreds of miles away in the Frankish kingdom the expatriate Northumbrian scholar Alcuin wrote in condolence to the bishop and monks of Lindisfarne.

When the community finally abandoned Lindisfarne after repeated Viking attacks in 875 they took their patron's remains with them and lived a wandering existence for the succeeding seven years. In 883 bishop and community settled at Chester-le-Street in Weardale, where they remained for a little over a century. In 995 they moved a few miles upstream to what has now been Cuthbert's resting place for over a thousand years – Durham. Our first glimpse of Uhtred as earl of Northumbria tells of his assistance to St Cuthbert's bishop and clergy on the occasion of the move.

But Cuthbert was not the only northern saint venerated in Northumbria a millennium ago. Wilfrid (d. 709) had been like Cuthbert both monk and bishop. After his death his mortal remains were deposited at one of his monastic foundations, Ripon, and there venerated. John of Beverley (d. 721), bishop successively of Hexham and of York, retired in later life to his monastery at Beverley where he was venerated as a saint after his death. Both these cults continued to be lively in the tenth and eleventh centuries, as did also other cults, lesser and more localized, at places hallowed by association with the heroes and heroines of early Northumbrian Christianity commemorated by Bede: the murdered King Oswin at Tynemouth, Bishop Acca at Hexham and many others.

It is important to grasp that these saints, though dead in the flesh, were considered to be spiritually alive. They were sources of holy energy which could be activated, 'switched on', by appropriately devout behaviour at their shrines. Seemly behaviour meant humility, supplication, propitiation. In a society where every variety of social transaction required by custom the lubricant of gift and counter-gift, saintly favour could best be secured by the giving of gifts, the more expensive the better. When King Athelstan visited the shrine of St Cuthbert at Chester-le-Street on his way to attack the Scots in 934 he is said to have presented the saint with gold and silver church plate, ecclesiastical vestments (some of which may still be seen at Durham), a cross of gold and ivory, luxury manuscripts, bells, candelabra, drinking horns chased in gold and silver, golden arm-rings, banners, a large quantity of cash and a big landed estate at Wearmouth. His subsequent campaign against the Scots was entirely successful.

Relics, then, attracted pilgrims, whether they were kings seeking victory in war who brought royal gifts, or the humblest labourer who sought a cure for sickness or disability, the widow who contributed her mite. The shrines themselves, and their settings of church and enclosure, were sacred places. Their sanctity was recognized and enforced by the public authority of Church and state. They became legal sanctuaries where asylum might be sought. Breaches of sanctuary were punished by exceptionally heavy fines and fearsome manifestations of saintly rage; their polluting effects required the ritual cleansing of the shrine that had been defiled. Special sanctuaries of this kind existed at Beverley and Ripon, at York Minster, at Durham and at Hexham. A twelfth-century writer described the holy of holies in the church of Hexham, the reliquary of its patron saints adjacent to the altar alongside which stood 'the stone chair which in English is called the *frith-stool*', which literally means 'peace seat'. This sanctuary chair, simple, solid and dignified, can still be seen at Hexham, as can a similar one at Beverley. They are tangible reminders of one of the ways in which a violent society sought to limit and control aggression.

After the saints it was the great aristocratic families who mattered in Northumbria. These people are elusive. The modern historian has pitifully inadequate sources for investigating them, their relationships, their doings. We can assemble all the references to them in the surviving narrative accounts which are without exception brief and often far from reliable. We can collect names from what are called 'diplomatic' as opposed to narrative sources. A *diploma*, often simply called a *charter*, was the formal written record of a grant of property made by a king. Its text was followed by a list of witnesses, prominent persons who attested the transaction and acted as its guarantors. Analysis of the names in witness lists allows us to draw inferences about the magnates of the English kingdom. Finally, we can attend to patterns of name-giving. Certain names, or name elements, tended to run in individual aristocratic families, in this period as in others more recent, over several generations. As a rough-and-ready rule of thumb we should be prepared at least to entertain the possibility that persons of similar name could have been kinsfolk. This is precious little to go on. As one historian has recently observed, 'there is much silence in the early history of Northumbria'.[1] We must grope our way as best we can.

'King Eric [Bloodaxe] was treacherously killed by Maccus in a certain lonely place which is called Stainmore, betrayed by Earl Oswulf: and then afterwards King Eadred ruled in these districts.'[2] So a typically laconic entry in one of our narratives. Stainmore – the name means 'rocky moor' – is indeed a lonely place, one of the bleakest spots in England, at the high point where the Roman road from Catterick to Carlisle (now the A66) swings across the roof of the Pennines before dropping down into Westmorland and the valley of the Eden. Maccus was a Norwegian enemy of Eric. After the latter's slaying, the whole of Northumbria fell under the notional authority of the king of Wessex, Eadred. An earl of Northumbria was appointed to administer it. That appointee was Oswulf, the man who had betrayed Eric to his death. Oswulf was also the grandfather of Earl Uhtred who was himself to die by treachery, as we know, some sixty years later.

Oswulf belonged to a very distinguished magnate family which was just possibly descended from one of the bloodlines that made up the tangled skein of the royal kin-groups of pre-Viking Northumbria. For at least three generations his forebears had ruled an Anglian principality which had held out against the Viking invaders in the northern half of what had been the kingdom of Northumbria. Their principal residence and fortress had been at Bamburgh, and it was as 'high-reeves' of Bamburgh that they were sometimes described in

GENEALOGICAL TABLE 2
THE HOUSE OF BAMBURGH

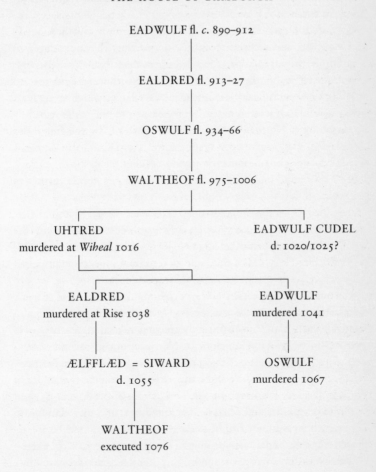

EADWULF fl. *c.* 890–912

EALDRED fl. 913–27

OSWULF fl. 934–66

WALTHEOF fl. 975–1006

UHTRED
murdered at *Wiheal* 1016

EADWULF CUDEL
d. 1020/1025?

EALDRED
murdered at Rise 1038

EADWULF
murdered 1041

ÆLFFLÆD = SIWARD
d. 1055

OSWULF
murdered 1067

WALTHEOF
executed 1076

our diplomatic sources. It's a puzzling title. The Old English term *heahgerefa*, 'high-reeve', is of very rare occurrence and in surviving tenth-century sources was only ever applied to members of this Northumbrian dynasty. A chronicler writing in Latin rendered it as *dux*, the usual term for 'earl', the highest-ranking nobleman below the king. As we shall see, some contemporaries judged that the high-reeves of Bamburgh were of even more exalted status than that.

Bamburgh is on the coast of modern Northumberland just to the south of Lindisfarne. The present-day village, which straggles a little way inland, is dominated by a rock at the sea's edge which is crowned by a Norman castle extensively rebuilt by the first Lord Armstrong, the armaments magnate, in the 1890s. The sea has retreated since the Anglo-Saxon period, leaving the castle on its rock lapped by sand-dunes. In Oswulf's day the sea penetrated further to the west, so that the rock would probably have been almost entirely surrounded by water at high tide.[3] The rock of Bamburgh is the strongest natural fortress on England's north-east coast. Before the development of sophisticated siege-engines it must have been well-nigh impregnable. No wonder the high-reeves chose it as their principal base.

It would be more accurate to say 'maintained' instead of 'chose'. Bamburgh had been closely associated with Northumbrian rulership from an early date; unsurprisingly, having regard to its defensive potential. The unitary kingdom of Northumbria in the pre-Viking period had been made up of two provinces, named Deira and Bernicia. Deira comprised Yorkshire and Lancashire, Bernicia the remainder of Northumbria to the north of the Tees. Deira and Bernicia were in origin two separate and often hostile kingdoms, and the relationship between them continued to be prickly even after they had been harnessed together under a single king in the seventh century. This sense of separation into two Northumbrian provinces, paired but distinct identities, long continued to be felt and significantly underlay the turbulent events of our tenth- and eleventh-century story.

Bamburgh seems to have been the principal centre of Bernician royal power in the shadowy sixth century when the Anglian invaders first established themselves in the north. It was one of the favoured residences of Bernician kings in the seventh century, and when they became

Christian they established their earliest bishopric and monastery at nearby Lindisfarne. After the Danish conquest of Deira in the 870s Bernicia remained in Anglian hands, a principality to all intents and purposes independent under its dynasty of high-reeves. A tenth-century annalist in Ireland could refer to them as 'kings of the Saxons [i.e. English] of the north'. A contemporary chronicler in Wessex revealingly numbered among 'all the *kings*' who submitted to Athelstan at the bridge over the Eamont in 927 Ealdred of Bamburgh, the father of Earl Oswulf. The spiritual needs of this effectively independent state were catered for by the successors of the community at Lindisfarne, the bishop and clergy of St Cuthbert's Land at Chester-le-Street. Relations between the bishops and the high-reeves were close and friendly. Indeed, it is likely that some of the tenth-century bishops were drawn from the ruling dynasty.

Oswulf's advancement from high-reeve of Bamburgh to earl of all Northumbria was presumably connected with the murky circumstances of the death of Eric Bloodaxe. By betraying Eric to his foe Maccus, Oswulf had rid King Eadred of a dangerous enemy and was rewarded by a grateful sovereign with the administration of that enemy's kingdom of York (or Deira). That is one way of looking at things. But not all the parties would necessarily have regarded the transactions in this straightforward way. The high-reeve of Bamburgh and earl of Northumbria was more a vassal prince than a mere royal official. This ambiguity in the relationship between kings of England and earls of Northumbria is an important element in our story. Having got rid of Eric by none too scrupulous means, did the vassal prince simply help himself to Deira? Could King Eadred in distant Winchester do more than acquiesce? From some perspectives – and especially perhaps from that of Oswulf's numerous, loyal and warlike retainers and clients – it could have looked like that. We must remember that Oswulf's family had been ruling for a century with little interference from outside; the kings of Wessex were interlopers whose fragile claims on the north dated back barely more than a generation. Who was most afraid of whom? To what limits might power be tested in this new relationship? Who had most to offer to the other? These were the unspoken questions that hung between king and earl in the years after Eric's death.

Here is another, related, area of uncertainty. When the high-reeves of Bamburgh found their sphere of authority enlarged by the acquisition of Deira they would have been confronted by the need to negotiate a new set of relationships through which to assert it. Of course, they would not have been complete strangers in southern Northumbria. They very likely owned estates south of the Tees. They would certainly have had to travel across Deira from time to time in paying visits to the royal court: our earliest sighting of Oswulf, indeed, shows him subscribing a royal diploma, in other words attending the royal court, at Nottingham in 934. Nevertheless, this was unfamiliar territory. There was not in Yorkshire the inherited, the carefully cherished, the intimately understood network of kin and dependants that there was up in Bernicia.

The most important person in tenth-century Yorkshire was the archbishop of York. The see of York was slightly older than that of Lindisfarne, and as an *arch*bishop, or metropolitan, its prelate was in a formal sense the most senior churchman in the north of England – though the bishop and clergy of St Cuthbert's see would have been reluctant to concede this. In one critical respect the fortunes of the church of York had differed from those of the church of Lindisfarne in the immediate past. Whereas for the clergy of Lindisfarne the Viking assault had meant several vexatious, damaging but essentially *intermittent* attacks, for the archbishop and cathedral community of York it had involved the *permanent* presence of conquerors and settlers in the city of York and nearby. York itself was the seat of the Scandinavian rulers of Deira from the 870s to the 950s. The contemporary poet Egil Skalla-grimsson memorably evoked Eric Bloodaxe in his hall at York,

> where the king kept his people cowed
> under the helmet of his terror.
> From his seat at York he ruled unflinchingly
> over a dank land.

Archaeologists have been able to pinpoint with some confidence where Eric's royal hall stood. Archbishop and Viking king lived side by side.

People who share space cannot for ever live at daggers drawn. From quite soon after the Danish conquest and settlement in the 870s there were signs of mutual accommodation. An early Danish ruler of York, Guthfrith, who died in 895, became a Christian of sorts and was buried beneath York Minster. Archbishop Wulfstan I (931–56) was viewed in southern eyes as a man who was all too accommodating to Eric Bloodaxe. A traitor to his lord the king of England? But it would depend (we must reiterate) on the angle from which you looked. Allegiance to a southern king was neither natural nor normal for such as Wulfstan. That southern political control had recently been imposed at the sword's point by King Athelstan and the turbulent events in Deira since his death had shown how fragile it was. No one could have told how long it might last. Archbishops, like secular lords, had to look cannily in all directions at once. A prudent man needed friends in every quarter.

In the event Archbishop Wulfstan seems to have been eased into retirement soon after Eric's death and the reimposition of West Saxon control in Deira. (Our fragmentary sources are particularly reticent about these probably uncanonical goings-on.) His successors were all men whose origins seem to have lain in the south-east midlands, in the Mercian/East Anglian region. They were evidently royal appointments. This is an important part of an answer to one of the questions posed above, because who had the loudest say in the appointment of the higher clergy was as clear a test of power, in this period, as any. The archbishopric of York was never allowed to become the pocket-bishopric of a magnate family (as that of Chester-le-Street had perhaps been, at any rate intermittently, for the high-reeves of Bamburgh). In addition to this, from 962 onwards every archbishop of York for the next sixty years held the southern bishopric of Worcester jointly with that of York. This highly irregular pluralism was winked at by the southern English bench of bishops, loyal to a man to their master the king, because it helped to peg York's loyalties firmly to the south. Kings often find it useful to have an ecclesiastical 'establishment' which is pliable.

Would the earldom of Northumbria become the pocket-earldom of the house of Bamburgh? It is another question surrounded by ambiguities. Kings wanted to control the succession to great offices in secular as in ecclesiastical affairs; of course they did. Yet it often made sense to grant the reversion to a kinsman of the previous incumbent. He would be the man on the spot, the man with local standing and influence, the man best placed to maintain the networks and relationships built up by his father (or uncle, or cousin, or brother). As we saw in the last chapter, East Anglia was run, under the crown, by a single family, father and then two sons, over a period of sixty years. But Northumbria was not East Anglia.

Earl Oswulf's sole governance of both Bernicia and Deira seems to have lasted about fourteen years. (Once more we face formidable problems of chronology which I pass over here.) In 966 a certain Oslac seems to have become ealdorman of Deira. It is possible that he was related to Oswulf in some way: so much is suggested by the 'Os' element in his name. A rival conjecture is that Oslac came from further south, seeing that his son can be connected in one surviving document with Cambridgeshire. Whether or not he was a kinsman of Oswulf, the important point is that the earldom of all Northumbria had been divided into a shared northern command, with Oswulf in Bernicia and Oslac in Deira; and this cannot have been effected by any other authority than the king.

Oslac seems to have been a loyal subject of King Edgar. A rough indicator to this effect is the frequency of his attestation of royal diplomas between 966 and the king's death in 975. But if, after the death of Oswulf at an unknown date, Oslac was permitted to govern all of Northumbria, he too was at some stage provided with a colleague. A certain Eadwulf, nicknamed 'Evil-child' – perhaps in allusion to a tearaway youth? – was given the ealdormanry of Bernicia, while Oslac presided over Deira. (One might suspect some connection of kinship here: an earlier high-reeve of Bamburgh, the father of Ealdred who submitted to Athelstan in 927, had been named Eadwulf.) We shall shortly encounter the two men, Oslac and Eadwulf, acting together on an important diplomatic mission in the year 973.

Two years later Oslac was broken, and sent into exile abroad.

The valiant man Oslac was driven from the country, over the tossing waves, the gannet's bath, the tumult of waters, the homeland of the whale; a grey-haired man, wise and skilled in speech, he was bereft of his lands.[4]

Why? We possess no further evidence relating to this episode and have to resort to guesswork. The year of King Edgar's death, 975, was followed by a disputed succession. It is tempting to connect the fall of Earl Oslac with the disturbances attendant upon it. Perhaps he supported the loser in the struggle over the succession. If this were the case, the king who won, Edward, was evidently able to intervene actively in northern affairs.

If Eadwulf Evil-child was swept from office in the same civil violence – for we hear no more of him – then Bernicia fell vacant too. The new incumbent there was Waltheof, son of Oswulf and father of Uhtred. In Deira, on the other hand, the new ealdorman was a certain Thored. We know nothing for certain of his family connections. He might have been the son of Oslac; he might have been the Thored son of Gunnar who is recorded ravaging Westmorland (in circumstances of which we know nothing whatsoever) in 966. We shall return to these questions in a later chapter. All that is certain about him is his name, which was not Old English but Old Norse.

In considering the secular élite of Deira or Yorkshire we are confronted at once by the problem of Scandinavian settlement in eastern England in the course of the Viking age. This has for long been the focus of lively, sometimes intemperate, controversy among historians. Was Scandinavian settlement a mass migration of land-hungry peasant farmers such as to effect a changed ethnic balance in the regions where they established themselves? Or was it the settlement of a much smaller number of Viking warlords who ousted the existing Anglian élite but left intact the lower ranks of society who continued to plough and reap as before, but for different landlords? Common sense (not invariably a conspicuous party to academic discussion) would suggest that any plausible answer is bound to be nuanced. Settlement took place over a long period of time in the course of the ninth and tenth centuries; it occurred across an enormous swathe of eastern England from Suffolk to North Yorkshire, and westwards in Lancashire, Westmorland and Cumberland, and in the Isle of Man; it embraced arable lowlands, upland sheep country, maritime and wetland where fishing was the prime source of livelihood, and (as we shall see in more detail shortly) thriving urban environments. Migrants of all epochs have tended to be a mixed bunch: the individual, desperate or enterprising as the case may be, will be balanced by the family group; there will be male and female, the adult, the child and the infant. Even had we all the evidence we might desire – and of course we haven't – generalization would be almost impossible.

About the lordly levels in Deira we can be reasonably confident. On the analogy with marginally better documented circumstances elsewhere, the Scandinavian rulers of York would undoubtedly have rewarded their followers with lands. The rulers wouldn't have lasted long if they had neglected to. The evidence of the names of these élite groups, where we can learn them, is decisive; for they are markedly Scandinavian in character. Here are three examples from the East Riding of Yorkshire. In 963 King Edgar granted an estate at Newbald to one Gunnar (conceivably the father of Thored who became ealdorman of Deira in or after 975); sometime between 978 and 1016 a certain Arnketel granted land at Lockington to the Fenland monastery of Ramsey; and not long afterwards a landowner named Ulf built a church at Aldbrough on the Yorkshire coast and had this fact recorded on an inscribed sundial. Gunnar, Arnketel and Ulf are all Scandinavian personal names. Other evidence supports the contention. For example, the sculpture of memorial gravestones in a Scandinavian artistic style suggests patrons as well as craftsmen of Scandinavian taste. A particularly fine collection of 'hogback' tombstones in the church of Brompton, just outside Northallerton, suggests the presence of such patrons in the vicinity. Or again, consider the place-names known as 'Grimston hybrids': that is, where an Old English suffix, -ton (from *tun*, 'a village') is tacked on to a prefix formed by a Scandinavian personal name in the genitive case. Even scholars are (nearly) all agreed that a place called 'Grim's *tun*' announces the takeover of an existing English estate by a new Scandinavian lord named Grim. There are plentiful examples in Yorkshire: Barkston, Flixton, Foston, Oulston, Saxton, Toulston and several more.

This is not to assert that all the aristocratic élite of tenth-century Yorkshire was of Scandinavian blood; of course not. There were cases of intermarriage between incomers and natives, probably far more than we shall ever know about. Ethnic mixture occurred. This was an Anglo-Scandinavian élite. The point is that the markers indicated above – personal names, sculpture, place-names – are of extremely frequent occurrence in Yorkshire, almost entirely lacking north of the Tees in Bernicia. The two halves of Northumbria were in this respect distinct.

The evidence of place-names suggests that Old Norse, the language of Denmark and Norway, became widespread in Yorkshire. This is evidence which makes it difficult to resist the conclusion that at least in certain areas the rural settlement of immigrants must have been fairly dense. It is not just that large numbers of Yorkshire villages have names terminating in the characteristically Old Norse suffixes -by and -thorp, such that Danby means 'settlement of Danes' and Bishopthorpe 'the [arch]bishop's estate'. Take the place-name Helperby in the North Riding of Yorkshire. It means the -by (or settlement) of a woman with the Old Norse name Hjálp. The people who called it that used the Old Norse inflexional genitive in -er, rather than the Old English genitive in -es, to define it: Hjálp-er-by rather than Hjálp-es-by. It surely follows that Old Norse was the language of everyday speech in the area round Helperby, and this is likely to indicate a fairly thick scattering of immigrants at a lowly social level. Other evidence would seem to point in the same direction. Minor topographical features such as fields, streams and woods often have Old Norse names in Yorkshire. Many dialect words also derive from Old Norse originals: some are still in use even today, as for instance the word ings, mentioned near the beginning of this chapter.

A definitively Scandinavian archaeology of rural settlement in Deira is oddly meagre, though not wholly lacking. By contrast, the celebrated excavation of the Coppergate site in York between 1976 and 1982 revealed the extent of the Scandinavian contribution to the economic life of the city in the tenth and eleventh centuries. Coppergate is itself a street-name derived from Old Norse, like so many others in the city of York: koppari-gata, 'the street of the wood-turners'. The sodden subsoil preserved the houses and workshops of the people who lived there a thousand years ago: their clothes and shoes, combs, tools, coins, cups and bowls, gaming-pieces and skates, all now to be seen in the Jorvik Museum. It also yielded up imported objects, evidence of trade across what the annalist who recorded Oslac's banishment called the whale's home or the gannet's bath. There were whetstones of Norwegian schist for sharpening the cooper's tools; handsome pitchers of the ceramic known as Badorf ware from Germany, presumably for the import of Rhenish wine; necklaces of amber from the Baltic; quernstones of the lava found at Niedermendig near Mainz. And there were too more exotic objects, indicators of more remote contacts: silk from Constantinople, a cowrie shell from the Red Sea, a coin from Samarkand which had travelled over three thousand miles before coming to rest in York. We need to ask ourselves how much that was perishable and leaves no archaeological trace was imported alongside the imperishable. Did spices as well as cowrie shells and coins make their way from the Middle East to York? Perhaps they did.

Coppergate and other sites in York furnish evidence of a crowded, busy, vibrant urban life. Wealth was being created in tenth-century York and we can see some of the uses to which it was being put. The urban bourgeoisie built parish churches in the city such as St Mary Castlegate, just next door to Coppergate, built by Grim and Aese, also a Scandinavian name, in about the year 1000, as its dedication stone records. Some of the more venturesome diversified into the money business: among the capitalists who ran the York mint under licence from the king were many with Scandinavian names. Sometimes they invested in landed property outside the city. Doubtless they bought all sorts of status trophies – fur coats, wine, gold and silver jewellery – which have left no trace because they perished, were consumed or were melted down for coin when times were hard. After their deaths they might be commemorated with one of the gravestones decorated in Scandinavian style which were discovered beneath the present York Minster in the 1970s.

The monk Byrhtferth of Ramsey, writing in about the year 1000, estimated the population of York at about 30,000. Modern historians have unanimously pooh-poohed this figure as grotesquely exaggerated. The trouble is that Byrhtferth was a noted mathematician who was careful with figures. If a witness of his character asserts that a given town had such-and-such a population he deserves to be taken seriously. If we cannot prove him right, neither can we prove him wrong.

Whatever might have been its population, York was a big, thriving city by the standards of the eleventh century. What needs emphasis is that it was, in Northumbria, unique. The characteristic Northumbrian settlement of that age that was a little bit more than a village – a

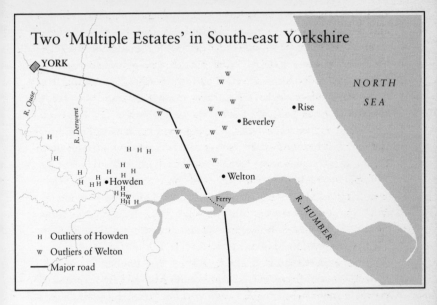

Two 'Multiple Estates' in South-east Yorkshire

YORK

R. Ouse

R. Derwent

NORTH SEA

Rise

Beverley

Welton

Howden

Ferry

R. HUMBER

H   Outliers of Howden
w   Outliers of Welton
──── Major road

necessary circumlocution if the word 'town' is to be avoided – was a centre for lordly consumption. Such a settlement was very frequently the central component of what is known as a 'multiple estate'. A multiple estate may be defined as a unit of agrarian exploitation organized round a central settlement to which the inhabitants of outlying subsidiary settlements, sometimes a considerable distance away, are required to render goods and services, and at which they must attend to observe legal and administrative routines. The map above illustrates two such multiple estates in the south-east of Yorkshire, based at Howden and Welton. Howden had been in royal hands in the middle years of the tenth century, and it is a reasonable guess that it had come into the king's possession in the wake of the imposition of West Saxon control after the fall of Eric Bloodaxe. After passing to other owners Howden was back in the king's hands by 1066; William I granted it to the bishopric of Durham in about 1080. Welton's history is less fully known but may have run along parallel lines; it too ended up in Durham's possession during the reign of the Conqueror. These were valuable estates, extending over several thousand acres apiece and comprising varied resources in arable, pasture, woodland, marshes and rivers. No less than ten miles separated the most north-westerly outlier of Howden, at Riccall on the River Ouse, from the most south-easterly at Yokefleet on the Humber. Both estates were notably well situated with regard to communications, with easy access to the principal ferry across the Humber and to the main road up to York, and ready-made waterways for travel by ship on the Ouse, Trent, Humber or North Sea.

Multiple estates went under various names in early medieval England. In Northumbria they were most commonly, if confusingly, known as *shires*, the word being often tacked on to the name of the central place as in Allertonshire, Howdenshire, Weltonshire, Richmondshire, Hexhamshire, Norhamshire and so on. They were not the only form of agrarian estate organization to be found in Northumbria: there existed large numbers of smaller and more compact landed units. But they were of very frequent occurrence in the north, thicker on the ground there than in England south of the Humber. An important point lurks here about social structure. Multiple estates required for their smooth running a range of what today might be called 'managerial' skills. The services rendered were often honourable rather than menial in character, such as escorting one's lord, providing facilities for hunting, carrying messages (always a highly responsible duty in largely illiterate societies). Participation in the administration of justice needed not only knowledge of law and custom but the ability to command respect for arbitrations, judgements and decisions. Enforcement required the rank and resources of men who owned horses and could bear arms. In other words, a multiple estate needed persons who came somewhere between the lord at the top and the slave or peasant cultivators at the bottom; persons of a certain weight and wealth, of the sort who would be called 'yeomanry' or 'gentry' in a later age. These were the sort of people who formed the network of clientage that clustered round the great magnates of Church and state such as the archbishops of York or the earls of Northumbria. They were men to be reckoned with.

It used to be thought that the distinctive forms of social organization generated and maintained by the multiple estates were a by-product of Scandinavian settlement. It is now clear that the multiple estate system – for it may well have been more systematic than now appears in the surviving sources – goes back to a very remote, possibly prehistoric antiquity. However, if the multiple estate can no longer be attributed to Scandinavian custom, there was plenty in the institutional life of tenth- and eleventh-century Yorkshire which can be. The three ridings – North, East and West – into which Yorkshire was divided for administrative purposes derived their name from an Old Norse term meaning 'a third part'. Subdivisions of the ridings were frequently if not invariably known as *wapentakes*, the word again deriving from Old Norse. For example, Wighill (if correctly identified with *Wiheal*), where Earl Uhtred was murdered in 1016, lies in the wapentake of Ainsty – another Old Norse name – which is the area to the west of York bounded by the rivers Ouse, Wharfe and Nidd. The legal peculiarities of those large parts of eastern England which had come under Scandinavian influence are reflected in the term 'Danelaw' which we met in chapter 2. The words employed for all sorts of social arrangements, from land measurement to indications of rank, were frequently drawn from Old Norse roots. One such term was the word *hold*, a designation of exalted social rank reckoned equivalent to that of high-reeve in one document which has come down to us. The district-name Holderness in south-east Yorkshire, which comprises the wedge-shaped territory between the Humber to the south and the North Sea coast below Flamborough Head to the east, is thought to mean 'the district subject to the authority of the *hold*'. Whoever was the lord of Holderness must have been a very great magnate indeed.

Now the only figure known to have held this rank in Yorkshire in the eleventh century was Thurbrand the Hold, Earl Uhtred's murderer. Thurbrand's descendants owned land in Holderness; it is a reasonable assumption that they had inherited it from him. It is therefore tempting to identify Thurbrand as the *hold* who gave his name to Holderness, and to situate the nucleus of his landed power in that territory at diametrically the opposite end of Northumbria from that of his victim, Uhtred of Bamburgh.

One way of interpreting the enmity between Uhtred and Thurbrand is as a tension between Bernicia and Deira, north and south within Northumbria, between Anglian and Anglo-Scandinavian, between rival families and their support networks in a contest for power.

Historians today like to debate the propriety of applying the term 'feud' to such contests. One such historian of eleventh-century Northumbria, William Kapelle, has suggested that the conflict which divided the families of Uhtred and Thurbrand was 'not a straightforward blood feud at all'.[5] It is not clear what significance the adjective 'straightforward' bears in this context. That puzzlement apart, however, the writer seems to have judged that because the conflict was about regional power in Northumbria it could not simultaneously have been a feud. But this is to misread the cultural context. There was no separation between social behaviour on the one hand and political action on the other. Disputes about honour could also be disputes about territory and power. Significantly, among the multifarious senses of the Latin word *honor* when used by writers from this period were such notions as 'lands' and 'office', as well as 'honour' in our modern sense and 'dignity'.

Be this as it may, it is not inconceivable that Thurbrand might have hoped that Canute would reward him for the slaying of Uhtred with the earldom of Northumbria. But Canute didn't: he gave it to a Scandinavian crony, his brother-in-law, instead. However, there was a further element in the enmity between Uhtred and Thurbrand which is revealed in a tantalizing sentence in our principal narrative, the Durham anonymous referred to in chapter 1. 'Uhtred married Sige, the daughter of Styr, the son of Ulf, a wealthy and prominent man; her father gave her to Uhtred on condition that he would slay his deadliest enemy, Thurbrand.' This thickens the plot considerably. To put it in another way, Uhtred was bought with a wife (who doubtless came with a handsome dowry) to act as a kind of contract killer on behalf of his father-in-law. Insistent questions at once crowd in. Who was Styr Ulfsson? Why was Thurbrand his enemy? Why did Styr invite Uhtred to act for him in this sinister and bloody bargain? Frustratingly, we simply cannot answer these questions from the sources at our disposal. The words that I have translated above as 'a wealthy and prominent man' are in the original Latin of our text *civis divitis* which literally means '(of) a rich citizen'. Successive historians have grasped at the urban connotations of the word 'citizen' and cast Styr Ulfsson as a citizen of York. But this is implausible. It is in the highest degree unlikely that a citizen of York, however rich, could ever have aspired to a marriage connection with so grand a figure as Earl Uhtred; or that Uhtred would ever have stooped to so humble a *mésalliance*. The word *civis*, from the pen of an eleventh-century writer, need not indicate 'citizen' in any urban sense. Writers of that epoch employed it also simply to indicate social prominence: that meant landed wealth and power. Styr the son of Ulf, in view of the Old Norse names borne by him and his father, is likely to have been a Deiran rather than a Bernician grandee. A man of this name attested royal diplomas conveying land in Derbyshire, contiguous to Deira, and he possessed estates in Teesdale, on the northern fringes of Deira, which he granted to the church of St Cuthbert at Durham. It is just faintly possible that another of his estates is commemorated in the village named Stearsby, 'Styr's settlement', some ten miles due north of York. Why Styr and Thurbrand should have been deadly enemies is anyone's guess. All one can say is that neighbouring magnate families often are at odds. Presumably Styr judged it advantageous to engage the assistance of the most powerful man in Northumbria to pursue his enmity with Thurbrand. Did Uhtred, the Bernician, see in the whole business – marriage, dowry, the violent removal of the lord of Holderness – a way of consolidating his influence in the southern half of his earldom, Deira? Perhaps he did. But Uhtred delayed and, as we know, Thurbrand struck first.

Uhtred owed his prominence not simply to wealth and descent but also to military prowess, and in particular to his exploits as a young man against the Scots. Here is the story as committed to writing by the Durham anonymous some sixty years or more after Uhtred's death.

In the reign of Ethelred, King of the English, King Malcolm of the Scots, son of King Kenneth, having gathered the army of all Scotland, devastated the province of the Northumbrians by fire and slaughter and surrounded Durham in a siege . . . Waltheof, who was Earl of Northumbria, shut himself up in Bamburgh. He was indeed of great age and so too old to be able to make a stand against the enemy . . . His son Uhtred [was] a young man of great energy and highly skilled in war . . . Seeing the land laid waste by the enemy and Durham besieged and his father unable to act, the young warrior gathered the army of the Northumbrians and the people of Yorkshire, no small force, and slaughtered almost all the Scottish host; whose king himself only just escaped by fleeing with a few men. Uhtred had the heads of the dead made more presentable with their hair braided, as was then the custom, and transported to Durham; there they were washed by four women, and fixed on stakes round the ramparts. They gave the women who had washed the heads a cow each as payment.

The battle took place, probably, in 1006. It makes a fine and gruesome yarn. The display of the heads of the enemy dead on stakes is credible. There was good biblical warrant for the practice in Judas Maccabeus' treatment of the head of Nicanor: 'He hanged also Nicanor's head upon the tower, an evident and manifest sign unto all of the help of the Lord' (2 Maccabees xv.35). In addition, we possess plentiful anthropological observation of this most public way of demonstrating the defeat and shaming of an enemy, as well as some near-contemporary medieval parallels.

The background to these events was the rise of a new and assertive monarchy in northern Britain in the course of the tenth century. If Northumbrian history is poorly documented, the early development of Scottish kingship is barely documented at all. Its evolution, of which we have no more than hints, runs something along these lines. In the heyday of Northumbrian kingly power in the seventh and eighth centuries, Anglian rule had stretched as far north as the Firth of Forth and as far west as Galloway and Ayrshire. It had extended, at any rate intermittently, over most of what is now Scotland to the south of the Forth–Clyde line, subjugating a Celtic principality, the British kingdom of Rheged or Strathclyde, which had its spine in the Annandale–Clydesdale corridor along the route of the present-day M74 motorway from Carlisle to Glasgow. Beyond the Forth–Clyde line there lay two further Celtic principalities. To the east there was the kingdom of the Picts, to the west the kingdom of the Scots. The Pictish kingdom had its centre of gravity in the region between the Firth of Forth and the Moray Firth. The Scots, originally immigrants from Ireland in the fifth century, were perched on the fringes of the western mainland and on its adjacent islands from Ardnamurchan south to Kintyre.

In circumstances of deepest, almost impenetrable, obscurity, the Scottish kingdom expanded eastwards at the expense of the Picts in the course of the ninth century, and that enigmatic people disappeared for ever from historical record. This expanding Scottish monarchy found its new territorial focus in the southern part of what had been the Pictish realm, in what is now Fife and Tayside. Royal patronage of the shrine of St Andrew, whose relics had allegedly been brought from Constantinople early in the ninth century, was an important part of the assertion of a royal identity in association with a cult based in the east (somewhat as Athelstan by his patronage associated West Saxon kingship with the northern cult of St Cuthbert). It is surely no coincidence that the name Constantine was taken up by the Scottish ruling dynasty at this time: the secular founder of the city of Constantinople remembered alongside the apostolic founder of the church of Constantinople, in a Scottish kingdom under the patronage of the same apostle whose relics rested at the place in Fife which still bears his name.

The Scottish rulers and their warrior-aristocrats looked with covetous eyes on the much richer lands which lay to the south of the Forth–Clyde line. There, on the west, the British kingdom of Strathclyde had obscurely revived after the Viking onslaught on Northumbria had fatally weakened her Anglian masters. Its rulers had even managed to push their authority down into present-day Cumbria: the choice of Penrith as the venue for the submissions to Athelstan in 927, mentioned in the preceding chapter, is most probably to be taken as indicating that the southern border of Strathclyde lay along the valley of the river Eamont. Over the next generation or so the British rulers of Strathclyde seem to have become clients or vassals of the Scottish kings and can be traced, just about, as such until the final extinction of their dynasty in 1018. Thereafter Scottish kings could and did lay claim to authority not only over Strathclyde proper but also over Cumbria. Who in practice, on the ground, ruled Cumbria was a different matter.

Over to the east, the Scottish kings also looked longingly at Lothian, the northern part of Bernicia. Again we are thwarted by an absence of documentation, but it seems reasonably probable that here once more the troubles of Northumbria at the hands of the Vikings presented opportunities which predators were not slow to grasp. During the tenth century Scottish royal authority crept southwards, little by little, unobtrusively, at the expense of the high-reeves of Bamburgh who were busy nearer home holding out against the Viking rulers of Deira/ York. At some point in the reign of King Edgar, probably in 973, there took place what has long been known, misleadingly, as the 'cession of Lothian'. What this seems to have been was a recognition by the distant English king of a *de facto* occupation of Lothian as far south as the Tweed by the Scots. The agreement was formalized at a meeting of the English royal court attended by King Kenneth II of Scotland: he had been escorted there by the two Northumbrian ealdormen, Oslac and Eadwulf Evil-child, and the bishop of Chester-le-Street.

In the fighting, encroaching, posturing and negotiating which would finally – after several centuries – bring an agreed Anglo-Scottish border into being, an important part was played by the earls of Northumbria in the tenth and eleventh centuries. The 'cession of Lothian' did emphatically *not* create a fixed and stable frontier. Scottish incursions into Bernicia, English incursions into Lothian went on after it just as they had before. Raiding to and fro for cattle and other loot was a part of the borderers' manner of life and would continue to be so for centuries to come: 'bloodthirsty shopping trips', as one modern historian has described the habit.[6] Had the Scottish invasion and siege of Durham in 1006 been successful, it could have resulted in a temporary, even in the longer term a permanent, shifting of the frontier to the line of the river Tyne, even perhaps of the river Tees. As things were, Earl Uhtred's defeat of the invaders served to keep the frontier on the line, apparently, of the Tweed. The earls were, thus, defenders of the northern marches against the king's enemies, or so no doubt they were viewed in far-off Wessex, at least at optimistic moments. Is that how they saw themselves? Uhtred was defending his own land, his own saint; he was relieving his elderly father cut off in Bamburgh. It was family business. It was also a question of the bickering of neighbours. The inhabitants of Lothian were of the same stock as the people of the rest of Bernicia to whom they had been politically linked for four centuries before the 'cession'. They spoke the same northern dialect of English. They farmed the same sort of countryside, fished in the same sea, raised the same sturdy cattle which they then stole from one other. St Cuthbert's church held properties in Lothian: perhaps Uhtred's family did too; perhaps many prominent northern families did as well. Which way did they face?

A fine story was told by our Durham cleric of Earl Uhtred's loyalty to his king. When Canute was attempting to enlist Northumbrian help against King Ethelred, Uhtred responded with the resounding words, 'No reward could persuade me to do what I ought not to. I will serve the king as long as he lives. He is my lord, by whose gift I enjoy riches and honour. I will never betray him.' The words may be the narrator's rather than Uhtred's own, and they may have been necessitated in the narrative context to provide a motive for Canute to compass Uhtred's end by allowing Thurbrand to set up his deadly ambush at *Wiheal*. But as a memory of Uhtred's political probity we cannot disregard the sentiments altogether. They serve to point up the theme of this chapter, the whole complicated and ambiguous matters of Northumbrian identity and Northumbrian loyalties. Who ran Northumbria? Who mattered? Who was answerable to whom, on what occasions, to what ends, for how long, on what conditions? We can feel these questions pulsing through our sources, fragmentary though those sources are. We can sense how troubling, intractable and in the last resort dangerous they were. It was these questions which lay behind Uhtred's murder in 1016.

4

Ethelred the Ill-advised

During the reign of Edgar's younger son, Ethelred, who ruled from 978 until 1016, Danish attacks on the kingdom of England were resumed in strength. After nearly three decades of warfare the English succumbed to the first of their eleventh-century conquests. Paradoxically, it was the very success of the West Saxon dynasty in the course of the tenth century that rendered their kingdom vulnerable. Reduced to its crude essentials, the formula for successful and robust kingship in that era was very simple: expand or go under. Victorious warlords gained lands, treasure, slaves and patronage; with these they could attract followers and reward loyalty. Providing that the rewards were doled out judiciously – and therein lay the art of the operation – kings could not really put a foot wrong. Difficulties would arise only when territorial expansion ceased, for then the stock of rewards would dry up. Of course, this is an oversimplification, which fails to take account of all sorts of adventitious variables: the instinct which makes us wary of historical formulae is a sound one. Nevertheless, one can see the recurrence of this fundamental pattern in other monarchies of that age.

Take the German monarchy. Under the stewardship of Otto I this kingship enjoyed several decades of expansion to the east at the expense of its Slavonic neighbours; after his death in 973 expansion came to an end and the reigns of his son Otto II (973–83) and grandson Otto III (983–1002) were troubled by internal discord. Or take the kingdom of León in north-western Spain. For some eighty years, from about 870 until the middle of the tenth century, it enjoyed a period of fairly consistent territorial expansion at the expense of its neighbours to the south, the Muslims, who had invaded and conquered Spain in the early years of the eighth century. In the second half of the tenth century the roles were reversed. Expansion came to a halt, and the kingdom fell victim to comparable sorts of internal strife.

In England, the heady expansion of the first half of the tenth century under Edward the Elder and his sons had carried West Saxon dominion from the Thames to Northumbria. The kings had ridden high, enriching their loyal warrior aristocracy, Athelstan Half-king and his like, with lands, treasure, office, power and renown. The fruits of this expansion could be enjoyed in the peace of Edgar's reign. But that same reign also generated the tensions which would poison the harmony of the Anglo-Saxon élite. When a king has less to give two consequences follow: a strain is placed upon loyalty; and there is more intense competition for such rewards as are left. Into this framework of mounting tension was inserted a royal determination to endow monastic foundations extremely lavishly with the only form of wealth that was secure and permanent – land.

All the evidence that we have suggests that there was an active land market in tenth-century England. Lands acquired by kings or others in the course of territorial expansion, or lands acquired by kings by way of confiscation from wrongdoers, were available for keeping or for distribution by way of gift, lease or sale: but those who had, or thought they had, a valid title to them, the dispossessed, were still there nursing their grievances. There is an additional point. This was a period when notions about legal title to land and the conventions governing inheritance of land were undergoing change. To put it simply, there was a tendency throughout western Europe for individual rights in land to gain ground at the expense of family rights; for father-to-son succession, a mode of transfer designed to safeguard the integrity of a landed holding, to replace the sharing-out of family land within a wider group of kinsfolk that had previously been a widespread norm. An individual heir may think that he can do as he wishes with his inheritance; his relatives may disagree. Here too can be an occasion of grievance. Grievances, like wounds, can fester and suppurate; if untended they can disperse their poison beyond the point of cure.

Suppose, for example, that a royal favourite such as that West Saxon nobleman Bishop Ethelwold of Winchester employed his characteristically hard-nosed business techniques to acquire an estate from a landed

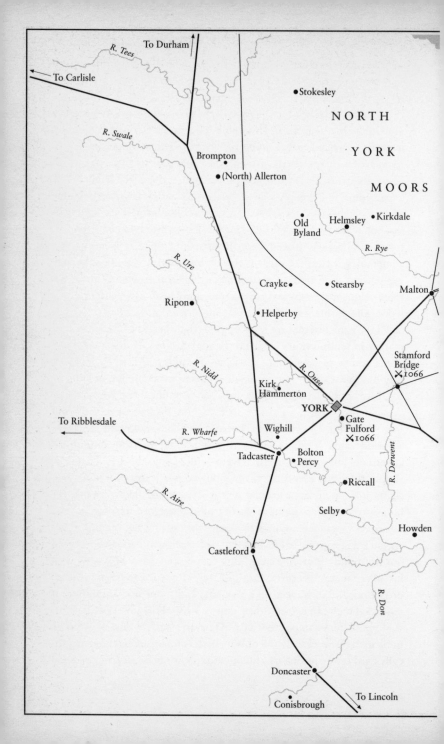

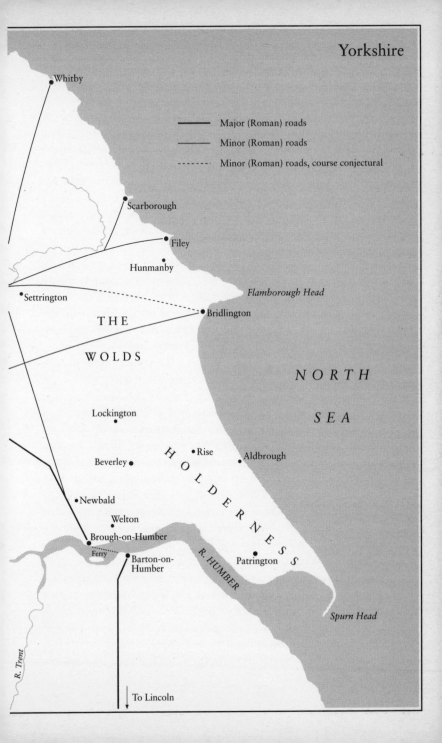

magnate of (let us say) Cambridgeshire named A with which to endow his monastery of Ely. Suppose further that A's kinsman B considered that he had claims to title in that estate which had been overridden by the purchaser. Suppose that at the same time B's ambition to become ealdorman of Cambridgeshire has been thwarted by the king's promotion of B's rival Z to that post. B is a big local figure with an extensive network of kinsfolk, relatives by marriage, friends, neighbours, clients and retainers who share his sense of grievance. They can make life very awkward for Z as he tries to govern the county on the king's behalf. So there you have a flashpoint. In no time at all the shire can spin out of the king's control, and all because of the escalation of a local dispute over land.

That was a hypothetical example: I invented it. Here's a real one. During the 980s a prominent Kentish landowner named Wulfbald seized much property, land and movables, from his stepmother upon his father's death: possibly the property had been settled upon the stepmother by the father, or perhaps she claimed that this had been done; we do not know. This was brought to the attention of the king, who ordered Wulfbald to make restitution. This he refused to do. For this defiance 'his *wergild* was assigned to the king', which means that he became liable to a fine amounting to the very considerable sum of his *wergild* or blood-price. This pattern of summons, defiance and assignment was repeated on no fewer than three subsequent occasions. Wulfbald apparently paid no attention whatsoever. Indeed he even compounded his crimes by seizing land from another kinsman. Then a meeting of the king's council was held in London at which more drastic steps were taken. The king's advisers unanimously agreed that all Wulfbald's property should be forfeit to the king and that he himself should be 'placed at the king's mercy, whether to live or die'. Wulfbald continued to pay no attention and held on to all his properties until his death not long afterwards. He left a widow and a son (both unnamed in our documentary source). At this point the family disputes over property escalated into bloodshed. The widow and the son killed another kinsman, Wulfbald's first cousin Eadmer, and fifteen of his retainers. Eadmer was a 'king's thegn', a man of high rank and weight in the service of the crown. The king seems to have been able to exert his authority then, though unfortunately we are not told precisely how. It seems to have involved the archbishop of Canterbury, who summoned a *mickle synod*, a great church council, at London. Perhaps it was the sanction of excommunication which did the trick. At any rate, all the property at issue came finally into the king's hands. In 996 he donated it to his mother. The document recording the donation rehearsed the tale of Wulfbald's crimes: that's how we know about them.[1]

This most instructive story shows how difficult it was for the king to give effect to decisions which were detrimental to the interests of a powerful local figure; and this in a south-eastern shire where the conjoint authority of king and archbishop was strong. Advanced governmental institutions coexisted with, had to operate in, a culture of lordly manipulation of or disregard for the king's law. It was a culture in which violence lurked in the wings, ever ready to step forth to centre stage and threaten widespread social dislocation.

King Edgar had kept the lid firmly on such simmering dissensions. As was hinted in an earlier chapter, the character of his rule was probably a good deal harsher than is suggested by his sobriquet, 'the Peaceable', and by the image of a devout young man cut off in his prime which was confected later on by grateful monastic chroniclers. After his death in 975 at the age of only thirty-two the dissensions boiled over.

The immediate occasion of turmoil was a disputed succession; not an uncommon occurrence in an era when the rules governing royal succession were much less rigid than they were to become in later centuries. Edgar had been married three times in the course of his short life. At his death he left two young sons. The elder, Edward, had been born to his first wife in about 962. The younger, Ethelred, had been born to his third wife, Ælfthryth, in about 968. The contested succession allowed the opening up of the fissures of tension among the secular and ecclesiastical élites. The partisans of the young Edward came out on top. But Ethelred's supporters had not given up. Their coup, when it came, was violent. Edward was assassinated at Corfe, in Dorset, on 18 March 978 while staying with his stepmother, the queen-dowager Ælfthryth. She was widely suspected of having instigated the murder. We shall never know the truth. At all events she, her son Ethelred and his supporters were the beneficiaries of the deed.

Excepting only 'Bad King John', Ethelred 'the Unready' has the worst reputation of any monarch in the history of England. This is less than wholly just. To begin with that nickname, Ethelred 'the Unready'. When it was coined, whether during his lifetime or not, we don't know: it isn't recorded in surviving sources until nearly two centuries after his death. It doesn't mean 'unready' in our modern sense of 'unprepared'. In origin it was a play on words. The name Ethelred is formed from the Old English words *æthel* and *ræd*, meaning 'noble' and 'counsel': *unræd* means 'no counsel' or 'lack of counsel'. *Æthelræd Unræd*, 'noble counsel, no counsel'. A more appropriate modern rendering might therefore be Ethelred 'the Ill-advised', rather than 'the Unready', meaning either that the king was himself foolish or that he was badly advised by his counsellors, or both.

The historical reality may have been misfortune rather than miscounsel. It was Ethelred's ill-fortune to be confronted by two intractable problems. One of these was the divisive inheritance from his father's reign and his half-brother's murder. The other was the emergence of a strong and aggressive monarchy in Denmark.

The growth of a more robust monarchy in tenth-century Denmark owed much to interactions with its very powerful neighbour, the German *Reich* under the Ottonian dynasty. In this, it was obedient to that tendency for satellite states to grow up on the fringes of imposing cultural and political systems. Danish rulers perceived that the God of the Christians had made their neighbour monarchs victorious, rich and powerful. So they embraced Christianity, and in so doing gave themselves a new orientation or alignment which involved a break with the past. The most tangible evidence of this exists at Jelling, in central Denmark. There, two enormous mounds were constructed for the burial and commemoration of King Gorm 'the Old' (d. 958) and his wife Queen Thyre. Shortly afterwards, in the reign of their son Harald 'Bluetooth', the bodies of his parents were exhumed and re-interred beneath a Christian church built between the two mounds. Outside the church an enormous triple-faceted stone portrays Christ crucified on one face, and on another bears a runic inscription proclaiming that 'King Harald ordered this monument to be made in memory of his father Gorm and his mother Thyre. That Harald won for himself all Denmark and Norway, and made the Danes Christian.'

It was the most public announcement possible of a new cultural and religious allegiance.

As a member of the community of Christian kings, Harald (958–87) grasped the techniques of rulership which they had inherited from a distant Romano-Christian past. Like them he issued coin bearing Christian symbolism, was rumoured to have promulgated laws (they do not survive), and founded churches, in one of which, Roskilde, he was buried. In addition, monuments of an entirely secular character continue to witness to his power. He enlarged and refurbished the *Danevirke*, the enormous eighth-century earthwork which defined a section of the frontier between Danes and Germans. He fortified the important trading town of Hedeby. He built an elaborate causeway and bridge at Ravning Enge near Jelling. Most impressive of all, it was Harald who was responsible for constructing the five military camps located in the northern mainland and eastern islands of Denmark, most likely for the purpose of maintaining control of the regions which he had brought under his authority – and their adjacent sea-lanes. King Harald's ability to 'win Norway for himself' obviously presupposed naval power. It seems likely, though it cannot be demonstrated, that he was able to call on his Danish subjects for levies of ships and their crews with which to forward his enterprises. It is practically impossible to understand his son Sweyn's conquest of England without some such system of ship-levies. Such was the formidable Danish monarchy whose attacks it was King Ethelred II's misfortune to have to face.

There is yet a third way in which Ethelred has been unfortunate, and that lies in the nature of the principal witness to the calamitous events of his reign. That witness is the annalistic work, already referred to more than once, known as the *Anglo-Saxon Chronicle*. This is not the place to enter into the extremely dense and difficult problems presented by the various manuscript versions of the *Chronicle*. Suffice it to say that for Ethelred's reign its narrative becomes detailed and full, so that we can know more about it than we can about the reigns of any others among his predecessors since Alfred a century beforehand. The character of the *Chronicle* as a set of year-by-year annals gives the impression of a compiler who set himself to render an account of each year as it ended. But – and this requires the strongest possible emphasis – such an impression is wholly false. The author of the principal version of the *Anglo-Saxon Chronicle* for the reign of Ethelred the Unready wrote up his account of the entire reign *after it was over*, early on in the reign of his conqueror and successor Canute.

This puts an entirely different complexion on the character and value of his testimony. He was writing with hindsight a story whose tragic end he already knew. He knew that Ethelred's reign would end in ignominy and defeat because it already had. He was writing precisely during that miserable aftermath. He organized his narrative in such a way as to give prominence to military blunders, divided counsels, treacherous dealings; to highlight scapegoats, the king himself and certain among his counsellors. Add to this his compelling stylistic art, his sombre vision, his sorrow and his anger and you have, in sum, a work of considerable literary power which has permanently coloured our interpretation of Ethelred's reign. The chronicler has skewed our image of the king, to his lasting disadvantage.

For a start, consider the phrase 'Danish conquest'. The author of the *Anglo-Saxon Chronicle* knew that Ethelred's reign ended in the conquest of England by Sweyn and his son Canute. He arranged his account of it so that all those troubled years could contribute to and culminate in that catastrophe. But the 'Danish conquest' was not until a very late stage an organized military operation. The renewal of Viking raids early in Ethelred's reign would not have been, could not have been, interpreted by those who experienced them as the beginning of a process that would have its end in the coronation of the as-yet-unborn Canute as king of England.

Even the phrase 'renewal of Viking raids' is a misleading one, implying as it does that this menace had somehow ceased after the expulsion of Eric Bloodaxe from York. Contemporaries knew better. King Eadred had left in his will, in 955, a very large sum of money to his people 'that they may redeem themselves from a heathen army if need be'; in plain words, to buy off the Vikings. It was an eventuality which it was realistic to anticipate. In about 966 or 967, in the middle of the reign of the powerful and peaceful Edgar, a Viking adventurer named Thorgils Skarthi, Thorgils 'of the hare lip', established himself on the Yorkshire coast at Scarborough, 'Skarthi's fortress'. His brother

Kormak Fleinn, Kormak 'the arrow', is said to have taken land at the same time a little way down the coast at Flamborough Head, 'Fleinn's stronghold'. Perhaps it was in the wake of these events that the prehistoric earthwork which cuts off the neck of the Flamborough peninsula acquired the name Danes' Dyke by which it has been known ever since.

We need also to bear in mind that not all seaborne Viking predators were necessarily in the strict sense Danes. There were nests of Viking pirates in other and nearer places such as Ireland and Normandy. The alliance sealed at Chester in 973 by the rowing of Edgar on the Dee could have been, for the princes concerned, as much about a common defensive front against pirates from the Norse settlements in Ireland as about the recognition of an English emperor. The Vikings who had settled in Normandy early in the tenth century – and given their name to it, 'Northmandy' – were capable of mounting piratical expeditions as far as the Atlantic coasts of Spain. How much easier to raid the coastline of southern England, nearer of access and with a much richer hinterland. When the chronicler tells us of a raid on Southampton in 980, we may suspect that the attackers came from Normandy. When he tells us that Cheshire was 'ravaged by a northern naval force' in the same year we may guess at raiders from Viking Dublin. When he tells us that St Petroc's monastery, then at Padstow, was sacked in 981 and the adjacent coasts of Cornwall and Devon plundered, we may suspect that the culprits came from southern bases of the Hiberno-Norse such as Waterford or Wexford. There cannot have been much on the inhospitable coastline of north Devon and Cornwall to attract more distant predators from Harald Bluetooth's Denmark.

Again, there were plenty of freelance warriors who were able to mount their own expeditions, attracting participants in search of booty from all quarters. One such was a certain Olaf Tryggvason, who may have been – we cannot be absolutely sure – among the leaders of the Viking force which was engaged in battle by the English on the coast of Essex in 991 and was there victorious. The encounter inspired one of the greatest of Old English poems, the *Battle of Maldon*, an elegiac celebration of the combat and lament for the slain (the interest of which for our understanding of a feuding culture was briefly alluded to in chapter 1). Three years later, Olaf was back, this time in alliance with Sweyn of Denmark. English diplomacy detached him from his royal ally. At a meeting of the English court at Andover Olaf, already baptized a Christian, was confirmed by the bishop of Winchester, King Ethelred himself being godfather. Loaded with treasure by his new spiritual kinsman, Olaf swore not to trouble England more – 'and kept his promise', as the chronicler observed. Olaf Tryggvason returned to his native Norway, where he became king. Later legend would remember his short and violent reign (995–9) as given over to the Christian evangelization of his subjects and neighbours by no-nonsense strong-arm tactics.

This is to indicate some of the ways in which the distortions of the chronicler may be corrected. What cannot be denied, however, is the sheer weight of enemy pressure upon England which he records. In 997 the south-west was again attacked. In 998 it was the turn of Dorset, in 999 of Kent, in 1001 of Sussex, Hampshire, Dorset and Somerset, in 1003 of Wiltshire, in 1004 of Norfolk, in 1006 of Kent, the Isle of Wight, Hampshire and Berkshire. Ethelred's responses do not indicate a king who was wholly ill-advised. Diplomacy was employed to neutralize individual leaders of warbands such as Olaf. Alliances were negotiated with Normandy to hinder Viking use of Norman ports as bases for cross-Channel raids on England. Ethelred's second marriage, to the duke of Normandy's daughter Emma in 1002, was the seal of this new policy. Military retaliation was attempted. Difficult though it was to pin down a seaborne enemy so elusively mobile, Ethelred could hit a static target effectively, as in the year 1000 when his army ravaged Cumberland and his fleet raided the Isle of Man, presumably in return for assistance to his enemies. He could meet atrocity with atrocity, as when he ordered a massacre of Danes within his authority in 1002.

Unfortunately for Ethelred's reputation, the response for which he is most notorious was the payment of what came to be known as Danegeld – paying the enemy to go away. In fairness to Ethelred one needs to bear in mind that this was a common early medieval response to enemy attack: Frankish, German, Italian and Spanish rulers had used the tactic; so had Alfred, and, as we have seen, King Eadred left money for this very purpose. It is easy to be wise after the event. Only time would tell, in the words of Rudyard Kipling,

That if once you have paid him the Danegeld
You never get rid of the Dane.

Neither was it the craven initiative of a feeble king. The policy of paying the enemy was advised by the archbishop of Canterbury at a council of the king's most senior and responsible counsellors. The *Chronicle* records payments of £10,000 in 991, of £16,000 in 994, of £24,000 in 1002, of £36,000 in 1007, of £48,000 in 1012. These were colossal sums of money by the standards of the day.

The author of the *Anglo-Saxon Chronicle*, to whose detailed if distorted record we owe so much of our knowledge of Ethelred's reign, was writing in southern England. His range of vision rarely strayed as far north as Northumbria. What little we know about Northumbrian affairs during the reign of Ethelred comes in the form of isolated fragments of information often lacking in background and context. To try to compose a history of England's northern provinces during that period is like doing a jigsaw puzzle most of whose pieces are missing. One famous historian of Anglo-Saxon England has even written in despair of 'the lost history of the north'.[2]

To begin with the basics of what is recoverable: the succession of bishops. The reader will recall that the unsatisfactory – from a southern point of view – Archbishop Wulfstan I of York had been removed from his see in obscure, not to say shady, circumstances probably between 952 and 954. His successor, Osketel, was a southerner and a king's man, a member of the Anglo-Danish aristocracy of East Anglia who had been given a bishopric under King Eadred in 949 or 950. That bishopric was Dorchester (Oxon.), whose enormous diocese comprised much of the eastern midlands. (In the following century the seat of the bishopric would be transferred to Lincoln.) His promotion to York indicates that he was regarded in governmental circles as a safe pair of hands. Osketel held the archbishopric until 970 or 971. His successor, Oswald, was not only kin to him – though we don't know precisely how they were related – but was also a nephew of Archbishop Oda of Canterbury (d. 958). Already bishop of Worcester, Oswald retained this see in plurality with York under the irregular arrangement already referred to (in chapter 3) until his death in 992.

He was a prelate of stature, closely associated with King Edgar's monastic policy and himself the founder of Benedictine communities at Westbury, Winchcombe and Ramsey. His successor Ealdwulf had previously served as the royal chancellor (or so it was believed in the twelfth century) and had been the first abbot of the monastery of Peterborough re-founded by that prominent royal servant Bishop Ethelwold of Winchester. He succeeded Oswald as bishop of Worcester in 992 and was promoted to York in 995. (There is a puzzling and unexplained hiatus at York between 992 and 995.) On Ealdwulf's death in 1002 he was replaced at York by Archbishop Wulfstan II, previously a monk (probably at Ely) and bishop of London from 996 to 1002. Wulfstan was archbishop of York from 1002 until 1023: a figure of seminal importance to whom we shall have to return shortly.

At York, then, the record is of a succession of archbishops over a period of nearly seventy years (954–1023) who were men of southern connections and of links with English governing circles. In the other northern see, the cathedral church of St Cuthbert, the pattern is less clear. During Ethelred's reign there were only two bishops. The connections of Bishop Ælfsige of Chester-le-Street (c. 968–90) remain unknown. His successor Ealdhun (c. 990–1018) was 'of noble descent', which presumably indicates connections among the aristocracy of Bernicia. He was certainly connected to them by marriage. His daughter Ecgfrida – presumably born to him before he became a bishop – was the first wife of none other than Earl Uhtred of Northumbria.

In turning from ecclesiastical to secular élites we move from the reasonably knowable to the all-but-irrecoverable. As we saw in chapter 3, Earl Oslac was sent into exile in 975. At the same time Eadwulf of Bernicia disappears from our view. It is a reasonable guess, though only a guess, that these changes had something to do with the faction fighting involved in the disputed succession to King Edgar. Eadwulf's successor in Bernicia seems to have been Waltheof, the son of Earl Oswulf and father of Earl Uhtred, a member therefore of the family of the high-reeves of Bamburgh who had been the uncrowned kings of northern Northumbria for at least a century. The new ealdorman of Deira/Yorkshire, though not securely attested in our records until 979, was named Thored.

Who was Thored? It is desirable to identify him for reasons which will shortly become clear. There are two possible Thoreds in the sources that have come down to us. Earl Oslac himself had a son named Thored, and some investigators have identified this man as Oslac's successor. On the other hand, it seems a little unlikely (though not, of course, impossible) that the son of a man who had just been exiled in the wake of what must have been a major political confrontation would have been preferred to his father's office. The other Thored seems to me to fit the bill a little more comfortably. This second Thored had proven Yorkshire landed connections. He was the son of Gunnar and is on record as having ravaged Westmorland in 966. This Gunnar had received a grant of land at Newbald, near Market Weighton in the East Riding of Yorkshire, from King Edgar in the year 963 to reward 'his most loyal service to the king'. We know that Thored also held extensive estates in the North Riding, three of which, at Crayke, Smeaton and Sutton-on-the-Forest, he gave to the cathedral church of St Cuthbert.

There is a further point of interest concerning the estate at Newbald. Possession of it was disputed between Thored and the archbishop of York. Newbald had been granted to Gunnar in 963. But at some point before 971 Archbishop Osketel bought it from the king for '120 mancuses [= £15] of red gold'. This information comes from a memorandum about the archiepiscopal estates drawn up by Osketel's successor, Oswald. In other words, at some point between 963 and 971 the estate at Newbald had come back into the king's hands. It is tempting to suppose that Thored was deprived of Newbald (and possibly other estates) by the king as a punishment for the ravaging of Westmorland in 966. Now 966 was the year of Oslac's appointment to the ealdormanry of Deira, an item of news suggestively juxtaposed in the text of the *Anglo-Saxon Chronicle* with the information about Thored's ravaging. Admittedly this entry remains, in the judgement of a distinguished authority, 'enigmatical', but a possible reconstruction of events might run like this: Thored, disappointed of the ealdormanry of Deira by the appointment of Oslac, laid waste Westmorland in retaliation, for which he was punished by the king with the dispossession of his estates. But that was not the end of the story. Thored fought back. Archbishop Oswald's memorandum went on to reveal that the Newbald estate had subsequently been seized by Thored. At this point the evidence peters out. We can sense the determination of the archbishops to regain their lost land, and we know that in the longer term they did so because Newbald was back in their possession by 1066. The story is a good example of the way in which local disputes over land underlay the high politics of the period.[3]

But this is not the end of our dossier on Thored. In some ways the most fascinating information of all is that his daughter was the first wife of King Ethelred II. Our source for this is very late – mid twelfth century – but the writer was well-informed and reliable on northern affairs. If it is prudent to repeat the caution of a historian of the Victorian age that Ethelred's first marriage is 'shrouded in some obscurity',[4] nevertheless the leading modern authorities accept the historical reality of the king's marriage to Thored's daughter, by name Ælfflæd. A royal marriage of this character – king to daughter of prominent nobleman – was evidently intended to achieve some political end. Kings marry for policy, not for love. Ethelred married Thored's daughter, as a modern expert on the period, Pauline Stafford, has urged, 'in an attempt to woo him'. In other words, Thored was unamenable to control by other means. It is even possible, as the same historian has speculated, that 'Thored may not even have been a royal appointment'.[5] We can go one cautious step further. There are hints in our sources of some sort of political crisis in Northumbria in the 980s which the king might have tried to calm by taking a northern wife. Whether this was so or not, there do seem to be grounds for supposing that the ruling élite down in Wessex was considerably less confident about the loyalties of the secular leaders of Northumbria than about those of the ecclesiastical. What we can learn and infer about Thored neatly exemplifies the difficulties that southern-based kings had in controlling Northumbria.

In the year 992 King Ethelred planned a large-scale naval expedition against his Viking enemies, 'to entrap them at sea' as the *Anglo-Saxon Chronicle* put it. Earl Thored was appointed one of its leaders. It was an abject failure owing, as the chronicler asserted, to treachery among the leadership. In the following year Northumbria was attacked. Bamburgh (of all places) was sacked and the regions to either side of the Humber were laid waste. An English army sent to disperse the raiders dissolved into ignominious flight. It was as a result of these failures, we may assume, that Thored was relieved of his office. His successor as ealdorman of Deira was Ælfhelm, who had been appointed by the summer of 993.

One chronicler alleged that the English army which failed to stand up to the raiders in Northumbria in 993 so acted because its three leaders 'were Danes on the father's side'. True or otherwise, the observation is valuable as shedding light on southern apprehensions about the loyalty of the Anglo-Scandinavian aristocracy of Deira. Ælfhelm's appointment seems to register a reaction. He was the first ealdorman of Yorkshire of whom we can be absolutely certain that he was not of a Northumbrian family. Not that he came from very far away. Ælfhelm belonged to a distinguished north Mercian family, of which we can learn something from the surviving will of his brother Wulfric (d. 1004), founder of the monastery of Burton-on-Trent, the northernmost foundation of the tenth-century monastic revival. Ælfhelm would remain in office until the year 1006.

Northumbria's difficulties were Scotland's opportunity. King Kenneth II seems to have respected the peace arising from the accord of 973 for some twenty years. But the Northumbrian embarrassments of the years 992–3 may have rendered action irresistible. It was perhaps in 994 that 'the Scots plundered Saxony [i.e. England] as far as Stainmore and Cleveland and the lakes of Deira'.[6] The information comes from a late and garbled source whose bearing is far from clear, and what the writer might have understood by 'the lakes of Deira' (if indeed that is what he wrote) is anyone's guess. But the reliably attested removal of St Cuthbert's clergy from Chester-le-Street to Ripon in 995 looks like a response to a threat from Scotland. Later in the same year they undertook their final move, to a new and immensely well-defended site on a high bluff above the river Wear – Durham, where St Cuthbert has reposed ever since. The move from Ripon to Durham implies a diminution in the danger from Scotland, suggestive in its turn of some successful retaliation for the raid of the previous year. It is probably right to attribute this action to the young Uhtred, 'with whose assistance', as the official historian of Durham was to put it a century later, the building of a new cathedral was begun.[7] If Uhtred did defeat Kenneth in 995, that would tarnish the renown of the king of Scots and render him vulnerable to domestic enemies. Perhaps it was no coincidence that he was killed later in the same year in the course of a bloodfeud. The bits and pieces of evidence, desperately fragmentary though they are, do suggest the outlines of a coherent story for the years 994 and 995. It is noteworthy that not one of them is transmitted to us by the southern compiler of the *Anglo-Saxon Chronicle*. The goings-on in the north took place a long way away from him, in a distant country of which he knew little.

He does, however, tell us of a campaign that took place in the year 1000. Taking advantage of the absence of the Viking army in Normandy, King Ethelred led an army to Cumbria to lay it waste. The operation was presumably in retaliation for assistance to the Scots in 994, or for some later and unknown hostilities. The next campaigning in the north of which we have notice belongs (probably) to the year 1006. This was the occasion alluded to in chapter 3 when King Malcolm II swept down into Northumbria, shutting up the elderly Earl Waltheof in Bamburgh, to besiege Durham, only to be repulsed by Uhtred who decorated the fortifications of Durham with the heads of the slain. The Scots 'left behind them a slaughter of their good men', as an Irish annalist observed.[8] There may also have been territorial changes. Uhtred's victory could have restored English dominion over at least parts of southern Lothian on the north bank of the Tweed.

It was in the wake of these operations that Uhtred was rewarded with the earldom of all Northumbria, Deira or Yorkshire as well as Bernicia. Yorkshire had become vacant owing to the violent removal from the scene of Ealdorman Ælfhelm. The leading modern authority on the reign of Ethelred the Unready has posited 'something approaching a palace revolution' among the royal associates who formed the governing circles of the kingdom.[9] The central figure in this revolution was a Mercian nobleman named Eadric who emerged at this time as the king's principal adviser and retained this position of influence for the remainder of the reign. In 1007 he was promoted to be ealdorman of the whole of Mercia and at about the same time was given the king's daughter Edith in marriage. Eadric's advancement required the fall of rivals: hence Ælfhelm's disappearance from the scene. According to our most detailed narrative, Eadric prepared a great feast at Shrewsbury to which he invited Ælfhelm. Nothing was done by halves; the festivities were stretched out over several days. On the third or fourth day, Eadric took Ælfhelm hunting. He had previously bribed a Shrewsbury butcher named Godwin *Porthund* ('Town-dog') to set an ambush. Ælfhelm was duly murdered. Shortly afterwards his two sons were blinded at the king's command – presumably at Eadric's instigation – again in treacherous circumstances: they were guests of the king at the time, staying with him at the royal estate of Cookham in Berkshire.

Uhtred therefore profited from Ælfhelm's fall, though there is nowhere any suggestion that he was implicated in it. Like Eadric, he too became a son-in-law of the king. It is time to turn our attention to Uhtred's marriages.

At this period marriage had not yet become subject to close ecclesiastical supervision. That was to be a development of the twelfth and thirteenth centuries. True, churchmen regarded it as desirable that marriage should be a lifelong and exclusive partnership between two persons unrelated to one another within the prohibited degrees of consanguinity. In practice, however, it is evident that all sorts of worldly considerations were likely to shape not simply the choice of a marriage partner but also the duration of any given union. 'A certain looseness in the marriage tie is long observable in northern Europe', as a gifted Victorian historian of the age long ago observed.[10] At the exalted social level with which we are here concerned, considerations of property and power tended to shape the strategy of marriage alliance.

Earl Uhtred was married three times. His first wife, Ecgfrida, was (as we have seen) the daughter of Bishop Ealdhun of Chester-le-Street/Durham. It is a reasonable guess that the marriage took place at or soon after the time when we first hear of Uhtred and Ealdhun acting in concert on the occasion of the founding of Durham cathedral in 995. This marriage signalled the reinforcement of a long-standing alliance between the leading aristocratic family of Bernicia and the most powerful spiritual force in the north, the community of St Cuthbert. In the exchange of possessions that accompanied the match, Bishop Ealdhun gave with his daughter the six estates in Teesdale whose recovery for the church of Durham was much later to prompt the composition of *De Obsessione Dunelmi*. Uhtred and Ecgfrida had one son, Ealdred. If there were any other children, we do not hear of them.

Uhtred subsequently 'sent her away', in other words divorced her.

GENEALOGICAL TABLE 3
THE MARRIAGES AND ISSUE OF EARL UHTRED

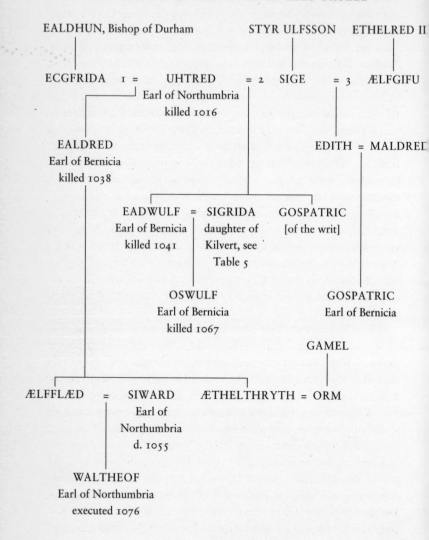

The occasion of the separation was presumably his wish to contract another marriage. His second wife was Sige, the daughter of Styr Ulfsson, and the condition of the marriage, as we saw in chapter 3, was that Uhtred should kill Styr's mortal enemy, Thurbrand. Can we date this second union? As we shall see in a moment, Uhtred's third marriage probably occurred in 1006 or 1007. There were at least two children of the second marriage, which means that it could hardly have taken place any later than 1004. This indicates that at least two years before his promotion to the governance of Deira Uhtred was already taking steps to build up influence there. We also know that Styr Ulfsson was a prominent loyalist, associated 'with my lord King Ethelred' in a grant of lands to the community of St Cuthbert,[11] so that in aligning himself with Styr and his Yorkshire connections Uhtred was simultaneously proclaiming his loyalty to the king (and underlining his suitability to be the earl of all Northumbria that he was soon to become). If we are correct about the date, we also learn that Uhtred and Thurbrand had been enemies for at least a dozen years before the earl's murder at *Wiheal* in 1016. Ecgfrida, meanwhile, married a Yorkshire nobleman named Kilvert by whom she had a daughter, Sigrida (whom we shall meet again), before being once more divorced. Summoned back to Durham by her father the bishop, she lived out the remainder of her life there as a nun.

Uhtred's third marriage, to King Ethelred's daughter the princess Ælfgifu, probably took place shortly after the palace revolution of 1006. As a rough check on this, we know that Uhtred himself gave his daughter of this marriage, Edith, to a man named Maldred, son of Crinan. If the girl had been born in 1007 she would have been rising nine at the time of her father's murder in 1016 – a not impossibly early age for an aristocratic betrothal in the eleventh century. We do not hear of any other children of this third union.

As far as concerns the north of England, then, the changes of the year 1006 indicate a new tack in royal policy. The employment of an outsider, in Ælfhelm, as ealdorman of Yorkshire had not worked out. Let Northumbria be united once more under a single command, a man of proven renown and worth who had shown that he could take steps to make himself acceptable in Deira as well as in his native Bernicia, whose loyalty to the king could be locked in securely by a royal marriage. Such was Earl Uhtred. The thinking was justified by the event. As we have already seen, Uhtred left behind him a reputation for loyalty that was still being talked of the better part of a century later. He was conspicuously loyal for the seven years that succeeded his appointment. But a testing time would come in 1013, for others as well as for Uhtred, when loyalties would be subjected to unendurable strain. A new king would feel that Earl Uhtred could no longer be trusted: that was where Thurbrand came in.

As it happened, roughly the same period of the second half of the first decade of the eleventh century also witnessed a change in the character of the Danish assault upon the kingdom of England. This was heralded by the invasion of Thorkell the Tall in 1009. Thorkell, a Dane who might have been a kinsman of King Sweyn, was one of the most renowned Viking commanders of the age. The army at whose head he landed in Kent in the summer of 1009 was of a different order from any of those which had raided England over the previous thirty years: bigger, better equipped, better disciplined. During the following year and a half, Thorkell's troops ravaged and plundered over much of eastern and southern England. In 1011 they returned to Kent, where they took and burnt the city of Canterbury, capturing a large number of high-ranking clergy including no less a person than Archbishop Ælfheah (or Elphege) of Canterbury (he who as bishop of Winchester had confirmed Olaf Tryggvason in 994). In the course of protracted negotiations during the winter of 1011–12 regarding the payment of a further levy of Danegeld, the elderly archbishop steadfastly refused to allow the payment of a separate personal ransom as the price of his freedom. His captors, exasperated by his stubbornness and inflamed by what the *Anglo-Saxon Chronicle* called 'wine from the south', eventually murdered him in a particularly brutal fashion on 19 April 1012: 'They pelted him with bones and with ox-heads, and one of them struck him on the head with the back of an axe, that he sank down with the blow and his holy blood fell on the ground and so he sent his holy soul to God's kingdom.' He was the first archbishop of Canterbury to die by violence.

A contemporary German chronicler, Bishop Thietmar of Merseburg, recorded that Thorkell had tried in vain to prevent his men from slaughtering the archbishop. This revulsion from barbarity and the associated loss of control over his troops are usually held sufficient to explain what happened next. One may suspect that in addition – as in the previous case of Olaf Tryggvason in 994 – English diplomacy had been quietly active behind the scenes. Whatever the reason, Thorkell himself with forty-five ships and their crews went over into the service of King Ethelred while the rest of his army dispersed.

The defection of Thorkell the Tall furnished King Sweyn of Denmark with a pretext, if one were required, for invading Ethelred's kingdom. Diplomatic niceties apart, however, it must have been clear for all to see that by 1012 the capacity of the English to resist had all but ebbed away. Sweyn could have made this appreciation for himself, for he seems to have campaigned in England on several occasions subsequent to the expedition of 994. His return to England at the head of a large army in August 1013 had a new objective: nothing less than outright conquest of Ethelred's kingdom.

Sweyn based himself at Gainsborough on the River Trent, on the border between Lincolnshire and Nottinghamshire. The choice of base indicates a new strategy. Instead of the hit-and-run raids of earlier years, or the great cross-country *chevauchées* of Thorkell's army, Sweyn was bidding for support in the Danelaw, with its booming Anglo-Danish towns such as York, Lincoln and Stamford and its disaffected noble families such as the kinsfolk of the murdered Ealdorman Ælfhelm. He found the support he sought. All of north-east midland England – the region to the north-east of Watling Street, the old line of division between 'English' and 'Danish' Mercia – submitted to him.

So did 'Earl Uhtred and all the Northumbrians', in the words of the *Chronicle*. Nothing whatsoever is known of northern affairs between Uhtred's promotion to the earldom of all Northumbria in 1006 and his submission to Sweyn in the late summer of 1013. Occasional appearances of Uhtred's name in the witness-lists of royal diplomas indicate his intermittent attendance at the court of King Ethelred. The last of these dates from not long before Sweyn's landing in England. The arrival of Sweyn and his army presented Uhtred with the hardest of choices. By family tradition he was a semi-independent Bernician grandee. By recent habit, reinforced by marriage, he was an Ethelredian loyalist. By office in Deira he was the lord of a thriving Anglo-Scandinavian city and the negotiator of friendships and enmities among an Anglo-Danish aristocracy consisting of such men as Styr Ulfsson and Thurbrand the Hold. Which way was he to jump?

In the event he joined Sweyn. Perhaps he did so with private misgivings, perhaps with public and ambiguous gestures of helplessness, even perhaps after striking some secret deal which might safeguard his free hand in Northumbria: we shall never know. All we know for certain is that he had to give hostages, some of them doubtless his kinsmen, for his good behaviour, just as did all those others who submitted to the Danish king.

Sweyn was in a hurry. The hostages were left in the charge of his young son Canute, then aged about eighteen. Sweyn pushed south with his army, ravaging across English Mercia, received the submission of Oxford, then of Winchester and the south-west, and finally, at the end of the year, of London. King Ethelred, Queen Emma and their children fled for safety to the queen's brother, Duke Richard II of Normandy. By the end of 1013 'all the nation regarded Sweyn as full king'.

He did not enjoy his triumph for long. On 3 February 1014 Sweyn died at Gainsborough. His followers chose Canute to succeed him as king. But the English élite had a different scheme in view. What happened next is best told in the vivid words of the *Anglo-Saxon Chronicle*:

Then all the councillors who were in England, ecclesiastical and lay, determined to send for King Ethelred, and they said that no lord was dearer to them than their natural lord if he would govern them more justly than he did before. Then the king sent his son Edward hither with the messengers, and bade them greet all his people, and said that he would be a gracious lord to them, and reform all the things which they all hated; and all the things that had been said and done against him should be forgiven, on condition that they all unanimously turned to him without treachery. And complete friendship was then established with oath and pledge on both sides, and they pronounced every Danish king an outlaw from England for ever. Then during the spring King Ethelred came home to his own people and he was gladly received by them all.

Immediately upon his return Ethelred gathered an army and proceeded to Lincolnshire. Canute took to the sea and went back to Denmark; but not before landing his hostages of the year before on the English coast shorn of their hands, ears and noses. We should not overlook the fact that, if they did include some of Uhtred's kin, this constituted an affront of the most serious kind to the honour of his family.

Whether or not Earl Uhtred was numbered among 'all the councillors' who negotiated the return of King Ethelred we do not know. But he evidently made his peace with the king, for he attested a diploma apparently issued in the summer of 1014, and a further one belonging to an unknown date in the year 1015. Not all were so fortunate. Under the year 1015 the chronicler recorded the treacherous murder of Sigeferth and Morcar, the leading men of the north-east midlands, and the confiscation of all their very extensive landed property by the king. Their killing itself he attributed, as he attributed all base acts, to Ealdorman Eadric of Mercia, the chief beneficiary of the palace revolution of 1006–7; but it is likely that Eadric was acting on royal orders. Now Sigeferth and Morcar were kin to Ealdorman Ælfhelm of Northumbria who had been butchered in 1006. They had been 'out' since then and were therefore among the disaffected who submitted to Sweyn in 1013. From one perspective, their murder was the penalty for disloyalty.

But this is not the only perspective. There was rather more at stake here than meets the eye. The complex politics of the year 1015 can be rendered intelligible only if we bear always in mind that behind the façade of kingly doings recorded in the annals of the *Anglo-Saxon Chronicle* there lay a cat's cradle compounded of the intertwining skeins of family rivalries and regional jockeyings for wealth, status and power. Consider those murders of Sigeferth and Morcar. They paid the penalty for disloyalty to their king, as stated above, and thus met their violent deaths in a context of national politics. But underlying this there was a *local* struggle for power within the bounds of Mercia. Sigeferth and Morcar, their kinsman Ælfhelm killed in 1006, and Ælfhelm's brother Wulfric who had died in 1004, were landed grandees in north-*eastern* Mercia. Their estates lay principally in Derbyshire, Nottinghamshire, Leicestershire, east Staffordshire, north Warwickshire and south Yorkshire. Their rival, Eadric, had his landed anchor in *western* Mercia, in Herefordshire, Shropshire, Worcestershire and western Staffordshire. The palace revolution of 1006–7 was not just about factions at court, about who had the ear of the king; it was also about who was in command in the Peak, or the Trent valley, or the Vale of Belvoir.

We must also remember that dissension could occur not simply between different families but also *inside* a single kin. This was indeed the most dreaded and bitterest kind of dissension, that on which the poets whose works were the staple diet of these aristocratic families dwelt with darkest brooding. The very worst conceivable kind of dissension that might occur would be dissension within the royal family itself. It had happened before, in the succession struggle following Edgar's death. It had happened, indeed, before that. And it had happened elsewhere, in Germany, in Francia, in Spain. This is exactly what occurred in England in 1015.

The fault-line here that could open up into a gaping fissure was that drawn by King Ethelred's two marriages. (By way of reminder: his first wife was Ælfflaed, the daughter of Earl Thored of Northumbria, to whom he was probably joined in about 985; his second wife was Emma of Normandy, whom he married in 1002.) It not infrequently happens – not just with royal families, and not just in the middle ages – that there is tension between the children of a first marriage, on the one hand, and on the other their stepmother and her children of the second. Where there is so much at stake, as in a royal family, there will the tension be most acute. There were no fewer than eleven children of Ethelred's first marriage, six sons and five daughters. For the immediate purposes of understanding the year 1015 we need focus on only one among them, the eldest surviving son, Edmund, nicknamed 'Ironside'. By 1015 he must have been aged at least twenty-two; well old enough to be king. There were three children of the second marriage, to Emma, two boys and a girl. The eldest son, Edward – later King Edward the Confessor (1042–66) – would have been at least ten in 1015, the age his father was when he succeeded to the throne in 978.

Everything that we know of Emma – actually quite a lot – suggests that she was a woman of energetic and ruthless ambition on behalf of her children, whom she had carried off to the safe haven of her family in Normandy as Sweyn of Denmark tightened his grip on the country in 1013. Her stepson Edmund, as heir to the throne, would have been right to be apprehensive; the more so when his young half-brother Edward acted as an ambassador, as a sort of deputy king, to negotiate his father's return in the following year, as we saw in the passage from the *Chronicle* quoted above. But there is a further complicating twist here. Could it not be that Edmund was now something more than simply *heir* to the throne? King Ethelred's flight to Normandy in the winter of 1013–14 could have been regarded as an abdication. The king had fled, leaving his kingdom a shambles. Long live the rightful king, his son Edmund!

Whatever sentiments might have been uttered or just pondered, the actions of Edmund Ironside in 1015 clearly amounted to a rebellion against his father. After the killing of Sigeferth and Morcar and the royal confiscation of their lands, King Ethelred had Morcar's widow, Ealdgyth, arrested and imprisoned at Malmesbury. Now Ealdgyth was the niece of Ælfhelm and Wulfric, doubly connected by blood and marriage to the kin-group ousted in the palace revolution of 1006–7, and therefore a woman of critical significance in the regional/matrimonial power struggle of those years. Edmund's actions in 1015 underline this. He went to Malmesbury, abducted Ealdgyth 'against the king's will' and married her. Immediately afterwards he went off to her family heartlands in the north-east midlands, appropriated her first husband's and her former brother-in-law's estates, 'and the people all submitted to him'. As in most texts of this era we must understand by 'people' the people who mattered, the aristocracy and gentry.

These actions could not fail to have had repercussions further north. Some of Morcar's lands lay in Yorkshire, quite probably some of Sigeferth's too: in other words, in Uhtred's earldom of Northumbria. Among the primary duties of an earl was responsibility for the administration of royal estates lying within his earldom. So when King Ethelred confiscated these lands they would have come under Uhtred's remit. Edmund must have put out feelers to Uhtred after his surprise arrival in the north with his new bride. Uhtred was, after all, not simply the most powerful man in the north of England but also Edmund's brother-in-law. The fact that Edmund was able to take over these estates indicates that Uhtred had showed himself willing to co-operate.

GENEALOGICAL TABLE 4
THE ANGLO-DANISH ROYAL FAMILY

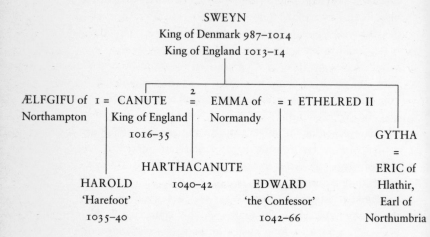

SWEYN
King of Denmark 987–1014
King of England 1013–14

ÆLFGIFU of 1 = CANUTE = EMMA of = 1 ETHELRED II
Northampton   King of England   ²   Normandy

King of England 1016–35   GYTHA
                                                                =
                    HARTHACANUTE   ERIC of
HAROLD   1040–42   EDWARD   Hlathir,
'Harefoot'   'the Confessor'   Earl of
1035–40   1042–66   Northumbria

In other words, he aligned himself with the rebel prince. They would campaign together in the following winter.

It was at this very confused and fluid juncture, in the late summer of 1015, that another actor reappeared upon the scene. Canute crossed the North Sea at the head of an invasion fleet and made landfall on the coast of Kent. Thence he proceeded down-Channel until reaching the mouth of the Dorset Frome where he disembarked his troops to ravage widely in Dorset, Somerset and Wiltshire. King Ethelred had fallen ill with what was to prove the onset of his last illness. He lay sick at Cosham, near Portsmouth, and could offer no resistance. Wessex submitted to Canute; so too did Ealdorman Eadric of Mercia.

In medieval Europe the campaigning season lasted, depending on the weather, from May to September. It was only in very exceptional circumstances that armies took the field in winter. The circumstances of the winter of 1015–16 were extremely exceptional. Shortly before Christmas Canute moved northwards into Mercia. Prince Edmund and Earl Uhtred busied themselves early in the new year in laying waste the heartlands of Ealdorman Eadric in Staffordshire, Shropshire and Cheshire. Then Canute pressed forward into Northumbria. Earl Uhtred hastened back and 'out of necessity' as the *Chronicle* put it, offered his submission to Canute. The place decided upon for the formal ceremony of submission was *Wiheal*. We know what happened next.

5

Millennium

The three years 1013, 1014 and 1015 were horrible ones for the upper ranks of the Anglo-Saxon aristocracy. They were faced by painful choices about the bestowal of loyalty in circumstances where consistency of behaviour was impossible if mere survival were to be ensured. Uhtred was not alone in his dilemma; nor was he the only casualty. Loyal to King Ethelred from his appointment to the earldom of all Northumbria in 1006 until 1013, in that year he went over to Sweyn of Denmark when Sweyn's victory over Ethelred seemed assured. In the wake of Sweyn's death he went back to Ethelred – and saw the hostages he had given, his retainers, possibly some of them his kinsmen, cruelly mutilated by a vengeful Canute. When Edmund rebelled against his father, Earl Uhtred joined him, abandoning his king for the second time in two years, experiencing all the agonies of dissension within the kin as he forsook a father-in-law for a brother-in-law. And then only a few months later he took the decision to throw over Edmund and submit to Canute.

On the face of it, not a pretty record. But it is all too easy to be judgemental a millennium after events of which we know only the barest outline. The contemporary who observed that Uhtred was driven by necessity showed a degree of sympathy that is perhaps revealing. Once again, the poetry of the age assists understanding. The morality of the heroic epic dwelt on the hard choices involved in conflicting loyalties. The poets knew their audience, and the realities of that audience's world.

Canute, that violent and ruthless young man, wanted Uhtred out of the way, and one can see why. How could he trust him? Thurbrand the Hold was there to be used as his tool, Thurbrand who had successfully eluded for a dozen years or more Uhtred's undertaking to kill him. The bloody imperatives of the national and the local intersected at *Wiheal* on that early spring day in 1016. Forty men dead beside their lord! It cut a huge swathe through the Northumbrian élite, made it the easier for Canute to leave the north in the hands of his brother-in-law, Eric of Hlathir, while he dashed south to continue his struggle with Edmund Ironside. What it didn't do was eliminate all Uhtred's kin. Thurbrand would one day pay a heavy price for this.

The details of Canute's struggle with Edmund Ironside form no part of our story. It will suffice to say that 1016 was a year of intense campaigning. Five considerable battles were fought, and London experienced a long-drawn-out Danish blockade. After the last battle, at Ashingdon in Essex, which took place late in the season on St Luke's day (18 October), both sides had fought themselves to a standstill. The country was partitioned, to Edmund going Wessex and to Canute the rest. But Edmund suddenly died (30 November) and Canute became sole king. He reigned over England until his death in 1035.

People who want to hold on to positions of high office, or indeed simply to remain alive, have to serve the regime which is in power. This unpalatable truth was as inescapable in the eleventh century as it remains in the twenty-first. Great secular noblemen like Uhtred were not alone in trying to manage the divergent tugs on their loyalty. Princes of the Church experienced the same agonies of conscience. What of Archbishop Wulfstan II of York, the leading prelate in the north of England, during those desperate years between 1013 and 1016? It looks as though his trajectory was suggestively similar to that of his secular partner in government, Earl Uhtred. After Sweyn's death at Gainsborough on 3 February 1014 his body was taken to York for burial there, presumably, though we are not explicitly told this, at York Minster. (It was subsequently removed to Denmark for reinterment at Roskilde.) This could have come about only with the archbishop's consent. We possess independent evidence to show that Wulfstan was in York at the time: on 16 February 1014 he consecrated a new bishop of London at York. In other words Wulfstan, like Uhtred, accepted Sweyn's authority. However, and again like Uhtred, he shortly afterwards made his peace with King Ethelred, for he attested those same two royal diplomas of 1014 and 1015. We have another and still more striking piece of evidence of his loyalty to Ethelred in 1014, as we shall see shortly. What might have been his leanings, his anxieties, his whereabouts and his actions during that critical winter of 1015–16 we do not know. What we do know is that very shortly after Canute's accession Wulfstan had thrown himself behind the new regime. Until his death in 1023 the archbishop of York remained one of Canute's most prominent and influential counsellors.

Wulfstan II of York was the most commanding figure in the life of the later Anglo-Saxon Church. He can be known to us better than any other owing to the body of writings attributable to him which has survived. These works comprise a number of sermons, several legal ordinances drawn up for Ethelred and Canute, and a work of what might be described as political theory, the so-called *Institutes of Polity, Civil and Ecclesiastical*. Wulfstan was a moralist and statesman who thought deeply about the ills of his day and how they might be remedied. As a devout Christian churchman he was convinced that the tribulations visited upon the English people should be interpreted as divine punishment for their sins and that only thoroughgoing moral reformation might avert God's displeasure.

His most famous surviving work is the homily known as *The Sermon of the Wolf to the English*. (Wulfstan used the literary alias or nickname of 'Wolf' in a play upon the first syllable of his name.) This was a sermon first delivered in 1014, almost certainly to an audience consisting of the royal court, probably not long after King Ethelred's return from Normandy. This extract gives the flavour of Wulfstan's oratory and embodies his most passionate convictions.

Understand well also that now for many years the devil has led astray this people too greatly and there has been little loyalty among men, though they spoke fair enough; and too many wrongs prevailed in the land, and there were never many men who sought after a remedy as zealously as one should; but daily evil was piled on evil and wrongs and many lawless acts committed far too widely throughout all this people; also we have on that account suffered many losses and insults, and, if we are to experience any improvement, we must then deserve better of God than we have previously done. For with great deserts have we merited the miseries which oppress us, and with very great deserts must we obtain relief from God if henceforward things are to start to improve. For lo! we know full that a great breach will require much repair, and a great fire no little water, if the fire is to be quenched at all; and great is the necessity for every man that he keep henceforward God's laws eagerly and pay God's dues rightly ... For it is clear and manifest in us all that we have previously transgressed more than we have amended, and therefore much is assailing this people. Things have not gone well now for a long time at home or abroad, but there has been devastation and famine, burning and bloodshed in every district again and again; and stealing and killing, sedition and pestilence, murrain and disease, malice and hate and spoliation by robbers have harmed us very grievously, and monstrous taxes have afflicted us greatly, and bad seasons have very often caused us failure of crops. For now for many years, as it may seem, there have been in this country many injustices and wavering loyalties among men everywhere.[1]

This was a message which Wulfstan had been hammering home for some time. He seems to have acquired a reputation as a pulpit orator before he became bishop of London in 996, and the theme was sounded in what appear to be among his earliest surviving sermons: 'Just as the Flood came once because of sin, so too because of sin will come fire upon mankind.' Later on, as a leading adviser of King Ethelred, he was responsible for putting in train the ritual measures designed to regain God's goodwill. When Thorkell's army invaded England in 1009 it was Wulfstan who drafted the ordinance (known as VII Ethelred) which required a general penitential fast.[2] The entire nation was called upon to fast for three days on bread and herbs and water from 26 to 28 September inclusive 'that we may obtain God's mercy and His compassion and that we may through His help withstand our enemies'. At every church throughout the kingdom priest and people were to process barefoot with their relics 'and call on Christ eagerly from their inmost hearts'. Compulsory levies of money were to take place for charitable purposes, with heavy penalties for non-payment. Even slaves – a notable concession, this, from so unbending an upholder of the social order as Wulfstan – were to be exempted from work during the three fast days so that they too could participate in the rituals.

One is bound to wonder to what extent this extraordinary attempt to mobilize the whole English people to a regime of severe religious discipline was realized in practice. As usual, we do not have the evidence which would enable us to offer any answer (though it is as well to remember that days of public fasting could be successfully imposed at later dates by English monarchs who had barely greater executive coercive powers than their late Saxon predecessors). What we can say, of course, is that calls to action of this sort are more likely to evoke a positive response if they are in tune with the mood of the times.

At this point it is all too fatally easy to slide into the trap of a circular argument. All our written sources emanate from churchmen. But we have to use those same sources to investigate 'the mood of the times'. Not surprisingly, therefore, churchmen like Wulfstan turn out to have been the very embodiment of 'the mood of the times'. QED. An escape route, of a sort, is provided if we look sideways across the Channel at Wulfstan's continental contemporaries (something that historians of Anglo-Saxon England have traditionally not been very good at doing, with a few distinguished exceptions). As a springboard into that wider world we could do worse than examine a quotation from one of Wulfstan's early homilies.

It was written and long ago prophesied 'after a thousand years will Satan be unbound'. A thousand years and more is now gone since Christ was among men in a human family, and Antichrist's time is now close at hand.

The words date themselves to shortly after the year 1000. Can we provide them with a context?

Christians had been taught by their Founder to await the imminent *Parousia*, the return of Christ to judge the living and the dead and to bring to an end the present world order. The fact that Christ's followers were early and expressly told not to attempt to predict the time of His coming (Mark xiii.32) suggests that this was precisely what they were prone to do. The *Parousia* would be preceded by the coming of Antichrist (I John ii.18), perhaps after a thousand years when Satan should be loosed upon the world (Revelation xx.2, 7). Antichrist would reign for a while, only to be slain by Christ at the inauguration of the Last Judgement, and the beginning of a new heaven and a new earth (Revelation xx.10–15; xxi.1–4). Such in briefest outline were the scriptural teachings upon which all sorts of expectations about The End have been erected over the last two thousand years (and still are being today, at the outset of the third millennium). The year AD 1000 marked the thousandth year since the birth of Jesus, and 1033 the thousandth year since His crucifixion.

There was eager interest in these apocalyptic matters among Wulfstan's contemporaries. In about 950 an abbot in eastern France, Adso of Montier-en-Der, had composed a treatise on Antichrist for a very exalted patroness, Gerberga, sister of Otto the Great of Germany and wife of Louis IV of France. Both her families had close contacts with England. Otto's first wife, Gerberga's sister-in-law, was the sister of King Athelstan of Wessex. Louis IV owed his nickname, *d'Outremer*, 'from across the sea', to his exile at Athelstan's court for a dozen years or so before he became king in 936. There existed a network of cross-Channel contacts at élite level which facilitated the transmission of ideas and concerns, and the books which embodied these in writing. Adso's treatise on the Antichrist was demonstrably known in England by the end of the tenth century. It was drawn upon by the other famous preacher of this period, Abbot Ælfric of Eynsham in Oxfordshire, in his first collected series of *Catholic Homilies* – known to Wulfstan – edited in about 990. It was copied into an English manuscript very probably at Worcester – Wulfstan's other diocese – shortly after the year 1000, the best possible evidence of a lively interest in the imminent End.

These concerns were not the recondite preserve of abbots, bishops and princesses. They were widely shared. At about the same time that Adso composed his treatise a bishop of Auxerre wrote a letter to his colleague of Verdun deploring that 'innumerable' people were convinced that the deadly raiding parties of Magyars from the east were the forces of Gog and Magog (foretold in Revelation xx.8), Satan's troops, heralding the end of the world. At the other end of Europe, in Spain, the Christian principalities which faced renewed onslaught from their Islamic neighbours in the last quarter of the tenth century interpreted their foes in a similar manner. Their arch-enemy Almanzor, the de facto ruler of the caliphate of Córdoba, was 'possessed by Satan' like Gog and Magog. Anxiously they scrutinized the book of Revelation and the commentary upon it by the eighth-century

Spanish monk Beatus of Liébana to make sense of their age. Intense interest in this text is shown by the number of luxury illustrated manuscripts of it that were copied in Christian Spain on either side of the year 1000. These same apocalyptic obsessions are attested by manuscript survivals from Germany and northern Italy dating from the same period; and we have already seen that they lay close to the surface of Wulfstan's mind. Ælfric saw in the Danish raids of the late tenth century similar portents of the onset of the End, nation rising up against nation exactly as Jesus had foretold. War was one of the four horsemen of the Apocalypse; Famine, Plague and Death were the others. Could it be coincidental that there was in the year 1005 'a great famine throughout England such that no man ever remembered one so cruel'?

The distinguished monastic leader Abbo of Fleury-sur-Loire recollected in later life that 'as a youth I heard a sermon preached to the people in a church in Paris to the effect that as soon as the number of 1000 years was completed, Antichrist would arrive and that, not long afterwards, the Last Judgement would follow'. The sermon that Abbo heard must have been preached at some point in the 960s, about a decade after Adso composed his pamphlet on Antichrist. Now Abbo's monastery of Fleury had contacts with the English Benedictine revival of the tenth century. Archbishop Oda of Canterbury had taken the monastic habit there. Oda's nephew Oswald spent a few years at Fleury in the 950s before he became bishop of Worcester and archbishop of York. Later on, Oswald invited Abbo to his own monastic foundation of Ramsey in the Fens. Abbo spent the years 985–7 at Ramsey supervising the development of the monastery school there, and in particular the study of what was called *computus*, the mathematics of the calendar (a subject of special relevance to apocalyptic investigation). Abbo's reminiscence quoted above occurred in a letter to the king of France composed in the 990s, but he could easily have shared it with the brethren of Ramsey a few years earlier. If the young Wulfstan were indeed a monk at nearby Ely, he too might have met Abbo and been influenced by him.

Of course Abbo, as an orthodox churchman, was scandalized by these attempts to find out 'that day and that hour' as expressly forbidden in St Mark's Gospel. What is notable about the continental evidence is that it suggests that apocalyptic anxieties were widespread within Christian society. 'Innumerable' people were affected by these disquieting notions; members of the clergy (who should have known better) were spreading them 'to the people' in sermons in church. A further testimony from the continent to widespread anxiety is furnished by the so-called 'Peace of God' movement. In its fundamentals this was a series of initiatives taken by leading local churchmen in the south-west of France to convoke assemblies at which a special peace, enforceable by ecclesiastical sanctions, was proclaimed over a region. At the most straightforward level this was a response to intolerable levels of disorder and violence in an area where traditional structures of civil authority had broken down. The clergy took steps to do what kings could no longer do. But there was more to it than just that. The peace assemblies were held in an atmosphere of heightened religious emotion. Very large numbers of people of every social rank attended them. They were often presided over by the saints, brought there in person in the guise of their relics by the clergy. Fiery sermons (of the sort that Wulfstan would have approved) were preached denouncing sin, naming and shaming sinners, urging repentance and social reconciliation in the face of the wrath to come. Processions were held, liturgies of public penance chanted, massed prayers poured forth. There were spectacular responses. Hardened knightly thugs would cast aside their arms and weep at the memory of acts of oppression. Families long divided by enmity would kiss and make friends. Quarrelling neighbours would patch up their differences. Oaths to keep the peace would be sworn. In this atmosphere of religious revivalism crowds would find redemption, a world made new by means of peace, a peace made, constructed, agreed upon, a peace deliberately entered into.

There seems to have been some connection of time and of tone between the peace movement and the apocalyptic anxieties of the age. The peace movement was at its most vital and intense in the half-century between c. 990 and c. 1040. The mass hysteria – for that is what it seems to have been – sprang from the expectation of imminence; people were in a hurry because there might not be long. What might be termed liturgical iconography began to display at about this time a preoccupation with the Lamb of God, so prominent, of course, in the apocalyptic book of Revelation. It was at this epoch that the final line of the *Agnus Dei*, said or sung at every celebration of mass, was changed from *miserere nobis* ('have mercy upon us') to *dona nobis pacem* ('grant us peace'). Cleansing in the blood of the Lamb became a favourite theme of peace sermons. The image of the cross-bearing Lamb started to become frequent in the sculpture and manuscript painting of the tenth and eleventh centuries.[3]

Against this backdrop consider what happened at Enham in Hampshire in the month of May in the year 1008. On the initiative of England's most senior prelates, archbishops Ælfheah of Canterbury and Wulfstan of York, a meeting of all the leading men in England was convened at Enham at the season of Pentecost or Whitsun, which in that year fell on 16 May. At a preliminary assembly of bishops a special peace was proclaimed. Then, at a plenary session consisting of king, clergy, magnates and 'people' (whatever that might have meant) Wulfstan preached on the need for national moral regeneration.

And every injustice is to be zealously cast out from this country. And deceitful deeds and hateful abuses are to be strictly shunned, namely, false weights and wrong measures and lying witnesses and shameful frauds, and horrible perjuries and devilish deeds of murder and manslaughter, of stealing and spoliation, of avarice and greed, of over-eating and over-drinking, of deceits and various breaches of law, of injuries to the clergy and of breaches of the marriage law, and of evil deeds of many kinds. But God's law henceforth is to be eagerly loved by word and deed; then God will at once become gracious to this nation.

The substance of his homily survives as the texts of the royal 'legislation' known as V and VI Ethelred.[4] It appears to have been shortly afterwards that a special issue of coinage was struck, unique not only to Ethelred's reign but to the entire numismatic history of early England. Each penny bore on its obverse an image of the Lamb of God and on its reverse the Holy Dove. The Dove would have had a special significance in connection with an assembly held at Pentecost, for it was at that season that the Holy Spirit, so frequently presented in the image of a dove, descended upon the apostles (Acts ii). As for the Lamb, we have already seen the links between this image and contemporary apocalyptic worries and the peace movement on the continent. It is of the greatest interest – and surely not coincidental – that the place-name Enham means 'a place of lambs' or 'a meadow where lambs are bred'. Neither can it have been coincidental that at the time of the meeting in mid-May the fields at Enham are likely to have been filled with young lambs.

So there are signs of widespread millennial anxiety in continental Europe round the turn of the year 1000, sufficient for us to regard this as a significant element in the mood of the times. The peace movement was not simply a response to disorder; it was also a call for moral reformation while there was yet time. Archbishop Wulfstan II of York shared in these millennial worries and sought to communicate them – if indeed this needed doing – to his fellow-countrymen in England. The assembly at Enham in 1008, with its sermonizing ordinances that Wulfstan drafted and its carefully staged references to lambs and doves, was the nearest thing to a French peace assembly that Anglo-Saxon England ever produced.

There were in addition two further strands in Wulfstan's thought which demand our attention. One concerned the righteousness of kings, the other the proper ordering of society. A king who rules unjustly will be punished by God: kingdom and people will suffer. In Wulfstan's eyes Ethelred was not simply foolish or badly counselled. Much more seriously, he was an unjust ruler.

Our best evidence for contemporary perceptions of the injustice of Ethelred's rule is furnished by the chronicler's report, quoted in the last chapter, of the constitutional pact which brought the king back to England in the spring of 1014. For all its brevity, the passage is of the utmost interest in recording an episode of considerable significance in English constitutional history (nowadays an imprudently neglected subject). This is the earliest recorded pact between an English ruler and his subjects, the first occasion (to our knowledge) on which a king was brought to agree to certain conditions before being permitted to resume his rule. We should dearly like to know more of the episode than we do. Who were 'all the councillors, ecclesiastical and lay'? Where and how did they deliberate? Did they, or did the king, have a written record made of demands and promises, or was all this weighty business transacted by word of mouth? What, precisely, did Ethelred undertake to reform? What, exactly, was sworn and pledged? We do not know the answers to these questions, though we can guess at the answer to one of them. It seems likely that the chronicler was summarizing or even quoting from a written document – which raises a further important (and insoluble) question about his means of access to this text.

The expectations which contemporaries held with regard to kings had provided the moral context of these negotiations. Over the preceding centuries a succession of formidably thoughtful churchmen had developed a body of theory about how secular rulers should govern themselves and their subjects. These luminaries ran from St Augustine of Hippo through Pope Gregory I, Isidore of Seville, Bede, Alcuin of York to Hincmar of Rheims in the ninth century. It was to their writings that the English churchmen of the age of Wulfstan of York were heirs. Royal obligations were encapsulated in the oath sworn by a king at his coronation and anointing, as we saw in chapter 2. It was administered by a leading prelate, usually the archbishop of Canterbury. The entire inauguration ritual, indeed, had a markedly ecclesiastical character. Whether the lay magnates of the kingdom entertained expectations of their rulers which differed in any way from those held by their clerical colleagues we cannot, for lack of evidence, be sure. The negotiations with King Ethelred in 1014 suggest their active role in formulating and pressing demands. This in turn raises questions and possibilities about the nature of the 'political nation' in eleventh-century England – and indeed in those other parts of Europe, such as Germany and Spain, where roughly comparable constitutional encounters occurred in the same century.

Heavy taxation was identified by clerical thinkers as a feature of unjust rule. We have already witnessed Wulfstan's denunciation of 'monstrous taxes' in his famous sermon. Kings should not burden their subjects with excessive and unreasonable demands. But this is just what Ethelred did in the form of the levies of Danegeld for which some figures were quoted in the last chapter. To appreciate how burdensome it was, how harsh in its side or indirect effects, we must examine this tax a little more closely.

The Old English word *geld* simply means 'payment' or 'tribute'; by extension, 'tax'. *Danegeld* thus means 'Dane-tax', 'tax paid to the

Danes'. The geld was a land tax. From a very early date Anglo-Saxon rulers had been accustomed to levy services and renders (at first in kind, later in money) from their landed subjects in accordance with assessments allotted to individual estates. The units of assessment were known over most of England as 'hides'. (There was some variation in terminology across the country which for simplicity's sake I leave to one side.) The word hide had once upon a time denoted the approximate area of land required to furnish the livelihood of a single family. By the later Anglo-Saxon period, however, the hide had long ago shed its earlier areal meaning and was simply a fiscal unit. Thus by King Ethelred's time an estate of ten hides did not denote an acreage of land sufficient for the support of ten families but simply an estate which was liable for ten units of service or tax at the behest of the king. When this mode of extracting services and commodities was made the vehicle for sustaining a national land tax paid in current coin of the realm, we do not know; and for present purposes the question does not matter. (It is tempting to guess at Edgar's reign and hazard some connection with the reorganization of the coinage in 973.) At any rate, by the time we get to Ethelred's reign the geld was evidently working efficiently, judging by its repeated yield of enormous sums of money.

About precisely how this tax, unique for scale and sophistication in the Europe of the day, worked in detail we should like to know a great deal more than we do. It is reasonably clear that large, round figures of assessment units were allotted to – or in the expressive Old English phrase 'thrown upon' – each shire. Within the individual shires these assessments would be shared out among the administrative subdivisions of the shire, the hundreds or wapentakes. Within each of these subdivisions liability for tax would be further shared out among the landholders. The local allotment of liability would have been expedited, therefore, in two stages: at the shire court, for allotment among the hundreds; and at the hundred court, for allotment among the landholders. The process would have fostered local negotiation and co-operation at the level of shire and hundred; doubtless it also gave rise to a good measure of local bickering and resentment.

So much for assessment. By contrast we know practically nothing at all about the mechanisms for collection and accounting. The geld had to be paid in current coin of the realm, the silver penny as periodically changed after the monetary reforms of 973. It is assumed that landlords collected the tax due from their villages and estates, and then passed the yield on to the reeve of hundred or wapentake. He in his turn would forward the entire yield of hundred or wapentake on to the shire-reeve or sheriff, the deputy of the ealdorman or earl in the administration of the shire. The sheriff would convey the entire yield from the shire on to some central collecting point, perhaps at Winchester, where one must presume that some sort of audit was held. This is guesswork, but it represents the only way in which the known administrative structure of later Anglo-Saxon England could have handled a tax of this complexity. It is noteworthy that in order to accomplish the necessary accounting at central and at shrieval levels, not inconceivably at hundredal ones also, it would have been necessary to keep records of payments made, arrears due, sums remitted, and so forth.

There were flexibilities in the geld. From the point of view of the king's government, there was flexibility in the rate of levy. As need determined he could impose a rate of one, two, four, six shillings per hide – and even more, as we shall see presently. There was the flexibility of regional variation in the incidence of the tax. A shire which had been devastated in the course of war, or which was experiencing famine owing to local drought or flood, might have its assessments temporarily reduced. Sensitive areas of the kingdom might be assessed at permanently lower rates than others. Northumbria, for example, was more lightly assessed than Mercia or Wessex. A different sort of flexibility altogether consisted in the phenomenon which historians call 'beneficial hidation'. What this means is that specially favoured courtiers might negotiate a reduction in their geld assessments. It was part of the treasury of royal patronage. (Of course, it did not mean that the tenants on the beneficially hidated estates were exempt from paying taxes; rather, that the lords did not have to pass on the yield to the king but could pocket it themselves.)

During the reign of Ethelred II the sheer weight of taxation became extremely heavy. Maitland, writing in the 1890s, wrote of it that 'no word but "appalling" will adequately describe the taxation of which [the chronicler] speaks'. Habituated as he was to a level of income tax of about 2 per cent, one can understand his sense of outrage. Take the year 1012. A sum of £48,000 was levied in Danegeld. This represents a rate of something like twelve shillings per hide (averaging out across the country in a rough-and-ready manner). It seems that a fiscal hide might be reckoned to stand for, give or take, an annual income of about £1. Twelve shillings on the hide therefore stands for a tax on income of something in the region of 60 per cent. These figures are very approximate, but approximations are the best we can offer. For all their statistical uncertainties, the figures do give the impression that Danegeld was a hefty burden to bear. But it was not all. In the same year of 1012 another tax was instituted known as the *Heregeld* or 'army tax'. The Danegeld was paid over to the Danes to get them to go away – for a time. The Heregeld was intended to fund an army with which to fight the Danes when they came back – which, as it turned out, was the following year. So there were two simultaneous impositions of direct taxation. (It is worth stressing that 'direct'. For let us not forget the modes of indirect taxation, most notably the fees paid for the compulsory changing of money at every periodic recoinage (not, as it happened, in 1012). Whatever the number of silver pennies you took to your local mint to be recoined, you came away with fewer than you brought. It was a completely visible, tangible, weighable stealth tax.)

What happened if you could not meet your tax bill? Evidence from the reign of Canute reveals a truly fiendish legal device; and we have no reason to suppose that it did not operate in Ethelred's reign also. If a landowner could not pay the tax due on his land someone else could come forward to pay it for him – and get title to the land in question as a reward. It is all too easy to imagine the consequences of such chicanery in the local societies of hundred and shire, the trickery it might engender, the anguish it might cause, the venom it might diffuse. We can point to one or two examples of those who seem to have profited spectacularly, most notable among them Earl Eadric of Mercia, whose nickname *Streona* means 'acquisitor'. The rich got richer and the poor poorer. As for the losers, we should remember that there was no safety-net for the destitute in Anglo-Saxon England. If the worst came to the very worst, they would have to sell all that they had left – themselves. Wulfstan was well aware that English people were being forced by poverty to sell themselves or each other into slavery and lamented and denounced this unpalatable truth in his

Sermon of the Wolf. There was nothing cosy about Anglo-Saxon society.

The other sanction that we know about was brute force. In the year 1041 two of the king's tax-collectors were slain in the course of their duties by the people of Worcester. The king at once dispatched an army containing his crack troops, the housecarls, under the command of no fewer than five earls,

> . . . ordering them to slay all the men if they could, to plunder and burn the city, and to lay waste the whole area. Arriving on 12 November, they began to lay waste both the city and the countryside, and did not stop doing that for four days, but they took or killed few of the townsfolk or the country people because, having received advance notice of their arrival, the country people had fled in all directions, and a great number of the townspeople had taken refuge on a small island called Bevere situated in the middle of the river Severn, and fortified it, and defended themselves so strongly against their enemies that when peace had been restored they were allowed to return home freely. On the fifth day, accordingly, when the city had been burnt, and all [the army] returned home with great booty, the king's anger was straightway slaked.[5]

The geld, then, was an extremely harsh imposition. For those who could pay, it was burdensome. For those who delayed or defied, reprisal would come in the form of armed thugs with licence to burn and pillage, beat up and rape. Those who could not pay might face dispossession of property and extreme social dislocation. The geld was a fiscal engine of elemental strength. To quote Maitland once more, it was 'an impost so heavy that it was fully capable of transmuting a whole nation'.

Small wonder that much ingenuity was deployed in attempts to seek exemption. The monks of Canterbury cathedral priory had already forged a number of charters attributed to early Anglo-Saxon kings of Kent which purported to free the church of Canterbury from all dues and services. The earliest surviving copy of one of these documents, claiming to free all church land in Kent from taxation, was made at Canterbury in the early years of the eleventh century. The date of the copying, and perhaps the 'improvement', of the text indicates the relevance of the issue. Small wonder too that saints who could be regarded as resisters of tribute-paying acquired a special veneration. Archbishop Ælfheah had met his grisly end in 1012 because he had stood out against the payment of a ransom which would have involved an even higher levy of Danegeld.

We may be reasonably confident that the geld was one of the features of Ethelred's government which the king promised to moderate in the constitutional pact of 1014. How sincerely and effectively he carried out his undertaking we have no means of telling. The two years that were left of Ethelred's life were too full of dissension and campaigning for the chroniclers to expend ink on financial matters. And then Canute became king by conquest, Canute who had entered into no constitutional pact with his subjects, who had a large army to pay off and fellow-conquerors with expectations of reward. Among Canute's earliest actions as king of England was to levy a geld at an unprecedentedly high rate; £72,000 was raised, in other words about £1 per hide, approximating to an income tax of something close to 100 per cent. In effect, Canute confiscated the earnings of the English people for the year 1017. It was the heaviest single levy of taxation which has ever been exacted from them. This enormous geld was accompanied by a special levy of £10,500 from the city of London. The Londoners had been consistently loyal to Ethelred: in this swingeing tax lay their punishment.

This first indication of the character of Canute's rule was soon followed by others. As a foreign conqueror, Canute needed an army of occupation. Although the evidence is fragmentary, there are some signs of the permanent garrisoning of Danish mercenary troops in London and some – possibly several – other towns, at least during the early years of the reign. These soldiers had to be paid. So too did the sailors who manned the ships with which Canute maintained his North Sea empire. English taxpayers had to foot the bill. The geld did not fade away. As with other emergency wartime taxes, it became an annual imposition in peacetime, a permanent feature of national life.

Canute rewarded his henchmen with land as well as bullion. This is another area of enquiry which is as obscure as it is important. It is clear enough that there was no wholesale dispossession of the English landed classes such as followed in the wake of the Norman Conquest in 1066 (as we shall see in chapter 9). On the other hand, the most acute modern investigator of the reign has been able to demonstrate the likelihood that Canute's followers received landed estates 'in nearly every shire in England'.[6] We learn about these people from the chance survival of records from a peculiarly ill-documented reign. For instance, one of the king's military retainers, or housecarls, bearing the Scandinavian name Urk received a seven-hide estate at Portisham in Dorset in 1024: we know of this only because Urk later donated it to the monastery of Abbotsbury so that Canute's diploma of donation, the principal title-deed, was preserved among the abbey's muniments. About some others we have only hints on which to base surmises. Was 'Sumerled the housecarl' (Danish name, Danish rank) who embellished the wooden church at Old Byland in the North Riding of Yorkshire with a stone sundial one of Canute's men, or descended from one such? Perhaps. About others we can only guess. It must surely have been the case that Canute's earl of Northumbria, his brother-in-law Eric of Hlathir, was granted lands in the north when he was appointed to the earldom in the wake of Uhtred's murder; but we know neither where they lay nor how extensive they were.

Heavy taxation, an occupying military presence, dispossession of at any rate some English landowners in every shire the length and breadth of England. The hand of government as wielded by Canute lay as heavy and harsh as ever it had in Ethelred's day. Furthermore, Canute was a cultural newcomer. He came from the very fringes of Christendom, from a society only recently introduced to civilized ways, where Christianity itself was an implant only a couple of generations old. Canute needed schooling in the ways of Christian kings. English churchmen, led by Wulfstan of York, were there to show him how to conduct himself.

Canute would have sworn the customary royal oath at his coronation and presumably have had its implications explained to him. The next important step was taken at a meeting of all the notabilities of the kingdom at Oxford in 1018. An 'agreement' was made which established 'peace and friendship between the Danes and the English' on the basis of a common acceptance of the laws of King Edgar. We owe our record of this to Archbishop Wulfstan, and it is likely that he had taken the initiative in bringing the agreement about. It sounds something like the constitutional pact of four years earlier. Canute agreed to accept Edgar's laws as a kind of standard of good government. This amounted to a promise to moderate the worst excesses of his regime.

Wulfstan's last major act in the schooling of Canute, and in many ways the crowning achievement of his life, was to draft the code of laws issued in Canute's name in the early 1020s. Canute's laws were the most comprehensive and sophisticated piece of legislation issued by any early medieval English king. They were more than just laws as we understand the term nowadays. Wulfstan, through the mouthpiece of Canute, sought to proclaim the standards of godly behaviour that a Christian people should observe and the nature of righteous rule that their king should exercise over them. Yes, the lawcode includes plentiful clauses on crime and punishment, on theft and murder, on fines and compurgation and outlawry, but looming over the here and now of the administration of justice is a far more exalted concern. Wulfstan wished to steer the English king and his subjects to righteousness, to make of them an acceptable people in the sight of the Lord. This high purpose accounts for the homiletic tone which permeates the code.

Wrong-doing is not permitted at any time; and yet it should be specially guarded against at festival seasons and in sacred places. And ever as a man is mightier or of higher rank, he must atone the deeper for wrong-doing both to God and to men.[7]

This is not the tone we associate with legislation today. But Archbishop Wulfstan thought it appropriate for his troubled epoch.

Did Wulfstan's admonitions bear fruit? How justly did Canute govern? He certainly went to great trouble to present himself to the world as a notably pious ruler who strove earnestly to reconcile English and Dane under his sceptre. As early as 1020 we find him founding a minster church at Ashingdon in Essex, the site of his last battle in 1016, 'for the souls of the men who had been slain there'. He offered a cloak decorated with peacocks – symbol of immortality – at the tomb of his former foe Edmund Ironside in the abbey church at Glastonbury. He honoured English saints. The mortal remains of Archbishop

Ælfheah were translated from London to Canterbury in 1023 in a carefully staged ceremony and enshrined alongside the high altar of Canterbury cathedral. When Canute visited the tomb of St Cuthbert at Durham he did so as a pilgrim, walking the last five miles barefoot. He commissioned a golden shrine for the tomb of St Edith at Wilton.

Canute was ostentatiously generous to other churches too. He and Queen Emma – Canute had married Ethelred's widow in 1017 – gave a magnificent processional cross of gold and silver to the cathedral church of Winchester. They may have given the luxury gospel-book known as the York Gospels (originally produced at Canterbury) to Archbishop Wulfstan. They certainly gave his successor, Ælfric, a handsome estate at Patrington in Holderness, where three centuries later archiepiscopal patronage yielded one of the most exquisite of English medieval parish churches. Neither did their generosity stop at the Channel. Among foreign churches we know that Chartres, Limoges, St Omer, Cologne and Bremen experienced Canute's largesse. We can be pretty confident that the tally is incomplete: it is surely only lack of evidence that excludes, for example, the churches of his native Denmark such as Roskilde, site of his father's burial, from the list.

The projection of an image was as important to eleventh-century kings and queens as it is to the presidents and prime ministers of our own day. Just such an image, in the literal sense, is preserved in the *Liber Vitae*, or 'Book of Life', of Winchester cathedral, the volume in which were listed the benefactors for whom the monks of Winchester offered regular prayers. King Canute and Queen Emma are pictured there offering the aforementioned processional cross to the cathedral church. Together they place a truly enormous cross upon the altar. An angel hovering above places a crown upon the king's head; another angel places a nun's veil, symbol of pious devotion, on the head of the queen. The angels point with admonitory fingers to where Christ sits in majesty above. Or again, the best-known story about the king is the moral tale about Canute and the waves. The point of the story (often misunderstood) is not an arrogant king's attempt to turn back the tide. It was the smarmy courtiers who told him that he could do that. Canute's action was in rebuke of their flattery, and a demonstration of Christian humility: only God can command the waves. Take, finally, his pilgrimage to Rome in 1027, carefully publicized by the king himself in an open newsletter to his subjects.[8]

I had long ago vowed this journey to God, but I was not able to perform it until now because of the affairs of the kingdom and other causes of hindrance. But now I give most humble thanks to my Almighty God, who has granted me in my lifetime to visit his holy apostles Peter and Paul, and every sacred place which I could learn of within the city of Rome and outside it, and in person to worship and adore there according to my desire. Especially have I accomplished this because I learned from wise men that the holy apostle Peter had received from the Lord great power to bind and to loose, and was the keeper of the keys of the kingdom of Heaven, and I considered it very profitable diligently to seek his special favour before God.

Canute was brilliantly successful in projecting an image of himself as a pious Christian king.

Naturally, given our source materials, it is pretty well impossible to get at the reality behind the image. In this regard we might care to consider the text just quoted in which the king reported on his Roman pilgrimage. It is extraordinarily fortunate that two twelfth-century historians chose to copy this letter, a richly fascinating and revealing document, into their works. It is, as I say, a newsletter; but it is also more than that. Consider these clauses:

Now, therefore, be it known to you all, that I have humbly vowed to Almighty God to amend my life from now on in all things, and to rule justly and faithfully the kingdoms and peoples subject to me and to maintain equal justice in all things; and if hitherto anything contrary to what is right has been done through the intemperance of my youth or through negligence, I intend to repair it all henceforth with the help of God. For this reason I implore and command all my councillors, to whom I have entrusted the councils of the kingdom, that from now on they shall not in any way, either for fear of me or for the favour of any powerful person, consent to any injustice, or suffer it to flourish in any part of the kingdom. I command also all the sheriffs and reeves over my whole kingdom, as they wish to retain my friendship and their own safety, that they employ no unjust force against any man, neither rich nor poor, but that all men, of noble or humble birth, rich or poor, shall have the right to enjoy just law; from which there is to be no deviation in any way, neither on account of the royal favour nor out of respect for any powerful man, nor in order to amass money for me; for I have no need that money should be amassed for me by unjust exaction.

In other words, the king had not kept, and admitted that he had not kept, the undertakings entered into at Oxford in 1018. Canute now promised amendment of specific shortcomings in the character of his rule. Promises of this nature are rarely, if ever, spontaneous. One may suspect that the king was responding to pressure of one sort or another. It seems that here we have a further example of a constitutional pact to set alongside the shadowy agreements of 1014 and 1018.

But this is not the end of the interest of this remarkable document. While in Rome Canute had attended the imperial coronation of Conrad II of Germany by Pope John XIX on Easter Day, 26 March 1027. (Canute's daughter Gunhild would later marry his son the Emperor Henry III.) This too was reported in the newsletter. And the announcement was coupled with something further.

I therefore spoke with the emperor and the lord pope and the princes who were present, concerning the needs of all the peoples of my whole kingdom, whether English or Danes, that they might be granted more equitable law and greater security on their way to Rome, and that they should not be hindered by so many barriers on the way and so oppressed by unjust tolls; and the emperor and King Rodulf [of Burgundy], who chiefly had dominion over those barriers, consented to my demands; and all the princes confirmed by edicts that my men, whether merchants or others travelling for the sake of prayer [i.e. pilgrims] should go to and return from Rome in safety with firm peace and just law, free from hindrances by barriers and tolls.

Here again, it is implausible to posit royal spontaneity. There is a whiff of negotiation in the background. English and Danish merchants were putting demands to the king to negotiate secure and toll-free travel on their behalf in the course of his Roman journey, in return for – what? The answer, surely, has to be money: what else could a king possibly want from the merchants? There is an intriguing contrast with the colossal levy of 1017–18. On that earlier occasion Canute had simply *taken* from the citizens of his biggest city; in 1027 he *bargained*. There are in addition insistent, and sadly unanswerable, questions which raise their heads. Who were these undifferentiated (in our text) 'merchants'? From London alone, or from other towns as well? How did they organize themselves? How did they lobby? On what occasion, and in what form, did they present their demands to the king?

If the business community (as we would call it today) of England in the first half of the eleventh century was sufficiently well organized to bring pressure to bear upon government, one is bound to ask oneself how long such a state of affairs had obtained. It has already been stressed that England in the tenth and eleventh centuries was a rich and well-exploited country. We can demonstrate from a variety of evidence, written, topographical, numismatic, archaeological, that the urban economy was in a state of something approaching permanent boom during the last century or so of the Anglo-Saxon state. This must imply a flourishing economy in the countryside too, given that towns are economically dependent upon their hinterlands. We know that many millions of silver pennies were in circulation at any one time in the England of Ethelred II and Canute – which raises tantalizing questions as to how such huge quantities of silver bullion ever got to a country whose native sources of silver are meagre. There are grounds for supposing the existence of an effective infrastructure of order, of markets, of transport, of steadily diffusing technologies of milling, metalworking, harnessing, shipbuilding. The leading authority on the period has gone so far as to state that 'the most important economic developments before the Industrial Revolution took place in the later Anglo-Saxon period'.[9] This is a bold and far-reaching claim, but it was made by a historian as judicious as he is learned; not a scholar to indulge in flights of fantasy.

If England really was an extremely wealthy country, then several features of the history of this epoch fall into place. We can understand why Sweyn and Canute were so greedy for conquest of it, as was William of Normandy a little later. We can understand how this burgeoning and blossoming economy could sustain very heavy levels of taxation. We can also begin to understand the anxieties of Archbishop Wulfstan of York about the proper ordering of society.

Among Wulfstan's minor works is a collection of brief observations about social ranks and status. Its opening sentences are revealingly nostalgic:

Once upon a time it used to be that people and right went by ranks. In those days the wise men among the people were entitled to respect. Each had his station, whether nobleman or commoner, retainer or lord.

We recognize at once the outraged cry of dismay of the conservative. Wulfstan was in no doubt that an ordered society, one in which all the people kept to their proper places, was pleasing to God. It was a theme that he developed in his *Institutes of Polity*. But in his own day something was going wrong. People were breaking ranks. There was a new fluidity in society. In his *Sermon of the Wolf* he put the blame on the presence of the Danish armies. Slaves were running away from their masters, joining the Danes, accumulating wealth, rising in social rank, sometimes even returning to enslave their former masters. The plight of the master enslaved by his own former slave was a *topos*, or literary convention, which was already many centuries old in Wulfstan's day. Though we do not have to take all his words literally, there is no reason to doubt the main lines of the archbishop's diagnosis.

As a bishop successively of London and of York, Wulfstan was of course well aware of what we call social mobility. Neither was he against it. In a celebrated passage he observed that 'if a merchant prospered, that if he three times crossed the ocean at his own expense, then was he afterwards entitled to the rights of a thegn'. And rights necessarily involved obligations, especially for the risen bourgeois who invested his profits in land. This social process, the passage of new wealth from town to countryside, which has been an immensely significant force in the shaping of English society over the centuries, was already at work in the eleventh. We can document it in the second half of the century and need not doubt that it was happening in Wulfstan's day. Like many another clerical conservative, Wulfstan approved of what later generations would call the 'landed interest'. Land gave solidity and respectability to new wealth. Its possession involved duties and responsibilities. The performance of these obligations buttressed the stable ordering of society. Coherence and hierarchy in human social order were pleasing to God.

What Wulfstan and others like him dreaded was the naked irresponsible wealth of the low-born adventurers who threw in their lot with the marauding Danish armies and made their money as military professionals. There were plenty of such people in eleventh-century Europe. This is not surprising: where there is plenty of money circulating, there you will find professionals, mercenaries, men who fight for pay and plunder. We come back to the root of the problem. Money is invariably a very powerful solvent of traditional social order. Wulfstan lived in times which were turbulent socially (as well as politically) *because* they were vibrant economically. These conditions were unprecedented. No wonder it was bewildering to clerical observers.

Wulfstan was not alone in voicing his anxieties. His contemporary Bishop Burchard of Worms (d. 1025) edited an ambitious collection of canon law known as the *Decretum*. To refer to it as 'canon law', as is conventional, is perhaps misleading as implying to a modern understanding a work exclusively ecclesiastical, churchly, in character. 'Christian law' might be a more appropriate formulation. In the many pages of his *Decretum* Burchard sought to proclaim, to restate to a society which was neglecting them, the moral norms which should regulate the life of Christendom in a manner acceptable to God. Burchard and Wulfstan never encountered one another's work (as far as we know): but they lived in the same moral and intellectual world, shared the same social and ethical concerns.

Other clergy indulged in social theorizing which hints obliquely at comparable anxieties. It was just at this time that a scheme for the threefold ordering of society was first widely committed to writing, which was to have a long currency throughout the medieval centuries and beyond. Christian society, wrote Bishop Adalbero of Laon in northern France in about 1026, is composed of three orders: those who fight, those who pray, and those who work. In modern parlance, these may be interpreted as the aristocratic and knightly classes, the clergy, and the vast majority who made up the rest. Adalbero may not have known this (any more than his modern French commentators), but he was only echoing a theme already sounded by English churchmen, Ælfric of Eynsham in a homily of perhaps *c.* 1005, and Wulfstan himself in the first draft of his *Institutes of Polity* a dozen or so years later. Why were churchmen on both sides of the Channel so interested in the theory of the Three Orders of society just at this time? One possibility suggests itself. Classifications of this sort are often a defensive reaction to unwelcome and bewildering change. So it may have been on this occasion. The Three Orders were prescriptive, not descriptive; they constituted a statement about how things ought to be, not how they actually were. The society which the threefold classification purported to encapsulate was no longer there.

England in the early years of the second millennium experienced the extremes of turbulence and distress, a prey to apocalyptic fears, to Danish raids and conquest, to unprecedentedly heavy levies of taxation. Yet in men such as Wulfstan of York it had leaders of courage and vision who sought, not without success, to moderate the worst excesses of predators, to temper the wind to the shorn lamb. And it had reserves and resilience, in its buoyant economy in countryside and town, in its creativity in the arts, above all in its institutions of orderly government. The English kingdom would come through.

6

Rise Wood

In the year 1018 a comet appeared for thirty successive nights in the skies above Northumbria in presage, so it was said, of some terrible future disaster for the region. The trouble, when it materialized, came from the north. Northumbria had been rendered vulnerable by Uhtred's death. Once again, the Scots seized their opportunity. That summer, King Malcolm II invaded Northumbria with a large army. English levies from between the Tees and the Tweed were called out to oppose him, only to experience overwhelming defeat at Carham-on-Tweed, between Coldstream and Kelso.[1] Victory at Carham enabled the Scots to reverse their disaster of 1006. The English authorities were forced to cede territory in southern Lothian to the Scots. The man held responsible for the cession, as presumably for the defeat which precipitated it, was Eadwulf, the brother of Earl Uhtred. Doubtless this accounts for his treatment at the hands of the Durham anonymous:

On Uhtred's death his brother Eadwulf, known as Cudel, succeeded to the earldom. He was a very slothful and cowardly man. Fearful lest the Scots whom his brother had slaughtered as aforesaid would avenge these deaths upon him, he surrendered the whole of Lothian to them by a firm treaty in order to make amends. In this manner was Lothian joined to the kingdom of the Scots.

Considered as history, this is of course misleading, as we have already seen. But it shows how a nobleman who failed in his primary task of defence would be remembered. Eadwulf Cudel seems to have held the northern, Bernician, half of Northumbria just as his father Waltheof had done. Canute's appointee to succeed Uhtred, Eric of Hlathir, though he may have enjoyed a primacy of honour over Bernicia, seems to have been first and foremost earl of Deira. Eric belonged to one of the many princely dynasties of a Norway which possessed as yet no settled royal dynasty. He had helped Canute's father Sweyn to defeat Olaf Tryggvason back in 999 and had subsequently governed Norway as Sweyn's nominal deputy. At some point he married Sweyn's daughter Gytha. He had campaigned with Sweyn in England, and it is possible that he and his men had been implicated in the murder of Archbishop Ælfheah in 1012. He must have played a prominent part in the conquest of England between 1013 and 1016: the earldom of Deira can only have been granted to him in recognition of distinguished and loyal service. He was presumably rewarded with lands in Yorkshire and perhaps elsewhere as well, though we do not know where they lay. Very little is known of his tenure of office. His name features among the witnesses of a number of royal diplomas, the latest from the year 1023. When Canute conquered Norway in 1028 he placed Eric's son Haakon as his regent over it. The implication would seem to be that the head of the family, Eric, was dead or incapacitated by then. At any rate, we hear no more of him after 1023. His successor as earl, Siward, cannot be traced before the year 1033 when he subscribed a diploma issued by Canute. The end of Eric's tenure as earl, and the beginning of Siward's, cannot therefore be dated more accurately than between 1023 and 1033.

There were ecclesiastical changes too. At Durham the elderly Bishop Ealdhun died of a broken heart after hearing news of the disaster at Carham. After his death the see of Durham was vacant 'for nearly three years', which takes us to the early part of 1021 before the next appointment, of a bishop named Edmund, was made. Such a long delay in filling a vacant bishopric was unusual at that period and is likely to have been occasioned by some sort of difficulty behind the scenes. Delay may in part have been caused by the absence of the king: Canute was in Denmark for much of 1019 until the spring of 1020. But that still leaves a further year or thereabouts before the new appointment was made. A strange story told by the monk Symeon of Durham, writing in about 1105, may be relevant here. According to Symeon, the choice of Edmund as bishop was insisted upon by a mysterious voice emanating from the tomb of St Cuthbert during mass.

1. A leaf from the single surviving manuscript of *De Obsessione Dunelmi* (see Chapter 1), Cambridge, Corpus Christi College, Parker Library MS 139, folio 51r. The murder of Earl Uhtred is described about three quarters of the way down the left-hand column: the place-name *Wiheal* may be read in the ninth line up from the foot.

2. Durham cathedral, one of the most majestic buildings in the world, stands on a high bluff above the River Wear, a site chosen by Bishop Ealdhun (not without regard to its defensive potential) in 995 to house the relics of St Cuthbert. Nothing now remains of the Anglo-Saxon cathedral. In this view from the south-west, the western towers were built between the twelfth and fourteenth centuries, and the mighty crossing tower between 1465 and 1500.

3. The Norman castle at Bamburgh, extensively reconstructed by the first Lord Armstrong between 1894 and 1905, a restoration described at the time as 'the acme of expenditure with a nadir of intelligent achievement'. The fortress of the tenth- and eleventh-century Earls of Bernicia is presumed to underlie the keep. At that period the North Sea at high tide probably lapped the foot of the rock on which the castle stands.

4. The sanctuary chair at Beverley Minster (see Chapter 3). Simple, dignified, unornamented (and therefore difficult for the art historian to date with precision), this stone *frith-stool* or 'peace seat' may have been made in the tenth century. It still stands, as it has always done, next to the altar of St John of Beverley, marking one of the holiest sanctuaries in Northumbria.

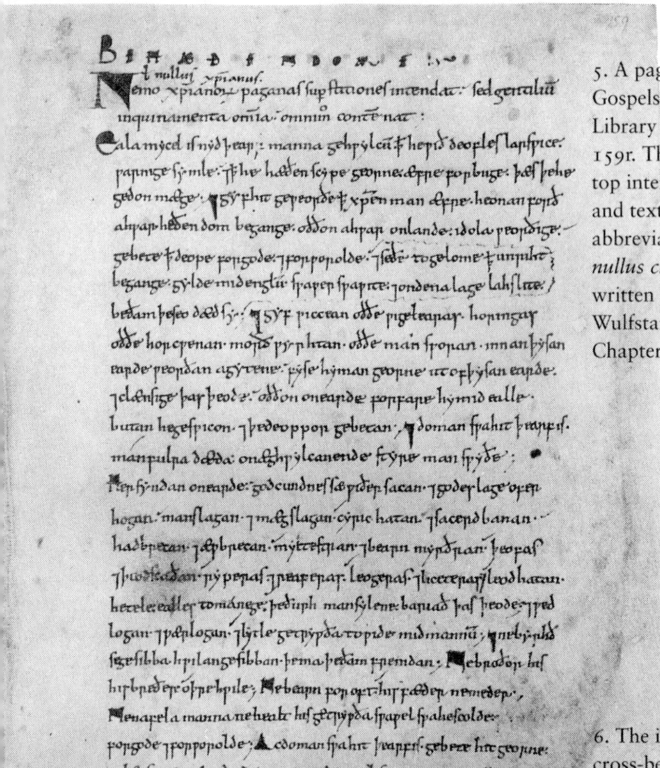

Beofod fofhnon fon

t nullus xpianus.
Nemo xpianorū · paganas supstitiones intendat · sed gentaliū
inquinamenta omnia · omniū contēnnat :

Ealamyed ıs noð þeah; manna gehyleð · þ hepıs ðeoples lapsþıce:
papınge symle · þ hy hæþen scıp oe gwynnæ oþþe popbuge: þæs þehe
geðon mæge · þ ıs þ he geþeopode þ xpen man oeþþe heonan fopð
ahpaþheden dom begange· oððon ahpan onlande: ıdola propodıge·
gebete ð deope þongode· �601poþpopolde· ıseðe tægelome þ unpihte
begange· gylde mıð englıſc þapen þpapıæ· �601ndena lage lahſlıæ· �
betan þeso dæð ſy· � syf þıcean oðer pigelaepar· hopingay
oððe hopepenan· moþe þypphtan· oððe man fpopan·mnanþyſan
eapde þeondan agypene· þyſe hyman gwopne·utopþyſan eapde·
�601clænſıge þap þeode· oððon oneapde· þonþaþe hymıd ealle·
butan hegeſpıcon· �601þeðeoppon gebetan· � doman þpahıt þpapeſ·
manþulþa deðða· onæðhp �601cleanende· ſtype man ſpyðe :•
þıep hyndan oneapde· godcundneſ ſcepdıp ſacan· �601godeſ lage oþep
hogan· manſlagan· � mæg ſlagan· cypıe hatan· � ſacepd banan·
hadbpecan· �601æþbpecan· mytceſtyan· �601þeapn myoðpan· þeopaſ·
�601þeoðſceaðan· þy þepaſ· � þeıp eapr· leogepaſ· �601lıecceþapſ· � laðhatan·
heteleceadleþ tomaneþ· þediuph manſlene· baptıað þaſ þeode· �601þed
logan· � þæþlogan· � þyrle �601eþypyðða tоþıðe mıð mannū· � unebpyhð·
�601eſıbba· hpılangeſıbban·þırma þeðam þpemdan: Þ ebnaðon hıſ
hıp þæðeip oſ þp hpıle· Þ ebeapn þonþeip· hıp þæðen· nemedeþ·
Þ enaþela manna nehæate· hıſ gecpyðða þapel þpahe ſcolde·
þonþode· �601þonþopolde· A codoman þpahıt· þ þapeſ· gebete hıt gwonne·
�601clænſıge þap þeode· gyf þ man godey mıltſe geunnan þılle :•

5. A page from the York
Gospels, York Minster
Library MS Add. 1, folio
159r. The three words at the
top interlined between title
and text, *t nullus xpianus* –
abbreviated form of *vel
nullus christianus* – were
written by Archbishop
Wulfstan of York (see
Chapter 5).

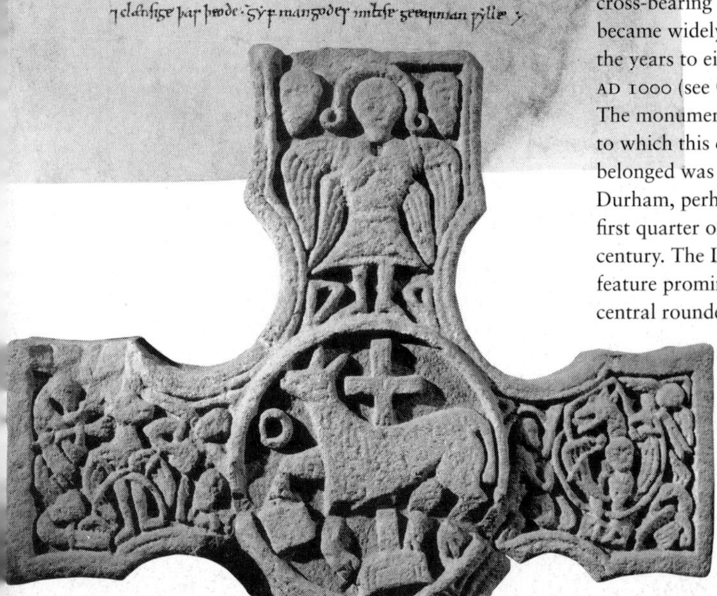

6. The iconography of the
cross-bearing Lamb of God
became widely diffused in
the years to either side of
AD 1000 (see Chapter 5).
The monumental stone cross
to which this cross-head
belonged was carved at
Durham, perhaps in the
first quarter of the eleventh
century. The Lamb and Cross
feature prominently in the
central roundel.

7. Another example of the Lamb of God iconography is to be found in the numismatically unique issue of the *Agnus Dei* penny from the reign of Ethelred II, probably 1008–9 (discussed in Chapter 5). This coin, British Museum CM 1955, 7-8, 81, was struck at the Derby mint by a moneyer named Blacaman.

8. The so-called Horn of Ulf from York Minster. An ivory horn, probably carved in southern Italy or Sicily in the early part of the eleventh century; the silver mounts and chain date from the seventeenth century. It is an example of the sort of exotic Mediterranean artwork so highly prized by the aristocracy of northern Europe. It could have been acquired in the course of a pilgrimage to Rome or Jerusalem such as that which Carl and Ealdred planned to undertake in 1038 (see Chapter 6). At York it was believed, by the fourteenth century at latest, that the horn had been given to the Minster as an act of piety by an eleventh-century landowner named Ulf. As it so happens, we do know of a prominent landed magnate named Ulf who went on a pilgrimage to Jerusalem in the 1060s: it is just possible that he was the donor.

9. Kirk Hammerton church, a few miles to the west of York. From this angle, the only structural feature which is not of eleventh-century date is the late-medieval square-headed window in the south wall of the nave. One can get a good idea of what a late Anglo-Saxon parish church might have looked like: it is probable, however, that the roof would have been covered in thatch.

10. A grave-marker from Auckland St Andrew in County Durham. The 'small stone cross' which marked the site of Ealdred's murder in Rise Wood (see Chapter 7) could have looked something like this.

11. An illustration of the Crucifixi[on] from the Gospel Book commission[ed] by Countess Judith, wife of Earl Tostig of Northumbria (see Chapt[er] 8), between 1051 and 1065, New York, Pierpont Morgan Library M[S] 709, folio IV. The female figure cl[ing]ing to the foot of the cross is held [to] be an image of Judith herself. The manuscript, which was probably written and decorated at Canterb[ury] is testimony to the remarkable tale[nt] of eleventh-century English artists.

12. Halley's Comet scudding acros[s] the skies of England in 1066, as re[p]resented on the Bayeux Tapestry. [The] caption above reads ISTI MIRANT[UR] STELLAM ('These people are wond[er]ing at the comet') as the designer h[as] made quite plain in their expressio[ns] and gestures. Comets were widely held to prefigure imminent tragic events. In the following scene, whe[re] King Harold is being told of the comet, the ghostly outlines of ship[s] in the lower border hint at what those events whould be.

13. The River Derwent at Stamford Bridge. The present stone bridge spans the river on the approximate site of the presumed wooden bridge which was the focus of the battle fought on 25 September 1066 (see Chapter). The slopes of the Wolds may be seen in the background.

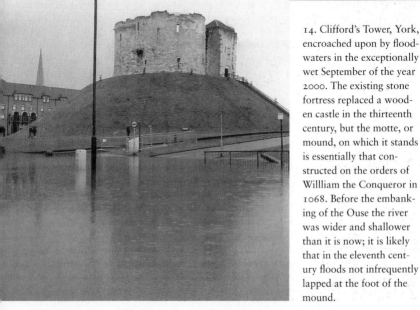

14. Clifford's Tower, York, encroached upon by flood-waters in the exceptionally wet September of the year 2000. The existing stone fortress replaced a wooden castle in the thirteenth century, but the motte, or mound, on which it stands is essentially that constructed on the orders of Willliam the Conqueror in 1068. Before the embanking of the Ouse the river was wider and shallower than it is now; it is likely that in the eleventh century floods not infrequently lapped at the foot of the mound.

15. Settrington on a sunny day in May 2000. The fifteenth-century tower of the parish church may be seen in the centre of the photograph. It is suggested in Chapter 9 that the hall in which the sons and grandsons of Carl were massacred may have stood to the left of the church among the trees which now conceal Settrington House. The photograph was taken from the rising ground to the east, from which quarter, it is suggested, the killers sent by Earl Waltheof came on that winter's afternoon in 1073–4.

16. The splendid south portal of Wighill church was probably commissioned by Geoffrey Haget and his siblings (see Chapter 10) and executed *circa* 1170–80. The same team of sculptors worked at other parish churches in the neighbourhood.

Symeon had heard this tale from an elderly priest whose grandfather had been the deacon assisting to serve the mass on that occasion. Such supernatural intervention was often a means of resolving conflict or controversy. In other words, there was a rival candidate for the bishopric of Durham. Symeon also tells us that Edmund was a member of the Durham community. It follows, in all likelihood, that the rival candidate was an outsider. A 'foreign' contender is most likely to have been the choice of the royal court. Evidently, however, king and court could not get their way: the local man won. So much we may infer from Symeon's story if we squeeze the evidence. Symeon tells us that Canute 'rejoiced' at Edmund's election. One cannot help suspecting that he might have done so through clenched teeth. Edmund's consecration at Winchester at the hands of Archbishop Wulfstan of York could have been a somewhat uneasy state occasion.[2]

It looks as though Canute's grasp on Bernicia was shaky. He could not get his man, whoever he was, into the bishopric of Durham. As for Earl Eadwulf – whatever his true character – he cannot have been well disposed towards a king who had perhaps instigated, certainly connived in, his brother's murder. And then there were the Scots. Who might guess where they would strike next? Malcolm's ally at Carham, his dependant the British princeling Owen the Bald of Strathclyde and Cumbria, had died later in the same year and his kingdom had fallen in to his overlord. Scottish royal authority now stretched as far south as the Lake District. That meant that Lancashire and the north-western parts of Yorkshire were vulnerable to Scottish raiding parties.

There was nothing surprising about this. The situation of Bernicia vis-à-vis a southern king was the same under Canute the Conqueror as it had been under his West Saxon precursors. Like them, he tried to make himself agreeable in the north. When he visited Durham at a later date he was, as King Athelstan had been before him, extremely generous. He gave St Cuthbert's clergy a handsome multiple estate at Staindrop in County Durham and confirmed many of their property rights in Yorkshire.

Down in Yorkshire the royal grasp lay a little more firmly. There was a brother-in-law in the earldom of Deira. When the great – and thoroughly reliable – Archbishop Wulfstan died in 1023 his successor was evidently a trusted king's man. Ælfric, nicknamed *Puttoc* ('the

Kite' or 'the Buzzard') for reasons unknown, was a monk of Winchester whose family origins may have lain in the eastern Danelaw (like those of several of his predecessors in the archbishopric of York). He was to hold the see of York for nearly thirty years, dying in 1051.

Nevertheless, we should not be far wrong to assume that Northumbria as a whole was in a fairly disrupted condition in the early years of Canute's reign. The opening years of any early medieval ruler's reign were invariably a testing time in which muscles were flexed, moves watched, networks reconnected, loyalties tested, weaknesses probed, in the complicated manoeuvring that personal monarchy entailed. Canute was not only a conqueror of England, with all a conqueror's initial fragility. He was in addition trying to maintain himself as king in Denmark. To these two horses a third would soon be added, in Norway. It was stretching the elasticity of personal rule to the very limits of tautness. In general terms, therefore, we might expect an English king's distant province of Northumbria to be uneasy. But there were particular terms as well. Northumbria's leading families had been scarred by the massacre at *Wiheal* and the slaughter at Carham. Family stability had been rent; enmities had been engendered. Archbishop Wulfstan would have found much to deplore in the Northumbria of his closing years. The disturbed state of Northumbria does not explain what happened next in our story, but it must have facilitated it.

Earl Eadwulf did not live long. He died, according to our Durham anonymous, *post modicum*, 'not long after' the last event mentioned, the battle of Carham in 1018. It's a vague phrase, which could mean anything from a few months to several years. Sometime in the early 1020s, at a guess, will have to do. He was succeeded in the earldom of Bernicia by his nephew Ealdred, the son of Uhtred by his first wife Ecgfrida, the daughter of Bishop Ealdhun of Durham.

'Ealdred killed Thurbrand, his father's murderer.' That's all we are told. We know neither when nor where, nor anything of the circumstances. We have simply the bare fact, a notice of telegraphic brevity about this second killing in our bloodfeud.

If Thurbrand had been acting with Canute's connivance, even encouragement, in slaying Uhtred, Ealdred was a spontaneous actor in avenging his father's death. Why was he not punished by due process of law for this murderous affray? But this is a modern question. It would not have made sense in eleventh-century England. A feuding culture, such as was sketched in chapter 1, accepted the indispensability of violence exercised in accordance with the recognized norms governing the conduct of a bloodfeud. In the words of one of the pioneers of Anglo-Saxon studies, John Mitchell Kemble,

This right of feud lies at the root of all Teutonic legislation; and in the Anglosaxon law especially it continues to be recognized long after an imperial power has been constituted, and the general conservancy of the peace has been committed to a central authority.[3]

The prosecution of feud was a matter of honour. Alcuin of York, writing to his patron Charlemagne in 801 to introduce some visitors from England, could present one of them, Torhtmund, as 'a man proved in loyalty, strenuous in arms, who has boldly avenged the blood of his lord'.[4] In killing, Torhtmund had acted as a man of honour. Alcuin's letters were widely read in eleventh-century England: Wulfstan of York's copy of the letter-collection, annotated in his own hand, survives to this day in the British Library. He would have known of Alcuin's commendation of Torhtmund. There is no reason to suppose that he would have dissented from Alcuin's judgement.

It should therefore be a little less surprising than some enquirers have found it that a feuding culture could coexist with an institutionally sophisticated monarchy such as that of tenth- and eleventh-century England. Royal legislation relating to feud is in this regard illuminating. Anglo-Saxon kings did not seek to abolish feuding; that would have been almost inconceivable. Guided by their churchmen they lamented indiscriminate violence, but they accepted the sanctioned, legitimate violence involved in feuding, seeking only to enforce a proper observance of customs designed to limit its spread. Alfred ruled that when a man has cornered an enemy in his house he should not immediately attack him: time must be allowed for mediation. If a man being pursued in the course of a feud should seek sanctuary in a church, the pursuers must respect it. A man may fight on behalf of his lord without becoming liable to feud with his lord's enemies. A husband who discovers his wife in bed with another man may use violence towards the adulterer without incurring feud.

Half a century later King Edmund issued a legislative ordinance almost entirely concerned with the conduct of feud. He shared the concerns which had preoccupied his grandfather: deferring violence, encouraging arbitration, limiting reprisal. A slayer must bear the burden of feud as an individual, should his kinsfolk disavow him. Those who kill in the prosecution of a feud are to be debarred from resort to royal courts until they have done penance under the direction of their bishop. 'Wise men' must act as arbitrators to settle feuds. The process of initiating compensation payments, in its carefully graded stages over nine weeks, is brought under the king's special protection; to breach it incurred heavy monetary penalties.[5]

Kings therefore sought to insert themselves into the feuding process in the role, so to say, of umpires or referees; and as time went by they did so, or wanted to do so, in a more assertive way. But we are still a long way from a legal culture in which all crime is crime against the king. And we need to remind ourselves that the king's *mund*, his peace or protection, lay more thinly and hesitantly – like his lands, his mints and his monasteries – the further one travelled from the Wessex heartlands.

Kings indeed did not, could not, regard themselves as being in some sense outside the conventions of feud. A conspirator against Otto I of Germany was killed by the king's men in 941. Twenty-seven years later his son was appointed to the Saxon bishopric of Halberstadt. When Otto invested him formally with the pastoral staff of episcopal office he said, 'Take this price for your father.' As a piece of badinage, we might judge it on the grim side. But, as Karl Leyser acutely pointed out, there was a serious edge to the king's remark. Otto was making reparation as convention demanded. 'The king did not regard himself as exempt from the social obligations which bound his nobles nor is he seen standing outside the ring of feud and revenge.'[6]

Prosecution of feud could be presented by kings, or their propagandists, as the pretext for what we should call acts of state such as declarations of war. When in 1058 King Fernando I of León-Castilla attacked the town of Viseu in central Portugal he acted so that 'the barbarians [i.e. Muslims] of that city should make due recompense for the death of his father-in-law', Alfonso V, who had met his end by the hand of an archer – the day being hot, he had removed his armour –

while besieging the town thirty years earlier.[7] Whether this really *was* Fernando's motive in attacking Viseu is irrelevant. What is interesting is that the writer, a monk in the city of León who was composing his chronicle at least half a century later, chose to present matters thus to his primary audience – just as the *Beowulf* poet chose to present his audience with God's feud with the kin of Cain. So these very different authors made sense of their world; so their audiences would have understood the stories they told.

Alfred and Edmund; Otto I and Fernando I; Uhtred, Thurbrand and Ealdred: all belonged to the very highest ranks, royal or aristocratic, of society. But feud involved men and women of lesser standing, and not simply in their role as retainers of the great. Round about the year 1000 a group of people describing themselves as 'the thegns of Cambridge', by which we should probably understand the local gentry of Cambridgeshire who would have been accustomed to gather regularly at Cambridge for meetings of the shire court, formed themselves into what they called a *gild* or guild. At that time the word 'guild' did not have the mercantile or craft associations which it later acquired. A guild in the eleventh century was simply an association, a club, a society, whose members met regularly for conviviality and who were bound together by mutual oaths of aid in times of sickness or trouble. The Cambridgeshire gentry were methodical men who had the rules of their guild written down. A copy of this document has survived; that is why we know about the Cambridgeshire thegns' guild. (There could have been many other such guilds in eleventh-century England of which we know nothing because no record of them has survived.) Necessarily, one of the kinds of trouble with which they concerned themselves was violence and its consequences. 'If anyone slay a guildsman, let £8 be paid in compensation. If the slayer refuses to pay the compensation, let all the guildship bear the feud and avenge the guildsman.' The members of the association undertook a collective responsibility for prosecuting a feud on behalf of one of their fellows. About half of the regulations concerned themselves with the conduct of feud. It was an ever-present possibility.[8]

Here is an example of the sort of flashpoint that could ignite a feud at thegnly level. It occurs as one of the 'mini-narratives' which sometimes feature in the texts of royal diplomas, in this instance a charter issued by King Ethelred II in the 990s, providing a tantalizing snapshot but no before or after. There were three brothers, landowners apparently in Oxfordshire. One of their retainers, a man named Leofric, stole a bridle. (The bridles and other riding accoutrements, such as saddles, stirrups, spurs and so forth, of the upper classes at this period were often richly decorated with gold and silver; objects therefore of considerable value.) The owners of the bridle attacked the brothers in retaliation. Two of the brothers were killed, but the third, together with Leofric, managed to escape to sanctuary in the church of St Helen at Abingdon. There the story fades out. But one may legitimately wonder what would be likely to have happened next. There was a double murder to be avenged.[9]

We should also bear in mind that feuding was no monopoly of the laity. The clergy belonged to the same moral and social universe. That great realist Archbishop Wulfstan of York was well aware of this. In Canute's lawcode, drafted as we saw in the last chapter by the archbishop, Wulfstan concerned himself with the respective obligations of cloistered monks and secular priests: 'No minster-monk may lawfully demand or pay compensation in a feud. He forsakes his kin-law when he bows to rule-law [i.e. accepts the discipline of a monastic rule].' Ordinary priests and deacons, on the other hand, should observe accepted customs: 'If a man in orders be charged with homicide, let him clear himself with his kinsfolk, who must bear the feud with him or pay compensation.'

As we have already seen, we cannot accurately date Ealdred's slaying of Thurbrand. Somewhere in the mid-1020s looks plausible. According to my very approximate chronology, which floats uneasily, a leaky vessel on a sea of speculation, Thurbrand could hardly have been born later than about 975. That would leave him, at about fifty years of age, a man of elderly – and therefore vulnerable? – fighting age in about 1025. Thurbrand left a son, Carl, whom it is tempting to identify with the *Karl, minister*, whose name appears in the witness-lists of royal diplomas from 1024 onwards. It has even been suggested that Carl was in effect if not in name earl of Deira in that awkward gap between Eric of Hlathir and Siward. At any rate, as heir to his father, he was a very imposing personage in Yorkshire.

The Durham anonymous tells us that Carl and his father's slayer,

Earl Ealdred, were extremely disturbed and roused to action (*exagitati*) by these shocking events. The action to which they were roused, of course, was the further prosecution of the feud. They laid ambushes for one another, but each man proved too wily to be trapped. How long this went on we are not told, but the implication seems to be that it was for some time. Perhaps, at a guess, we should reckon some years rather than months. Eventually, Ealdred and Carl were brought together by the intervention of friends. This is a classic episode of feuding convention, arbitration by mediators acceptable to both parties. It has been suggested that the mediators were none other than the king and his courtiers. Canute is known to have visited the north of England at about the right time, in 1031 according to one version of the *Anglo-Saxon Chronicle*. But there is no need to ascribe this peacemaking to the king. The friends who mediated could have been other northern noblemen or the archbishop of York and his clergy. Whoever they were, their arbitration was successful. So successful was it, indeed, that Ealdred and Carl entered into a sworn brotherhood – a bond of the closest possible kind creating an artificial kinship – and vowed to go on pilgrimage to Rome together.

It is all too easy to forget that these violent men and women were also pious. Violence and piety coexisted in them in a manner which may initially surprise us. It was not an interior piety, though we have the testimony of Ælfric of Eynsham, the homilist, that some at any rate among the laity did ponder their Christian faith. One of his biblical treatises was composed at the request of an Oxfordshire landowner, and his translation of six books of the Old Testament into the vernacular was commissioned by a nobleman of high rank. These indications aside, however, it is broadly true to say that the piety of the laity was a piety of performance, of visible public actions. Almsgiving, manumission of slaves, grants of land or treasure to the Church, building of churches, going on pilgrimage: these were the ways in which wealthy men and women of the eleventh century set about the business of pleasing God. He was a great lord, a triumphant king, a just judge, a figure of awful majesty such as we can see, for example, sculpted in stone in Barnack church near Peterborough in one of the most accomplished artworks of the late Anglo-Saxon period. Though far above all earthly kings, God needed to be approached, like them, with all the prudent rituals of pleasing. It was a world, as we have already seen, in which all relationships were lubricated by gift and counter-gift. So too the relationship with God. Pious generosity might dispose him to have mercy on the erring and straying sinner.

'I grant that every penally enslaved man whom I acquired in the course of jurisdiction be freed ... and I wish that every year one hundred poor people be fed at the monastery of Ely on the feast-day of St Etheldreda.' These words are quoted from the will of King Ethelred's eldest son who died young, predeceasing his father, in 1015. At about the same time a noblewoman in Bernicia was making similar provision:

Geatfleda has given freedom for the love of God and for the need of her soul: namely [to] Ecceard the smith and Ælfstan and his wife and all their offspring, born and unborn, and Arcil and Cole and Ecgferth and Ealdhun's daughter, and all those people whose heads she took for their food in the evil days [i.e. those whom she had accepted as slaves to rescue them from starvation]. Whosoever perverts this and robs her soul of this, may God Almighty rob him of this life and of the heavenly kingdom, and may he be accursed dead and alive ever into eternity. And also she has freed the men whom she begged from Gospatric, namely Ælfwold and Colbrand and Ælfsige and his son Gamel, Ethelred Tredewude and his stepson Uhtred, Aculf and Thurkil and Ælfsige. Whoever deprives them of this, may God Almighty and St Cuthbert be angry with them.

This is the language of late Anglo-Saxon piety. It also serves to remind us of some of the harsher realities of life in England a thousand years ago: people were entering into slavery to stay alive; slaves were being passed from owner to owner.[10]

Many parish churches were being built in eleventh-century England. It is likely that most of them were paid for by the lords of the estates they served. Sometimes we are explicitly told as much. 'Ulf ordered the church to be erected for himself and for Gunwara's soul.' So runs the inscription on a sundial in the church at Aldbrough in Holderness. Or again, more ambitiously, 'Orm the son of Gamel acquired St Gregory's church when it was completely ruined and collapsed, and he had it built anew from the ground to Christ and St Gregory in the days of King Edward and Earl Tostig.' This text flanks a sundial at St Gregory's minster in Kirkdale, at the southern fringe of the North York Moors. Both Orm and Ulf are known to us from other sources as prominent Yorkshire landowners.

The surviving fabric of the churches at Aldbrough and Kirkdale is not that commissioned by Orm and Ulf. Both buildings have undergone major structural change in later centuries. Sometimes, however, we can get a sense of what a late Anglo-Saxon parish church looked like. At Kirk Hammerton, some nine miles to the west of York, it is possible to view the church on the south side from such an angle that only the Anglo-Saxon fabric is visible, not the later additions. It is a simple two-cell building of nave and smaller chancel, with a western tower. Yet it makes an impressive ensemble: all the more so when one considers that this stone church, with its very large blocks, was built in an area not supplied with good nearby building stone. Kirk Hammerton church was underwritten by heavy investment in tackle and transport – presumably along the river Nidd, which runs close by – as well as in quarrying and building work.

Pilgrimage was nothing new in eleventh-century England. The shrines of the northern saints, above all Cuthbert, had been attracting pilgrims for centuries. Pilgrimage not to local but to distant shrines, however, to Rome or to the Holy Places, seems to have been rare before the eleventh century. Quite suddenly we have record of a whole succession of distinguished pilgrims from the British Isles. One may suspect that this new fashion in piety was set by a king. In 1027, as we saw in the preceding chapter, King Canute had made his way to Rome. Over the next generation or so we learn of Roman pilgrimages by, among others, King Macbeth of Scotland, Earl Thorfinn of Orkney and Earl Tostig of Northumbria. One of the few surviving Anglo-Saxon wills was made by a testator named Ketel, a prominent East Anglian landowner, before he set out for Rome in the 1050s. There was, thus, a context for Ealdred's and Carl's resolve.

They planned to set out on the first leg of their journey to Rome by sea. They were to sail from one of the harbours in Holderness where Carl's landholdings principally lay, probably the port of Brough-on-Humber, presumably to make landfall in one of the many anchorages in the Rhineland, Flanders or north-eastern France. Unfortunately the

English weather let them down. They were held up in port for a long time by storms at sea. Eventually they gave up waiting, presumably deciding to postpone their pilgrimage, and returned home. The home to which they returned was a manor house or hunting lodge belonging to Carl's family at Rise, a village about seven miles east of Beverley. Rise stands on very slightly rising ground in that flat area – though this is to suggest a completely false etymology: Rise actually means 'a place of brushwood'. It commands long views down the plain of Holderness and across the Humber to the Lincolnshire Wolds. It would have been a convenient place to watch and wait for a change in the weather before taking to the sea. To the west of the church at Rise, in an angle formed by a sharp bend in the present B1243 road, there stands a mound known as Mote Hill, the site of a moated dwelling possibly of the twelfth century. Mote Hill could, earlier on, have been the place where Carl's hall stood.

Carl was a generous host and entertained Ealdred splendidly. But something went terribly wrong. We shall never know what it was: an incautious jest, perhaps, uttered at a juncture when conviviality (a word used by our source) had reached a fairly advanced stage? Something of that sort, no doubt. Carl resolved to slay his guest. Later on, perhaps the next day, Carl offered to show the unsuspecting Ealdred round the estate. When the two men were concealed from view in the depths of Rise Wood – which is still there today, though it was probably much more extensive in the eleventh century – Carl killed his sworn brother Ealdred. This, the third murder in the cycle of feud, occurred in 1038.

7

Ecgfrida's Dowry

We should like to know more than we do of the immediate circumstances surrounding Carl's murder of Ealdred. Eleventh-century noblemen were rarely alone. If the two men were unaccompanied as they strolled in Rise Wood, there would have been retainers and servants not far away. What Ealdred's men were told, how they reacted, how they were treated, are all matters on which we should value information. Was there, for example, further bloodshed? But the trail of evidence goes cold. Ealdred's body would presumably have been taken back to his northern heartlands for burial, at Durham perhaps, or at Bamburgh. However, we are told by our principal source that he was also commemorated at the place where he fell. 'Still today the place of his murder is marked by a small stone cross.'

This was not just hearsay. Our anonymous author at Durham was in a good position to be well informed on the matter. The bishopric of Durham possessed two large and valuable multiple estates in south-east Yorkshire, at Howden and at Welton (see the map on p. 49), the latter next door to Brough-on-Humber. (It is a fair guess that the bishop kept a ship there, to enable him, when need arose, to get as quickly as possible to meetings of the royal court in the south – a reminder that at this period travel by water was a good deal quicker and cheaper than travel overland.) One of the outlying components of the Welton estate was at Walkington, just to the south-west of Beverley, only an hour's ride from Rise. The tenants of Welton and Howdenshire could have supplied reliable local information to their corporate lord, the cathedral community of Durham.

The cross at Rise does not survive but we can form a good idea of what it might have looked like from the numerous stone crosses which have come down to us from tenth- and eleventh-century Northumbria. The Rise cross was presumably commissioned by Ealdred's daughters – (of whom more presently); he had no son – and its erection there must have required the permission of Carl, perhaps granted in a mood of subsequent remorse. It was expressive of the daughters' piety, of their affection for their father, of their family solidarity. But it could have had an additional function. 'Largely pre-literate feuding societies have created a number of crude devices which serve to record the events of feud and to "awaken" successive generations to take vengeance for their forefathers.'[1] Such devices could include the marking of the place of a death or an affray; the preservation and subsequent display of items closely associated with a victim, such as weapons, jewellery, bloodstained garments; funerary dirges, laments which could be learned by heart and repeated years later. Markers, objects, dirges, had a mnemonic function. They were a reminder to the kinsfolk and retainers of the victim not simply of a death but of a duty too. The Anglo-Saxons were acquainted with this cultural convention. In *Beowulf*, when the son of Hunlaf placed a sword in the lap of Hengest, the latter knew that it was his duty to slay Finn. The cross in Rise Wood mutely proclaimed unfinished business, a feud that was not dead.

It is also of great interest that the cross at Rise was put up by women. Anthropologists have repeatedly observed that in those societies in which women do not normally have a role as active combatants – that is, in most Indo-European cultures – they play an important part in the process of urging their menfolk to action.

The soul of her dead husband has cried to her night after night . . . Her son must go out to slay or be slain for his father's sake. For this she has kept in a bottle a blood-soaked piece of his garment, and again and again shown it to him. It is a treasure hidden in her dower-chest; and a day comes, so all declare, when the dry blood becomes moist and forms bubbles – the blood boils. The soul of the dead man can no longer wait; blood must be taken.[2]

This is Albania *c.* 1900, not Northumbria nine centuries earlier. But we may not unreasonably guess that Ealdred's daughters would have sympathized with the Albanian widow.

Thus far, our investigations have concerned a man's world, of warfare, bloodshed and politics. But it was a woman's world too. The recent upsurge of interest in women's history has prompted a number of studies of women in Anglo-Saxon England. For the most part such studies remain unsatisfying. This is not owing to any lack of skill and dedication on the part of modern enquirers – far from it – but is because the shortage of evidence renders Anglo-Saxon women almost invisible. Leaving to one side a certain amount of legal material, which presents the usual problems of prescriptive evidence (as we shall see shortly), there is really extraordinarily little documentation to illumine the activities, let alone the thoughts, of half the population of England in the course of the tenth and eleventh centuries. Only two women in the entire Old English period are documented in any depth, and they are two eleventh-century queens, Emma, the wife of Ethelred II and subsequently of Canute, and Edith, the wife of Edward the Confessor.[3]

Queens are not as other women. Especially is this so in an epoch when, as has been argued, western European queens in general were coming to enjoy more enhanced dignity and greater power than had previously been theirs. As against this, neither Emma nor Edith had been nurtured as 'princesses of the blood'. They were members of the aristocracy, daughters respectively of a rudimentary territorial princeling in northern France, Count Richard I of Normandy, and of an upstart man-on-the-make, Earl Godwin of Wessex. (The contrast to draw would be with Byzantine brides such as Theophanu, who married Otto II of Germany, or Anna, who married Vladimir of Kiev. Nurture in the imperial palace in Constantinople was an entirely different experience from an upbringing in the household of a Norman count or an English earl.) In upbringing, tastes, skills and expectations a young woman like Ecgfrida, daughter of an aristocratic bishop of Durham, need not have differed from Emma or Edith. The difference lay in subsequent fortunes. Emma and Edith married kings; Ecgfrida married an earl, Uhtred. There was a big gap between a king and even the biggest, most wayward, most independent of his earls.

Marriage was, in effect, the only option available to aristocratic women in tenth- and eleventh-century England, with what it brought in its train – child-bearing and child-raising, the smooth running of a large and frequently itinerant household. A very few who would not or could not marry might become 'religious' in the technical sense of that word, that is living a formally religious life as nuns or anchoresses. On the whole it seems likely that the small number of religious women was recruited from the ranks of those who had been widowed or otherwise abandoned by their husbands rather than from the unmarried. And marriage, let there be no misunderstanding about it, was a *business* for the two families concerned. It was not a matter for individual choice. Still less was it a matter for romance, though surviving Old English poetry makes it abundantly clear that love might grow within a marriage. Girls of marriageable age were pieces – I do not say pawns – in a network of family relationships. Brides might, in a famous phrase, 'weave peace' between hostile kins. They might initiate or strengthen local alliances. They might consolidate a family's relationship with a king. They might bring dowries to extend their husbands' landholdings.

A little tract survives, apparently from the time, and just conceivably from the pen, of Archbishop Wulfstan II of York known as *Wifmannes Beweddung*, 'Betrothal of a Woman'.[4] It is our principal guide to what the churchmen of that age considered seemly in the arrangements attendant upon the union between husband and wife. That rather cumbersome phrase is used here because it is necessary to stress that in the Anglo-Saxon period it was betrothal, i.e. the preliminary agreement to marry, rather than the marriage ceremony itself, which was the socially and legally decisive element in the bargain. 'If a man wishes to betroth a maiden or a widow,' runs the opening clause of this tract, 'and it so pleases her and her kinsmen, then it is right that . . .' The phrase 'and it so pleases her' constitutes the only indication in this document that an element of consent on the woman's part was considered desirable. The same point was made in Canute's lawcode, drafted by Wulfstan: 'neither a widow or a maiden is ever to be forced to marry a man whom she herself dislikes'.[5] It is hard to persuade oneself that high-born girls of strong character – and the high-born girl who became Queen Emma was most emphatically of strong character – were incapable of expressing likes or dislikes when it came to the choice of a partner. To what extent preferences might be realized in practice is entirely a matter for guesswork. Legislators would not have stressed the desirability of consent, one might surmise, were not consent frequently disregarded.

The succeeding six clauses (out of nine altogether in Dorothy Whitelock's translation) are entirely concerned with arrangements relating to the exchange of properties between the contracting parties to the betrothal. Neither should this surprise us. Betrothal, at whatever social level, created a new economic unit of husband and wife to which the families of both bride and groom contributed the resources necessary for its maintenance. Careful negotiations about these respective contributions took place between the two kins concerned and the arrangements agreed upon would have been clearly spelt out in front of witnesses. At the more exalted social levels they would have been committed to writing. As it so happens, only two such betrothal agreements in written form have come down to us from the Anglo-Saxon period. By a remarkable chance, one of them concerns the betrothal of none other than the sister of Archbishop Wulfstan II of York. Wulfstan's sister (we are not told her name) was to marry a man named Wulfric, evidently a considerable landowner in Worcestershire. Wulfric undertook to settle upon his bride four landed estates, a large quantity of gold, thirty slaves and thirty horses: a substantial dower. The document was witnessed by an impressive group of notables; a Mercian ealdorman, the bishop of Hereford, an abbot, a priest who later became an abbot and then a bishop, 'and many good men besides them, both ecclesiastics and laymen'. The parties had two copies of the text made, to be preserved in the episcopal archives of Hereford and of Worcester.[6]

The marriage ceremony itself features only in the penultimate clause of *Wifmannes Beweddung*. The writer observed, a shade hesitantly, that 'at the marriage there should by rights be a priest, who shall unite them together with God's blessing in all prosperity'. The consent of husband and wife made a marriage. Priestly blessing was desirable but not necessary. This was a world in which the church had hardly yet started to embark upon the difficult path of claiming control of Christian marriage.

The final clause of *Wifmannes Beweddung* concerns itself with consanguinity and separation: 'It is also well to take care that one knows that they are not too closely related, lest one afterwards put asunder what was previously wrongly joined together.' Consanguinity means descent from a common ancestor. Within how many 'degrees' of consanguinity, i.e. number of generations of shared descent, a man and a woman might or might not marry was a matter of keen debate. Legal niceties apart, one senses that in practice consanguinity, unless blatantly close, was unlikely to impede an aristocratic union but was available as a card that might be played to secure a separation. This circumstance is perhaps what was envisaged in the clause quoted above. High-minded churchmen taught that the marriage bond should be indissoluble: 'If anyone abandons a living legal wife, and wrongly takes to wife another woman, may he not have God's mercy, unless' – a saving clause – 'he atones for it.' The word for 'atones' is *gebete*, whose primary meaning was 'pays compensation'. Those who could afford it, then, could unscramble their marriages. This last ruling features not in *Wifmannes Beweddung* but in another legal tract known as the *Northumbrian Priests' Law*, long attributed to Wulfstan, perhaps more plausibly to one of his successors such as Ælfric Puttoc or Cynesige.[7]

This same tract implicitly concedes that priests were likely to be married too: 'If a priest leaves a woman and takes another, let him be anathema.' Though sacerdotal celibacy had been regarded as desirable and praiseworthy from a very early epoch in the history of the Christian Church, in practice before the twelfth century ecclesiastical authority made little attempt to enforce a requirement of celibacy. Priests were one thing; bishops, however, quite another. Although examples can be found of discreetly married bishops, in general when we learn of bishops' children the assumption should be that these were the issue of unions that had been terminated before advancement to episcopal office. The Durham anonymous displayed no embarrassment in referring to Ecgfrida as the daughter of the saintly Bishop Ealdhun. She must have been born well before he became a bishop in 990.

Ecgfrida's marriage to Uhtred was an entirely suitable one in the context of Bernician local alliances: promising young earl marries bishop's daughter. The match was underpinned by appropriate property transactions. These transactions were indeed the starting-point of the narrative composed by our Durham monk, because they were to be the cause of so much trouble later on. Bishop Ealdhun gave with his daughter a dowry of six estates which belonged to the endowments of the church of St Cuthbert and lay in the region between Durham and the river Tees. Five of them lay a little to the north of Darlington: Aycliffe, Barmpton, Carlton, Elton and Skirningham; a sixth (Monk) Heselden, lay near the coast just to the north of Hartlepool (see the map on pp. 34–5). All were situated in the fertile agricultural plain of lower Teesdale: in a crudely material sense they were properties worth having. Uhtred and his kin would have given a counter-gift of property to the bride. These transactions would almost certainly have been recorded in writing like the marriage agreement concerning Archbishop Wulfstan's sister referred to above. Indeed, it is not impossible that the Durham anonymous had copies of these texts before him as he wrote.

Did the bishop have any right to alienate in this fashion the patrimony of St Cuthbert? It is a troubling question. It is no adequate answer, though it is not irrelevant, to observe that one could cite scores of well-attested cases of early medieval prelates who used the endowments of which they were the stewards to enrich their kinsfolk; the great Wulfstan of York, for example, among them. Our Durham writer asserts that there was a condition: Uhtred was to hold Ecgfrida's dowry 'on condition that he should always deal honourably with his [the bishop's] daughter for as long as he should live in marriage [with her]'. Whether this condition was present in the original document we shall never know. It could have been an 'improvement' on some words in the text, it could indeed have been invented in its entirety by the later writer, using his knowledge of what happened to the marriage and in order to save the reputation of a bishop looked back to as a saintly man.

Earl Uhtred's marital career gave dismay to the Victorian editor of the anonymous narrative from Durham:

The loose notions and practice which then prevailed on the subject of marriage are very noticeable; a Turkish pacha could hardly consult his own inclinations in this matter more unscrupulously than was done by Uhtred, the English earl of Northumbria.[8]

Dismayed or not, we are likely to find the marital sagas to be recounted in the next few pages confusing: it is hoped that Genealogical Tables 3 (see p. 76) and 5 (see p. 132) will prove helpful. As we saw in an earlier chapter, after Ecgfrida Uhtred married successively Sige, the daughter of Styr Ulfsson, and then Ælfgifu, the daughter of King Ethelred II; and we saw that each of these unions could best be interpreted in the context of regional or national politics. In order to marry Sige, Uhtred had to divorce Ecgfrida. It is possible that a divorce was justified on the grounds of consanguinity. Although we cannot prove this, it is not unlikely that a common ancestor of the pair could be found, or alleged, back in the mists of the ninth or tenth centuries. Following upon her divorce Ecgfrida returned to her father's household, taking back with her the six estates of her dowry.

She did not remain single for long: 'A certain thegn in Yorkshire, Kilvert the son of Ligulf, took to wife the daughter of Bishop Ealdhun whom Earl Uhtred had divorced.' Kilvert cannot be identified with certainty, nor the whereabouts of his landed estates. The marriage is perhaps best understood as part of the bishop's strategy to win friends in Yorkshire. The Teesdale lands once more accompanied Ecgfrida as her dowry. A daughter named Sigrida was born to Ecgfrida and Kilvert. And then, according to the Durham anonymous, the marriage was terminated, in unknown circumstances.

Kilvert son of Ligulf dismissed Ecgfrida, daughter of Bishop Ealdhun, upon which the bishop told her to come back to Durham at once. Obedient to her father's orders she returned, bringing with her Barmpton, Elton and Skirningham, which she was retaining under her own control. She gave back her own lands, together with herself, to the church and the bishop. Later on she took the veil [as a nun] and lived well until the end of her days. She was buried in the cemetery of Durham where she awaits Judgement Day.

Ecgfrida's return to Durham evidently preceded the death of her father the bishop on hearing the news of the disaster at Carham in 1018. We do not know when she died.

The other three estates which had formed part of Ecgfrida's dowry passed into the hands of her daughter Sigrida. She proved to be another much-married woman. Her first husband was a certain Arkil, the son of Fridegist, of whom no more is known. Her second husband was named Eadwulf. Now this Eadwulf was the second son of Earl Uhtred (Sigrida's mother's first husband) and thus the younger brother of Earl

Ealdred who was killed by Carl in Rise Wood in 1038. Eadwulf succeeded his brother as earl of Bernicia but was himself to meet a violent end in 1041. Whether Sigrida's second marriage was ended by Eadwulf's death, or whether it had been terminated upon some other occasion earlier on, she entered into a third union with, confusingly, yet another Arkil, the son of Ecgfrith. (The name Arkil is a contracted form of Arnketil. In order to reduce the chances of confusion it will be as well to refer to this second Arkil by the uncontracted form of his name.) This Arnketil was a very important figure in Northumbria in the middle years of the eleventh century: we shall meet him again in a different context. Sigrida predeceased Arnketil, and upon her death he gave back to the church of Durham the three Teesdale estates of Aycliffe, Carlton and Heselden, 'which the church still possesses'.

In this manner the cathedral church of St Cuthbert was repossessed of the estates which had been alienated by Bishop Ealdhun at the time of his daughter's marriage. It's a complicated story. But the reader's patience must be put under further strain; for it's even more complicated than this. We must go back to Earl Ealdred who fell victim to Carl in Rise Wood. By a wife or wives of whom we know nothing at all, Ealdred fathered five daughters but no son. These were the women who commemorated their father with a stone cross at the site of his death. One of these daughters, Ælfflæd, married a husband named Siward.

We have already met Siward. He it was who was chosen by King Canute to succeed Eric of Hlathir as earl of Northumbria. Eric, as we have seen, might have been dead or incapacitated by 1028; Siward's tenure as earl is not securely attested until 1033. Siward's origins are unknown. His Old Norse name, Sigvarðr, suggests a Scandinavian, presumably Danish, origin. Only a trusted henchman of Canute would have been given so exalted and sensitive an office as the earldom of Northumbria. Siward was nicknamed *Digera*, an Old Norse term meaning 'strong'. Later legends about him would claim that he was descended from a bear, his great-grandfather having been the son of a union between a white bear and a noblewoman. This does not quite make him 'a Danish warrior of primitive type' in the curiously dismissive words of Sir Frank Stenton,[9] but we may be sure that Siward the Strong was a man of formidable physical presence who possessed the

GENEALOGICAL TABLE 5
ECGFRIDA AND HER KINSFOLK

Holders of or claimants to the disputed Teesdale estates are in capitals.

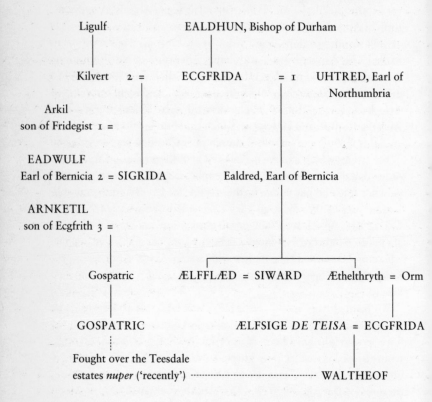

muscle to enforce his will, should words fail, by blows. His tenure of the earldom of Northumbria would last until his death in 1055.

Siward's marriage into the family of the earls of Northumbria was presumably intended to strengthen his position in northern England. Necessarily it also involved him in family politics. Prominent among these were territorial claims. His wife, Ælfflæd, laid claim to the six estates in Teesdale as hers 'by hereditary right' in view of her descent from Earl Uhtred. Evidently within the family a somewhat different view obtained about the terms on which the estates had come into Uhtred's hands from that which was held by the churchmen of Durham. Ælfflæd succeeded in gaining possession of the estates because 'her husband Siward gave them to her'. But how did Siward get his hands on these six estates, three of which were in the possession of the bishopric of Durham and three in that of Sigrida and her husband Earl Eadwulf, Ælfflæd's uncle?

Any answer must necessarily be speculative. Here is a suggestion. Let us recall that the six contested estates were in Bernicia, Northumbria's northern half. Now Siward, like his predecessor Eric of Hlathir, though he may have been entitled Earl of Northumbria, initially exercised direct power primarily over Deira, the southern part of Northumbria. If we can identify a time when Siward extended the earl's effective power over Bernicia as well as Deira, we might reasonably suppose that that would have furnished opportunity for pressing wifely claims; perhaps for pressing them none too scrupulously. And this, by good fortune, we can do.

The elements in this new *conjoncture* of circumstances are already familiar: Anglo-Scottish relations, the fortunes of the bishopric of Durham, the intermittently looming presence of a southern English king. We left King Malcolm II rejoicing in his victory at Carham in 1018, pushing his lordship down into Cumbria and threatening Northumbria's western flanks as well as its northern marches. Counter-measures were called for. A king of England would want to intervene personally, if only to assert his authority over a bishop at Durham whom he had not chosen (Edmund) and a northern earl (Ealdred) whose father he had had killed. Canute campaigned twice against the Scots. The earlier of these expeditions, a shadowy business, was referred to by a chronicler writing in Burgundy, called Rodulfus Glaber or Ralph the Bald. Glaber's notice is vague and confused, but he was a strictly contemporary witness, usually reliable, whose testimony cannot simply be set aside. The leading modern authority on Canute's reign has accepted it, albeit cautiously.[10] Glaber tells us that Canute set out with an enormous army to subjugate the Scots, that Malcolm successfully resisted him, and that arbitrators brokered a peaceful settlement between them. This inconclusive campaign, if anything a win on points for Malcolm, seems to have occurred in about 1024. It cannot have boosted Canute's standing in Northumbria.

In 1031 Canute made a second appearance in the north. Invoking the supernatural aid of St Cuthbert, possibly of other northern saints too, with gifts, the king seems to have been more successful. 'King Canute went to Scotland, and Malcolm king of Scots surrendered to him, and two other kings, Mælbæth and Iehmarc,' according to one of the annalists who compiled the *Anglo-Saxon Chronicle*. The first of these is probably to be identified with Macbeth, ruler of Moray, of whom more presently. Iehmarc might be an English scribe's shot at Echmarcach, a member of a Hiberno-Norse dynasty who in 1031 may have been ruling parts of Galloway. One of Canute's panegyrists, Sigvat the Skald, celebrated the expedition: 'the most famous princes in the north from the midst of Fife have brought their heads [i.e. submitted] to Canute to buy peace'.[11] In actual fact the submission was as ephemeral as some of those earlier submissions back in the tenth century, as another version of the *Anglo-Saxon Chronicle* recognized: 'Malcolm the king of Scots surrendered to him and became his man, yet he observed it but little time.'

Malcolm II died on 25 November 1034 and was succeeded by his grandson Duncan I. Canute died a year later (12 November 1035) and was succeeded by his son Harold 'Harefoot'. In both England and Scotland the instability attendant upon a change of ruler prevailed. In Scotland the new king was much preoccupied by the opposition of northern lords to him. With Duncan's attention thus distracted from his southernmost marches, Earl Eadwulf of Bernicia was able to 'ravage the Britons', that is of Strathclyde and Cumbria, 'pretty savagely' (*satis atrociter*).[12] This action might explain in its turn why Duncan mounted a counter-raid in 1039:

King Duncan of the Scots came with immense forces, besieged Durham, and expended much labour to conquer it, but in vain. For when the greater part of his cavalry had been killed by those who were being besieged, he fled in confusion, and in this flight he lost all his foot soldiers who were killed and their heads taken to the market-place and stuck up on stakes.[13]

GENEALOGICAL TABLE 6
THE SCOTTISH ROYAL FAMILY

In this much simplified family tree the kings who ruled over Scotland are in capitals.

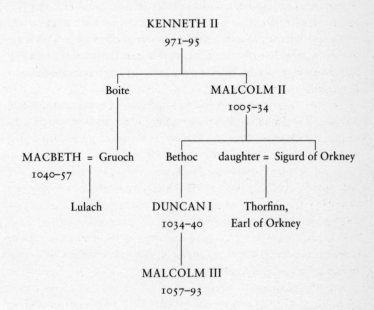

The writer connected this military reverse with Duncan's end soon afterwards: 'And not long afterwards, when he had now returned to Scotland, the king perished, slain by his own people.' Shakespeare has ensured that everybody knows that Duncan was killed by Macbeth: the historical reality which underlies the play is less familiar. Macbeth belonged to a family who were the hereditary *mórmaers* of Moray. The term *mórmaer* meant something like 'high steward' and – like the comparable Old English term *heahgerefa*, 'high-reeve' – is suggestive of an office held under the king. This is deceptive. The *mórmaers* of Moray were as independent as the high-reeves of Bamburgh had been, and indeed like them were sometimes alluded to as kings. They seem to have descended from a magnate family of Scottish Dalriada who migrated north-east up the line of the Great Glen and established a kingdom for themselves at the expense of the northern Picts in the middle years of the ninth century. The very fragmentary records of the tenth and early eleventh centuries reveal a seemingly constant state of hostility between these northern rulers and the kings 'of the Scots' whose realm was anchored further south in Angus and Fife. In Macbeth's day the Moray of the *mórmaers* extended over much of the north-east of modern Scotland, from Deeside northwards to the Moray Firth and onward to the shores of the Dornoch Firth and the valley of the Oykel where the *mórmaers*' zone of influence marched with that of the Norse earls of Orkney.[14]

So there was rivalry between what had once been the northern and southern districts of the Pictish kingdom. Macbeth used marriage to exploit his enemies' divisions. His wife belonged to a branch of the Scots' dynasty which had long been embroiled in an internecine feud with the branch represented by Kenneth II (d. 995) and his son Malcolm II (d. 1034). The historical 'Lady Macbeth', whose unlovely name was Gruoch, may or may not have 'awakened' her husband to a duty to kill Malcolm's grandson Duncan. Neither do the sources, such as they are, make any play with treacherous breach of the rites of hospitality. Macbeth and his wife owe their evil reputation to the imaginations of later chroniclers.

The immediate consequence of Macbeth's seizure of a kingship of all Scotland in 1040 was the shift of its centre of gravity away from the fringes of the Forth and the Tay to the shores of the Moray Firth. This had the effect of making its southern regions more vulnerable to English attack.

Further to destabilize the northern scene, Bishop Edmund of Durham died in the course of a visit to the English royal court at Gloucester. The leader of the cathedral community – the title 'dean' was not yet widely used – by name Eadred, helped himself to cathedral funds, went off to the king and bought his succession to the bishopric from him. Such highly irregular behaviour, the sin of simony indeed, could not go unpunished: 'Divine vengeance did not allow him to exercise episcopal office.' Before Eadred could enter the cathedral church thus unlawfully acquired he was struck down by illness, took to his bed and died ten months later. His successor was Ethelric, formerly a monk of Peterborough, who had been employed at Durham by Bishop Edmund as an instructor in the monastic life. Ethelric was consecrated at York on 11 January 1042, our solitary fixed point in a morass of chronological uncertainty. Symeon of Durham, our early twelfth-century source for these goings-on, seems to imply that Earl Siward was somehow implicated in Ethelric's advancement. Siward it certainly was who came to Ethelric's aid when in 1044 he roused the opposition of his cathedral community and had to seek safety in flight. Ethelric appealed to Siward for help, and Siward reinstated him in his bishopric – but at a price: *munere oblato*, 'a gift having been given', as Symeon coyly put it.[15] Could this gift have been the three estates at Barmpton, Elton and Skirningham which Siward's wife Ælfflæd was claiming as hers 'by hereditary right'? It is tempting to guess that it was.

Siward could help a bishop of Durham because by this time he was earl of all Northumbria, Bernicia as well as Deira. He had achieved this position at the expense of his wife's uncle Eadwulf who, it will be recalled, had governed Bernicia since his brother Ealdred's murder in 1038. Eadwulf met his death by violence in a manner reminiscent of his father Uhtred's end twenty-five years beforehand. He was treacherously slain while on a visit to the royal court under promise of safeconduct. The king who perpetrated the deed was Canute's son by Emma, Harthacanute, who had succeeded his brother Harold in 1040. One of our sources tells us that Earl Eadwulf had come under safeconduct 'to be reconciled', which points to some previous enmity between king and earl.[16] We do not know what this was, though it is a fair guess that in the struggle for the succession between Harold and Harthacanute the earl had made a wrong or mistimed choice. As we saw in the instance of his father Uhtred, this was perilously easy to do. Symeon of Durham, a usually reliable authority, informs us that none other than Earl Siward was responsible for the death of Earl Eadwulf. Why there should have been enmity between Siward and Eadwulf we do not know, beyond the fact that they governed respectively Deira and Bernicia. At any rate, if Symeon is correct, Siward allowed himself to play Thurbrand to Eadwulf's Uhtred: but with this difference, that Siward's victim was his wife's uncle. What may plausibly be surmised is that this could have been the occasion for Siward to lay hold on the three Teesdale estates – Aycliffe, Carlton and Heselden – which Sigrida had brought to her marriage to Eadwulf.

This is simply to suggest an answer to the question posed several pages back as to how Siward was in a position to give his wife Ælfflæd all six of the Teesdale estates which long ago Bishop Ealdhun had settled on her grandmother Ecgfrida. However, that is still not the end of the story, for as we have seen Sigrida's third husband, Arnketil, was in a position to give three of the estates back to the church of Durham after her death. The Durham anonymous could explain that too.

On the death of Earl Siward and Countess Ælfflæd, disorder broke out and the estates became vacant. Afterwards Arnketil the son of Ecgfrith who had married Sigrida . . . seized those vacant lands for himself and occupied them.

(The words which I have translated 'became vacant' and again 'vacant' literally mean 'were laid waste' and 'devastated'. There is much disagreement among historians about the precise significance of the terms 'waste' or 'wasted lands' in eleventh-century England, a problem to which we shall return in a later chapter in the context of the Domesday survey of 1086. One possible meaning is 'unoccupied', which seems to make good sense here.) After Sigrida's death Arnketil gave three of them back to Durham, presumably retaining the other three in his own hands. Arnketil ended his life as an exile, fleeing in 1069 from the wrath of William the Conqueror. At this point yet another claimant appeared. Another of Earl Ealdred's five daughters, Æthelthryth, had married a Yorkshire landowner named Orm the son of Gamel – he who rebuilt St Gregory's minster in Kirkdale. Æthelthryth and Orm had a daughter, Ecgfrida – named after her great-grandmother, Bishop Ealdhun's daughter – who claimed the estates by right of her descent from that earlier Ecgfrida. She and her husband, Ælfsige *de Teisa*, Ælfsige 'of the Tees' – presumably a landowner in Teesdale – helped themselves to Barmpton and Skirningham. (The fate of the sixth estate, Elton, is not mentioned.) But this usurpation, as it was in some eyes, did not go unchallenged. In the following generation the grandson of Arnketil and Sigrida, by name Gospatric, claimed the lands from

Waltheof, the son of Ælfsige and Ecgfrida. Gospatric and Waltheof fought about this 'recently'. That tantalizing 'recently' provides one of the few hints as to the date when *De Obsessione Dunelmi* was composed – or (which is not the same thing) edited. The date referred to can hardly be earlier than the last decade of the eleventh century. It would appear that Waltheof successfully fought off – literally – this claim, for when we next hear of Barmpton and Skirningham they were still in his hands. But with a very significant difference. Waltheof the son of Ælfsige was no longer their owner. He was a tenant; and his new lord was a Norman baron, Nigel d'Aubigny. That was in the early years of the twelfth century.

The lands had been in contention for a hundred years. In the labyrinthine tale of their changing tenure, it seems that it was often the women who took the initiative. Ecgfrida retained the estates 'under her own control'. Ælfflæd 'claimed the aforesaid lands by hereditary right'. Sigrida took her dowry to three husbands. The second Ecgfrida 'laid hold on' Barmpton and Skirningham – true, 'with her husband Ælfsige', but the writer left the verb in the singular, clearly betraying his judgement that Ecgfrida was the prime mover. Perhaps noblewomen played a role in reactivating property disputes not unlike the part they played in reawakening feuds. One senses formidable personalities among these Northumbrian aristocratic ladies of the eleventh century: no mere pawns in men's games.

Waltheof son of Ælfsige was in the fifth generation of descent from Bishop Ealdhun. That claims to land could be pursued over at least such a span of time tells us something about the tenacity of the Anglo-Saxon nobility. (We have to say 'at least' because we haven't the faintest idea what sort of tangled history the estates might have had *before* the bishop bestowed them on his daughter.) Why were they so tenacious? The estates were worth having, covetable; so greed comes into the equation. But it was not just a matter of naked rapacity – unwise though it would be to underestimate aristocratic greed at any epoch or fail to allow for the proclivity of the very rich always to want more. Family honour was at stake, a much more powerful force than mere covetousness. So too was individual reputation within a family. Call to mind the slothful and cowardly Earl Eadwulf, Uhtred's brother, remembered as the giver away of Lothian to the Scots. (No matter that the memory was historically inaccurate: what matters is that it was held.) Who would want to be remembered like that? The Teesdale estates were but Lothian writ small. Slights to honour, sagging reputations, would be held in the collective memory of kin and neighbours, brooded upon, talked of over the mead at family gatherings in the feasting season of winter. What else was there to talk of, what other diversions? Even the most mustard-keen sportsmen and warriors cannot spend *all* their time talking about dogs and horses and weapons. (The force of boredom in human history is one that historians have underestimated.)

But conflict could never be straightforward in that inextricably tangled aristocratic world where brides went from husband to husband and where everyone seems to have been kin to everybody else. Ælf-flæd's insistence that all six estates be restored to her hands – did even Siward the Strong, her husband, quail before that imperious will? – was guaranteed to cause the discord that followed. And this was discord within the kin. Counter-claims came from her aunt Sigrida and her niece Ecgfrida. They could as easily have come – and not inconceivably *did* come, though we don't know about it – from several other cousins. So where did an individual's loyalty lie? Whose side should you take? There were painful dilemmas here, divergent tugs on allegiance, occasions of severe mental stress. As James Campbell has remarked of a slightly earlier but morally similar age, 'no wonder they drank so much'.[17]

Whether dispute over landed estates could remain within an acceptable level of muted violence was yet another anxious issue. In the 'recent' fight between Waltheof the son of Ælfsige and Sigrida's grandson Gospatric, Waltheof came off best. It need not have been a fight to the death. The point is that fighting, whether or not lethal, inflicted humiliation, a slur on honour, upon the defeated. That could ignite a feud. And feuds, as we now know, could last a long time, involve a lot of people, stain with fear a whole region.

Lastly, let us remember that our narrative of the descent of the Teesdale estates is the *only* one of its kind that has come down to us from eleventh-century Northumbria. It cannot be too heavily emphasized that this tract stands wholly alone. Given that this century of quarrelling over land took its rise from a commonplace, everyday transaction, the provision of landed dowry for a bride, it is reasonable to suppose that there were numerous comparable transactions which brought similar contention in their wake, transactions and contentions about which we shall never know anything at all. Of course, it would not do to suggest that *all* dealings in land provoked dissension: there must have been many in which all parties were satisfied with the arrangements proposed and witnessed. But we should do well to remember that this was a legal climate in which uncontested title was rare and the right of individuals to bequeath landed property was circumscribed; a moral climate in which offence was easily taken and insult long brooded upon. It would come as no surprise to learn that most of the prominent aristocratic and gentry families of eleventh-century Northumbria – of England indeed, of western Europe as a whole – were embroiled in comparable disputes. If we are to understand these men and women we must bear in mind that they were helplessly ensnared in familial conflict of their own making.

8

Siward and Tostig

The early part of the 1040s saw changes among the principal authorities in the north. Macbeth became king of Scotland in 1040, Siward became earl of all Northumbria in 1041, Ethelric was in place as bishop of Durham by January 1042, and upon the sudden death of the young Harthacanute (aged about twenty-four) his older half-brother Edward, later to be known as 'the Confessor', became king of England in June 1042.

Edward was the eldest son of the marriage of Ethelred II and Emma of Normandy. He had been born soon after the union, perhaps as early as 1002, certainly by 1005. (Most unusually, we know the place of his birth, Islip in Oxfordshire.) His childhood was overshadowed by the ever more intense Danish assault upon the kingdom of England. As we have seen, when Sweyn of Denmark mounted his final invasion in 1013 the royal family took refuge with Emma's kinsfolk in Normandy. After the tumultuous events of the years 1014–16, which brought the young prince briefly back to England, Canute emerged as sole king in the autumn of 1016, and Edward went into exile once more.

Edward spent the following twenty-five years as an exile in northern France. It was a formative period in his life. We have seen evidence already that periods of exile were a common enough hazard in the careers of eleventh-century noblemen. On the whole, such periods tended to be fairly short: a few years, perhaps only a few months, time that could be usefully employed in, say, a pilgrimage to Rome or Jerusalem or Santiago de Compostela, a journey which might directly or indirectly yield profitable martial encounters as well as spiritual merit. (The Norman conquest of southern Italy began with the hiring of pilgrims as mercenary soldiers in about 1018.) Edward's quarter-century of exile was exceptionally long. He left his homeland as a youth of about twelve; he returned in his late thirties, a man of fairly advanced age by the standards of the time. (The average age at death of his seven predecessors on the throne of England had been just under thirty.) His return in 1041 apparently occurred at the invitation of Harthacanute and his advisers. It is not clear on what terms it took place. No one could have foreseen Harthacanute's death a year later, of a sudden seizure at a wedding:

While at a feast at a place called Lambeth, at which Osgod Clapa, a very powerful man, married his daughter Gytha, with great joy, to Tofi, surnamed the Proud . . . Harthacanute king of the English, merry, in good health and in great heart, was standing drinking with the aforementioned bride and certain men when he suddenly crashed to the ground in a wretched fall. He remained speechless until his death on Tuesday 8 June.[1]

Unexpectedly, his next-of-kin Edward found himself king of England.

Edward's long exile had two critically important consequences. One of these was temperamental. After long, lean years as an impecunious suppliant not invariably (one may guess) wholeheartedly welcome at the princely courts of northern France, he had suddenly in middle age become the second most powerful ruler (after the German emperor) in western Europe with all the unmatched resources of the most institutionally sophisticated monarchy in western Christendom at his beck and call. It must have been a heady change. His most acute modern biographer, Frank Barlow, has persuasively likened him to Charles II. Like Charles, Edward was determined not to go on his travels again. The stilted conventional literary commonplaces of early medieval chroniclers are always difficult to penetrate to the flesh-and-blood humans they purport to delineate: but there is some reason to suppose that Edward shared traits of character with Charles. They both had an easygoing charm, a certain laziness about state business, a wish to avoid trouble, and a devotion to the pleasures of the chase – in Edward's case in the hunting field rather than, as with Charles, in the bedchamber.

A second consequence, not unconnected with the first, was political.

Edward's long exile made it almost unavoidable for him to accept a *fait accompli* in the workings of the English monarchy as it had developed in the previous generation under Canute and his sons – even supposing that he had had a will for change. In terms of the way in which eleventh-century personal, itinerant government worked, that meant accepting the people who were currently keeping the show, quite literally, on the road. As we have already seen, the fundamental unit of local government in Anglo-Saxon England was the shire, administered by its royally appointed ealdorman and his deputy the 'shire-reeve' or sheriff. In the course of the tenth century a tendency had gained ground for the grouping of several contiguous shires under the control of a sort of 'super-ealdorman'. An early example is furnished by Athelstan 'Half-king' whom we met in chapter 2. It became gradually customary to give these super-ealdormen the title of 'earl' (Old English *eorl*).

This is to simplify a gradual institutional evolution. What is clear is that by the beginning of Edward's reign in 1042 there were three big earldoms in England, of Wessex, Mercia and Northumbria.* Wessex was under the rule of Earl Godwin. Godwin's was one of the great success stories of his age. The son of a landowner in southern England of no particular prominence, the young Godwin seems to have prospered in service to the royal family. Seeing which way the wind was blowing he adroitly switched his loyalties to Canute and evidently at once distinguished himself in some markedly impressive way for in 1018 he was rewarded with the earldom of Wessex. At about the same time he married Gytha, the sister of Canute's cousin and brother-in-law. Godwin was, thus, governor of the richest province of England which stretched from Kent to Cornwall and by his marriage a member of the royal kin. He would retain this earldom until his death in 1053, excepting only a period of twelve months in 1051–2. During his long tenure of Wessex Godwin was able to enrich himself and his family

---

* These were not absolutely fixed and immutable entities. Part of the armoury of royal patronage was the ability to create new earldoms, for instance of East Anglia, or to split up the large ones into, say, Western and Eastern Mercia. The king could also effect subsequent coalescence into the larger units. The history of the earldoms during Edward's reign is fairly kaleidoscopic and not always clear in detail. Once more I simplify.

GENEALOGICAL TABLE 7

THE FAMILY OF EARL GODWIN OF WESSEX

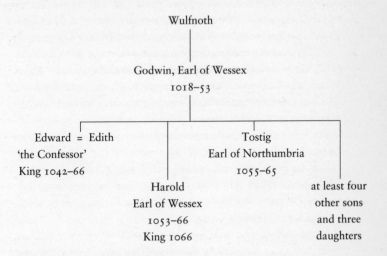

Wulfnoth

Godwin, Earl of Wessex
1018–53

Edward = Edith
'the Confessor'
King 1042–66

Tostig
Earl of Northumbria
1055–65

Harold
Earl of Wessex
1053–66
King 1066

at least four
other sons
and three
daughters

prodigiously. In 1045, furthermore, his connection with the restored royal family was strengthened when the returned exile, King Edward, married Godwin's daughter Edith. Godwin's son Harold would become king of England on Edward's death in 1066, only to lose both throne and life at Hastings.

The other two earls at the beginning of Edward's reign were much smaller fry by comparison with this colossally overmighty subject. Leofric had been earl of Mercia since 1032 at the latest. He belonged to a locally prominent family which had held high office in the midlands from the 990s. He was married to an aristocratic lady named Godgifu – the 'Lady Godiva' of legend – and the couple left a reputation for piety. The magnificent church at Stow in Lincolnshire still stands as a testimony of it. If Leofric faced in any particular direction it was westwards. As the principalities of Wales became more robust and assertive – like the kingdom of the Scots – an earl of Mercia's first duty was to guard his marches. There was no love lost between the house of Leofric and the house of Godwin.

Much the same could be said, *mutatis mutandis*, of Siward of North-umbria. As far as we can tell, Edward the Confessor never visited the north of England. The furthest north that his – admittedly, patchily recorded – itinerary ever took him was Gloucester. Earl Siward, there-fore, was left to govern Northumbria with a pretty free hand. That does not mean that he never appeared at the king's court; his subscriptions of royal charters show him to have been a regular attender. King Edward evidently trusted his loyalty. Not only did the king let sleeping dogs lie in Northumbria, he even added two Mercian counties, Northampton-shire and Huntingdonshire, to Siward's earldom. This was done partly to boost the revenues of the poorest of the earls, partly to lock his loyalty even more firmly into a southern orientation – as with the simultaneous holding of the see of Worcester by the archbishop of York. On two critical state occasions Siward may be traced loyally at Edward's side: in 1043 when the king despoiled his mother of her property, and in 1051 during the course of the confrontation between Edward and Earl Godwin.

If Siward's path to the earldom of all Northumbria – Bernicia as well as Deira – was a bloody and violent one, we can see him trying to integrate himself into northern aristocratic society. Not only did he marry into the traditional ruling dynasty of Bernicia; he even acqui-esced in naming the son of that marriage Waltheof, after the boy's great-great-grandfather on his mother's side, the Waltheof son of Oswulf who had been earl of Bernicia back in the 970s and 980s. In addition, he took steps to provide for the last surviving son of the great Earl Uhtred, as we shall see presently. Though his relations with the cathedral community of Durham may have been a little guarded, we have no reason to suppose that his dealings with two successive archbishops of York, Ælfric Puttoc (1023–51) and Cynesige (1051–60), were anything but cordial. It was presumably with the latter's encouragement that Siward founded a minster church just outside the city of York dedicated to St Olaf. Olaf Haraldsson had been king of Norway from 1015 to 1028 when he was dethroned by Canute; attempting to reclaim the kingship in 1030 he was defeated and killed at the battle of Stiklestad near Trondheim. During his reign Olaf had been a vigorous promoter of Christianity in a country where the faith had as yet made little impact – despite the efforts of his predecessor and namesake Olaf Tryggvason – and though his death was entirely a matter of secular politics he was regarded as a martyr. His cult spread with great rapidity not just within Norway but across the North Sea in the British Isles as well. In expressing his devotion to this martial northern evangelist Earl Siward was in the forefront of the fashionable piety of the day. On his death in 1055 Siward was buried in his new minster church. It lay just on the northern edge of the city in an area known as Galmanho, also as Earlsburgh because that was where the earls had their principal residence and headquarters. The present church of St Olave in Marygate is presumed to stand on the site of Siward's minster.

Siward won fame in his dealings with the Scots. He continued Earl Eadwulf's aggressive stance towards the Britons of Cumbria and Strathclyde – after 1018, it will be recalled, under the dominion of the kings of Scotland. Siward's actions resulted in a spectacular expansion of Northumbrian power over Cumbria. The evidence for this is furnished by an enigmatic document known as Gospatric's writ. What this text, which survives only in a late copy, garbled in transmission, seems to record is the formal confirmation of some fiscal and legal privileges by a certain Gospatric, who appears to associate himself with Earl Siward, to a group of landowners, identified as men 'who used to be Cumbrian', dwelling in the northern parts of modern Cumbria bounded by the Pennines, the mountains of the Lake District and the Solway Firth. It is exactly the sort of guarantee that would be sought by persons who had experienced a recent change of overlordship. The reference to Siward dates the document to the period 1041–55.[2] The Gospatric who issued the writ is very probably – as usual we can't be absolutely certain – to be identified as the sole surviving son of Earl Uhtred's second marriage to Sige, daughter of Styr Ulfsson; the younger brother of Earl Eadwulf who had been killed in 1041. It is a plausible surmise that Siward had sought to buy off any claims that Gospatric might reasonably have entertained to the earldom of Bernicia by granting him an alternative command in newly conquered Cumbria.

Early in the twelfth century it was believed at York that Archbishop Cynesige had consecrated two successive bishops, named 'Magsuen' (Magnus?) and John, for the people of Cumbria.[3] If this information is correct, we are probably to envisage a 'district bishopric' without a fixed urban seat. (The diocese of Carlisle was not founded until 1133.) At the village of Morland, near Penrith, there are substantial remains of what must have been a fairly ambitious late Anglo-Saxon church, architecturally speaking. Morland could have been the base, or one of the bases, for these bishops' pastoral activity.

Strathclyde–Cumbria was rendered vulnerable to Northumbrian aggression because of the northward shift of the Scottish monarchy's centre of gravity under Macbeth, as we saw in the last chapter. Another consequence of Macbeth's seizure of power was the flight of princely Scottish refugees to the safety of English Northumbria. These included the sons of the murdered Duncan, Malcolm and Donald, and Duncan's brother Maldred. Now Maldred had married Edith, daughter of Earl Uhtred by his third wife Ælfgifu, the daughter of King Ethelred II. Maldred was thus the kinsman by marriage of Earl Siward and the husband of King Edward's niece. The Scottish princes in exile in Northumbria were kin as well as guests, with a double claim upon Northumbrian assistance.

With Siward's help the refugees mounted an invasion of Scotland in 1046, but it was defeated. Macbeth must have felt himself secure, for in 1050 he went on a pilgrimage to Rome where he was long remembered for his largesse: 'He scattered silver like seed to the poor.'[4] Anglo-Scottish relations continued tense after his return. In addition to the usual raids to and fro, in 1053 Macbeth offered his hospitality to prominent English exiles from King Edward's court who sought asylum in Scotland. Earl Siward's last campaign took place in 1054. As commander-in-chief of a combined land and sea force – like King Athelstan in 934 – he invaded Scotland and defeated Macbeth in a hard-fought battle. (Its site is not known: Dunsinane, properly Dunsinnan, is a later improvisation.) Malcolm was installed as king. Macbeth survived, but fled northwards to his homeland of Moray where he was brought to battle and killed by Malcolm three years later. Siward returned to Northumbria loaded with booty and glory. But victory had been won at a heavy personal cost. Siward's eldest son Osbeorn had been killed; so too his nephew, another Siward. It was a chronicler writing about a century later, Henry of Huntingdon, who first set down in writing the story of the father's enquiries about his son's wounds, which Shakespeare would draw on several centuries later.

Perhaps grief hastened Siward's death. He must in any case have been a fairly elderly man by the standards of the day at the time of his last campaign. He died, as we have already seen, in the following year and was buried in his minster church of St Olaf outside York. He is commemorated still in the name Siward's Howe which has become attached to an Iron Age burial mound to the south-east of the city of York, perched on what passes for a hill in that part of the world.

Siward's successor was a wholly surprising appointment. Tostig, who was to hold the earldom of Northumbria for the next ten years, was the son of Earl Godwin. Though he had a Danish mother and bore a Danish name, his upbringing had been wholly southern, in his father's earldom of Wessex. The wife whom he married in 1051 was from across the Channel. Countess Judith was the daughter of Count Baldwin IV of Flanders and his wife Eleanor (the daughter of Richard II of Normandy, and thus first cousin of King Edward). Tostig was the first southerner ever to be appointed to the earldom of Northumbria. There had been outsiders before, Ælfhelm at the turn of the century, then Siward. But Ælfhelm had been a near neighbour from northern Mercia, Siward a Dane who was acceptable to the Anglo-Danish aristocracy of Yorkshire and who sought by marriage to enter the ruling circles of Bernicia. Tostig was a complete stranger.

His appointment needs to be considered in the context of the almost unassailable power of the house of Godwin during Edward's later years. After a sharp crisis in the relations between the king and his earl of Wessex in the years 1051–2 Godwin had emerged with undiminished power. On his death in 1053 his eldest surviving son, Harold, became earl of Wessex. With the promotion of Tostig to Northumbria in 1055 and of another brother, Gyrth, to East Anglia in 1057, the only part of the English kingdom not under the direct control of the sons of Godwin was the earldom of Mercia. Not surprisingly, there was enmity between the family of the elderly Earl Leofric of Mercia and the family of Godwin. How this enmity might be contained was one of the major political problems of King Edward's later years.

Another factor behind Tostig's appointment could have been that the king wanted an earl who might bring a measure of stability to his turbulent Northumbrian province by aggregating it to the West Saxon system of royal authority. This may be to read royal intentions which were not operative in 1055 back from Tostig's actions as earl over the next ten years; so the case must not be pressed. Tostig was certainly a tough figure. We possess a character sketch of him in a strictly contemporary work, the *Vita Ædwardi Regis* ('The Life of King Edward'). This is a richly fascinating and puzzling work, composed in the years 1065–7 by a Flemish monk living in England. The anonymous author, who had probably met Tostig and admired him warmly, regarded him as 'a man of courage, and endowed with great wisdom and shrewdness of mind'. In an extended comparison between the brothers Harold and Tostig, he had this to say of the latter:

Earl Tostig himself was endowed with very great and prudent restraint – although occasionally he was a little over-zealous in attacking evil – and with bold and inflexible constancy of mind. He would first ponder much and by himself the plans in his mind, and when he had ascertained by an appreciation of the matter the final issue, he would set them in order; and these [plans] he would not readily share with anyone. Also sometimes he was so cautiously active that his action seemed to come before his planning; and this often enough was advantageous to him in the theatre of the world. When he gave, he was lavish with liberal bounty and, urged by his religious wife, it was done more frequently in honour of Christ than for any fickle favour of men. In his word, deed, or promise he was distinguished by adamantine steadfastness. He renounced desire for all women except his wife of royal stock, and chastely, with restraint, and wisely he governed the use of his body and tongue. Both [brothers] persevered with what they had begun: but Tostig vigorously, Harold prudently; the one in action aimed at success, the other also at happiness. Both at times so cleverly disguised their intentions that one who did not know them was in doubt what to think. And to sum up their character for our readers, no age and province has reared two mortals of such worth at the same time.[5]

With Harold and Tostig as his senior earls, the writer optimistically concluded, King Edward could live a life free from care, 'for the one drove back the foe from the south and the other scared them off from the north'.

Alas, this was just what Tostig did *not* do. We left Scotland with

Malcolm installed as king by Earl Siward in 1054 and his defeated rival Macbeth in retreat to the north. Macbeth was down but not quite out, and Malcolm's early years were doubtless tinged with the apprehension that he might pick himself up and fight again. But Macbeth was killed in 1057, and his son Lulach in 1058. King Malcolm was able to turn his attention to his southern marches.

Scottish raids began once more. 'The Scots, since they had not yet tested Tostig and held him more cheaply, harassed him often with raids rather than war.' Tostig's response was 'to wear them down as much by cunning schemes as by martial courage and military campaigns'.[6] This would appear to be the most tactful phrasing which a writer favourable to Tostig could devise to indicate that in his dealings with the Scots the earl preferred diplomacy to war. We get a glimpse of this diplomacy in another source which tells of a state visit made by Malcolm to King Edward in 1059 escorted by Archbishop Cynesige of York, Bishop Ethelwine of Durham and Earl Tostig. We don't know what was agreed at this meeting, though it is likely to have been the occasion when Malcolm and Tostig, like Carl and Ealdred twenty years earlier, entered into a sworn brotherhood, a bond of special intensity which artificially created a new and close kin relationship. We may suppose that it ranked as one of the earl's 'cunning schemes'. One wonders what the ruling families of Northumbria had to say about Tostig's tactics. Were unfavourable comparisons drawn, in conversations over the mead tankards, with Siward or the great Uhtred?

Worse, much worse, was to come. In 1061 Tostig and Judith set off on a pilgrimage to Rome. It was during their prolonged absence that 'King Malcolm of the Scots savagely harried the earldom of his sworn brother, Earl Tostig, and violated the peace of St Cuthbert on the island of Lindisfarne'. It was most probably at the same time that a serious territorial loss occurred. Cumbria, laboriously brought under English rule by the campaigns of earls Eadwulf and Siward, its notables reassured by Gospatric's concessions, was 'violently subjugated' by the Scots.[7]

There is a chilling footnote to this story. Malcolm and his men expelled the Northumbrian ruling class from Cumbria, and this would have included the ecclesiastical as well as the secular élite. Bishop John, the second prelate consecrated by Archbishop Cynesige, suddenly found himself unemployed. His next move can be traced with the unexpected aid of a contemporary chronicler in north Germany. Adam of Bremen, writing in about 1075, tells us that a certain bishop called John, 'from Scotland', turned up on the doorstep of Archbishop Adalbert of Hamburg-Bremen (1043–72) and was by him appointed to the missionary see of Mecklenburg on the frontier between Christian Germans and pagan Slavs. Adam offered no date but seems to place the posting sometime in the early 1060s. It is hard to believe that these two bishops named John were not one and the same person. Neither need it be wholly surprising that a cleric should migrate from Britain to the shores of the Baltic. The secular ruler of the Mecklenburg region, a Christian Slavonic prince (though with a German name acquired during his upbringing in the Saxon monastery of Lüneburg) called Gottschalk, had spent time in England while in exile from his native land between 1029 and 1042. He may have been a distant kinsman of Canute through the latter's Slav mother. Archbishop Adalbert claimed jurisdiction over the churches which ministered to the spiritual needs of the Norse settlers in the Orkneys and Shetlands. When Earl Thorfinn of Orkney – a pious man who built the handsome church at Birsay whose remains may still be seen – went on a pilgrimage to Rome about the year 1060, he travelled by way of Denmark and had a meeting with Archbishop Adalbert. Malcolm III of Scotland had sought an alliance with Thorfinn against Macbeth and to seal it had married his daughter Ingibiorg. Contemporaneously, English clergy were working as missionaries in Norway. In short, the connections across the North Sea were in place which might assist an exiled bishop from the northwestern marches of England to find a niche for himself in the remote and dangerous north-eastern fringes of Christendom. John laboured in the bishopric of Mecklenburg until 1066. In that year there occurred an uprising of the pagan Slavs against their Christian and Germanized master, Prince Gottschalk, and the clergy associated with him. Bishop John had the misfortune to fall into the hands of the pagan rebels. He was tortured but steadfastly refused to deny his faith. On 10 November 1066 his hands and feet were cut off and then he was beheaded. His severed head was offered as a sacrifice to the pagan god Redigast.

Among the secular élite who would have been expelled from

Cumbria by the Scots must have been numbered Gospatric. This member of the house of Bamburgh thus owed his exclusion from power, command and wealth to the negligent absence of the upstart earl from the south. Tostig had inflicted dishonour on the family. It is just conceivable that relations between Tostig and Gospatric were already so strained that the earl had taken the precaution of keeping a relative of Gospatric in his entourage as a hostage. The case for this supposition rests on a curious tale told by the author of the *Vita Ædwardi Regis* relating to Tostig's pilgrimage. Among the very distinguished party which made its way to Rome in the company of the earl was a young man named Gospatric (yet another), a kinsman of King Edward. When the returning pilgrims were attacked by robbers in the Roman Campagna this Gospatric courageously employed a ruse to save Tostig from harm.

For as he [Gospatric] rode in the very van of the pilgrims, he was asked by the robbers which of them was Earl Tostig. Realising immediately what was their trade, he said that he was, and signalled to the earl with all possible signs to ride away. He was believed because of the luxury of his clothes and his physical appearance, which was indeed distinguished; and so he was taken away, in vain hope indeed, with the rest of the booty. When, however, he thought the earl far enough away to be safe, during his interrogation on various matters he confessed at length that he was not the man they thought they had captured. Although when the robbers first understood the case they put his life in jeopardy, finally, however, some of them treated his behaviour more generously, and not only was he allowed to depart, but, marked with these soldiers' great esteem and praise, and restored to the possession of his own things, he was escorted back in peace, followed by the good wishes of all.

This Gospatric is very probably to be identified with a Gospatric who was the grandson of Earl Uhtred by his third wife, the daughter of King Ethelred II. Not only was he kin to King Edward, he was also a member of the house of Bamburgh, nephew of Gospatric of Cumbria, he of the mysterious writ. Of course we cannot *demonstrate* that he was in Tostig's company as a hostage. His presence there might have been entirely innocent. He might have joined the pilgrims simply as an act of piety. But we are permitted to surmise, as we so often have to do in the study of Anglo-Saxon history. Kings and great magnates usually had a few hostages in their entourages at any given moment. Tostig's younger brother Wulfnoth, for instance, seems to have spent all his adult life as a hostage in the grip of William of Normandy. It is striking that Tostig should have had in his retinue a man who belonged to the clan of his rivals.

Be this as it may, the loss of Cumbria to the Scots can only have exacerbated tensions between the earl and the north's foremost family. It also rendered southern Northumbria vulnerable once more. Scottish raiders coming from Cumbria down into Teesdale or over Stainmore and down Swaledale were within reach of the rich estates of the plain of York such as Allertonshire, were even within striking distance of the city of York itself. Cumbria would remain under Scottish control, and Yorkshire correspondingly vulnerable, until 1092.

Tostig, therefore, was failing in an earl's primary duty, of defence, and simultaneously making some dangerous enemies. How did he get on with the others who mattered most in Northumbria? Of his personal piety, and that of his wife, there can be no doubt. Their Roman pilgrimage was one expression of it; another, the 'no few' gifts which they offered to the church of St Cuthbert. Judith's consisted of 'various ornaments for the church', which could indicate plate or ivories, books or textiles.[8] Her discernment as a patron can still be sensed in the *Gospels of Countess Judith*, now preserved in the Pierpont Morgan Library in New York, which she commissioned from English scribes and artists. It contains some of the most exquisite illustrations produced by the brilliantly talented school of artists who were active in England in the last generation or so before the Norman Conquest. It is only from Durham, we must remember, that narrative records survive to tell of Tostig's and Judith's munificence. It is likely that the other great churches of the north benefited from their pious generosity: York, Beverley, Hexham, Ripon . . .

And yet a critical note was sounded even by the grateful clergy of Durham. We can hear it in a brutally misogynistic story told about Countess Judith. She conceived a desire to enter the church of St Cuthbert in order to pray at the saint's tomb. This was something that no woman had ever been allowed to do. Judith did not quite dare to do it herself, but conceived the following stratagem. (Like her

husband, she seems to have been good at hatching 'cunning schemes'.)
She would send one of her maidservants on this risky and unprecedented venture and if *she* survived the experiment her mistress would
know that it would be safe for her to follow in the same footsteps. No
sooner had the luckless girl who was chosen set foot in the cemetery
of St Cuthbert's church than she was turned back and struck down by
a violent gust of wind. Gravely injured, she took to her bed and died
in agony shortly afterwards. Judith, terrified, commissioned a sculpture
of the Crucifixion, and another of St Mary and St John the Evangelist,
which she ordered to be encased in gold and silver. She presented them
to St Cuthbert in reparation. It's a curious, and to modern sensibilities
a distasteful, story. What is striking in the present context is that it was
remembered and written down. Judith left an ambivalent reputation at
Durham.

So did her husband, for this was not the only story about intrusion
into sacred space that has come down to us. Tostig had arrested a local
brigand named Aldan-Hamel and imprisoned him at Durham. With
the miraculous assistance of St Cuthbert Aldan-Hamel contrived to
escape, and fled to the sanctuary of the saint's church. Tostig's retainers
pursued him there, and paused. But their leader, Barcwith, uncon-
trollably angry, cried out, 'What are we waiting for? Let's break down
the doors!' and was just about to do so when he was struck down 'by,
as it were, an arrow from on high' and died horribly three days later.[9]
Violation of the holiest sanctuary in the north of England was an
extremely serious crime; nothing less than sacrilege. It put the per-
petrator beyond the pale. In English eyes it was the sort of thing that
the Scots did, as King Malcolm had at Lindisfarne in 1061. Sacrilege
of this order had to be compensated by a fine of £96. This was an
enormous sum of money; more than double the annual render (£40)
of the bishop of Durham's multiple estate at Howden. The violator,
Barcwith, was not just any old rank-and-file member of Tostig's
entourage: 'In power he came before all others in the [earl's] household.' If Tostig's right-hand man was guilty of breach of sanctuary in
the course of duty it must have looked as though he had the tacit
licence of his master. The earl's establishment was insulting God and
his saints, affronting cherished local sentiment, tearing down one of
the struts with which a violent society sought to build peace.

Matters were not helped by Tostig's exercise of ecclesiastical patronage. It will be recalled that Bishop Ethelric of Durham, that outsider from Peterborough, did not get on with his cathedral chapter. At the root of the trouble lay rows about property. We have seen that Ethelric may not have been above alienating St Cuthbert's estates in order to repay a favour. We are on firmer ground with the reputation for personal rapacity which the bishop left behind him. Matters came to a head with the rebuilding of a church. The bishop planned to replace the old wooden church at Chester-le-Street with a new one of stone. While digging the foundations workmen unearthed a buried treasure – presumably a Roman coin hoard. The bishop appropriated the treasure for himself and sent it to his home down south at Peterborough. This high-handed act evidently provoked much resentment in the north. For the bishop it proved to be the last straw. In 1056 he followed ignominiously in the wake of the treasure, 'voluntarily' emphasizes one source, which prompts one to suspect that this was just what it was not. Ethelric was no longer welcome at Durham.

Ethelric had a brother named Ethelwine who had been his accomplice in the fleecing of St Cuthbert's patrimony. It was this very brother who was appointed to the bishopric upon Ethelric's ignoble 'resignation'. Formally speaking, the appointment was made by the king; but Edward acted 'on the prompting and advocacy of Earl Tostig'. It was the earl of Northumbria who was held responsible for inflicting this second bad lot upon the church of Durham. Indeed, Ethelwine proved to be much worse than his brother.

With Archbishop Ealdred of York (1061–9) Tostig's relations appear to have been cordial. Ealdred was an immensely grand figure, 'the nearest to a prince-bishop that the Edwardian church produced', as he has been justly termed.[10] Long remembered in his diocese of York as a builder and embellisher of churches on a lavish scale, he moved also on a wider stage. A courtier and man of the world, he had served King Edward on an embassy to the German Empire to transact important and delicate business. He had travelled as far as Jerusalem as a pilgrim. He was in the party of very imposing figures who accompanied Earl Tostig to Rome in 1061: it included three more bishops. (As to the character of one of these bishops, Walter of Hereford, there were evidently more facets than piety. He met a dreadful end several years later, stabbed to death with a pair of scissors wielded in self-defence by a seamstress to whom he was making improper advances.)

The limitations of the sources are such that much less can confidently be said about Tostig's relations with the secular aristocracy, apart from the house of Bamburgh. There is one straw in the wind at which we can grasp. Tostig seems to have delegated much of the earldom's routine business to a Yorkshire thegn named Copsig. Symeon of Durham described him as a *familiaris* of Tostig, which we might translate as 'crony', and tells us that 'under Tostig he managed the business of the whole earldom'. Now Copsig was a rather lesser landowner in Yorkshire. He held some land at Marske in Cleveland which he gave to the church of Durham, together with a silver goblet. He owned two further estates, at Coxwold and Danby Wiske, which were together worth £8 per annum. These were very modest possessions compared to the amply spreading acres of such as Arnketil son of Ecgfrith or Orm the son of Gamel. People like this would have looked on Copsig as an upstart. It would be part of their count against Tostig that he set such a man to lord it over his betters.

Given the terms on which noblemen conducted their dissensions in eleventh-century Northumbria, of which we have now seen plentiful evidence, it will come as no surprise to learn that blood was shed. Three victims in particular who fell foul of Earl Tostig are mentioned in our sources. In 1063 Gamel son of Orm and Ulf the son of Dolfin were killed in Tostig's own hall at York. They had come there under promise of safe-conduct. Shortly after Christmas 1064 Gospatric was killed at the king's own court. The murder was said to have been contrived by Queen Edith at the instance of her brother Tostig.

Who were these prominent victims? Gospatric is presumed to have been the son of Earl Uhtred, he who had administered Cumbria under Earl Siward and had been unceremoniously expelled when Malcolm III's Scots swept down in 1061. He and Tostig were old enemies. Ulf the son of Dolfin is less easy to identify. An Irish annalist preserved the information that a leading Northumbrian named Dolfin was slain in 1054 in the course of the battle in which Earl Siward defeated Macbeth. Our Durham anonymous tells us that the (unnamed) daughter of Dolfin married Gospatric (still one more), the son of Arnketil and Sigrida. If these two Dolfins were the same one, Ulf could plausibly be claimed as the brother of the unnamed wife. Gamel the son of Orm is irresistibly to be connected with Orm the son of Gamel, husband of Æthelthryth the daughter of Earl Ealdred and restorer of St Gregory's minster, Kirkdale. We may suppose that the Gamel who was killed by Earl Tostig in 1063 was his son. (It is just worth noting that a Gamel was listed among the *kynling*, the kinsmen, of Gospatric in the text of Gospatric's writ.)

Now it has to be said, in all candour, that the names Dolfin, Gamel, Gospatric, Orm and Ulf were fairly common names in eleventh-century Northumbria. Our identifications have to be tentative. However, if – *if* – they are correct, these victims were all members of the house of Bamburgh by blood or marriage. Frank Barlow has commented that 'it is quite clear that Tostig had become involved in feuds'.[11] For an earl of Northumbria in the eleventh century it must have been well-nigh impossible not to become 'involved in feuds'. Was Tostig in some sense the continuator of the feud between the houses of Uhtred and Thurbrand? So he might have been perceived by members of Uhtred's clan. The suggestion would gain force if we could show that Tostig was aided and abetted by the Yorkshire descendants of Thurbrand, that is to say Carl (who might by now have been dead) and his sons. But we can't. As so often, the evidence fails us. The only supporters of Tostig whom we can identify by name are Copsig, who had no traceable connections with Thurbrand's family, and the two Danish leaders of his mercenary troops, Amund and Ravenswart, who would be lynched in 1065.

So Tostig failed to defend Northumbria against the Scots; he made powerful enemies; he was treacherous in his dealings; and he alienated the community of St Cuthbert. But that was not all. When revolt against him finally broke out in 1065 the rebels had three sorts of complaint about the character of his rule. First, they objected to 'the enormous tax which he had unjustly levied upon Northumbria'.[12] The surviving evidence shows that the tax assessments for the king's geld in Northumbria were a good deal lighter than those laid upon the Southumbrian shires of, say, Wessex. Why this should have been so we can only guess. Northumbria was a poorer province than Wessex, colder, less fertile, less populous, less monetized, less urbanized; in a word, less taxable. It was also a province but recently and uncertainly brought under West Saxon royal authority, whose continuing loyalty to a southern king was not to be taken for granted. Prudent rulers would not stretch this loyalty by oppressing the Northumbrians with burdensome levies of taxation. But this is exactly what Tostig did. No one likes tax increases. Tostig managed to anger the entire tax-paying population of Northumbria.

The rebels complained, second, of the quality of the justice administered by Earl Tostig: 'He oppressed the nobles with the heavy yoke of his rule because of their misdeeds . . . and he was accused of punishing wrongdoers more from a wish to confiscate their property than for love of justice.' Severe justice could simply mean effective justice. As for corruption, it was a common charge, and in the light of what we know of the administration of justice in Anglo-Saxon England, not a surprising one. As it happens, we have an interesting hint about what were perceived as Tostig's methods in the single surviving reference to a lawsuit during his tenure of the earldom of Northumbria. It concerns the case of Aldan-Hamel, the grisly fate of whose pursuer Barcwith we encountered a few pages earlier. When Aldan-Hamel, accused of robbery, arson, rape and murder, was arrested 'his kinsfolk and friends offered much and promised more [to the earl] to ward off his execution'. It would of course be unwise to read too much into a single piece of anecdotal evidence of this nature. That said, one can well believe, in the light of what we know of his character, that Tostig's justice could be harsh. And we can be confident that the earl and his subordinates would have done nicely for themselves out of its administration. After all, when men of modest estate like Copsig start giving silver cups to the church they've got to pay for them somehow or other.

Third, the rebels sought, and got from King Edward, a 'renewal of Canute's law'. The sense of this piece of information seems to be that Canute's lawcode of nearly fifty years earlier had come to assume the character of a standard or yardstick of good government. (Just so after another half-century would King Henry I 'restore the law of King Edward' in his coronation charter of 1100.) In their minds Canute's laws stood, in Patrick Wormald's words, 'for the days before Tostig brought intrusive southern government to the north'.[13]

In the spring of 1065 the mortal remains of St Oswin, king and martyr, were disinterred and publicly displayed at Durham. Oswin was an early Northumbrian ruler who was treacherously betrayed and killed by his kinsman King Oswy in the year 651. The 'epiphany' of saints, their 'shewing forth', was not an innocent act in eleventh-century Christendom. We have already seen how their ghostly presence helped to incite the revivalism of the Peace meetings across the Channel. The relics of Oswin were displayed as rapidly as possible – as soon as the worst of the northern winter was past – after the treacherous murder of a Northumbrian magnate at the court of King Edward engineered by Earl Tostig. The parallel was there for all to see in the carefully staged ceremony at Durham.

The Northumbrian rebellion of 1065 did not start until after the harvest was over. It had evidently been well prepared under able leadership. So much is suggested by the organized hurry of the rebels' movements and the coherence of the demands they put forward. On 3 October 1065 a force of two hundred soldiers entered York. Their leaders are named as three prominent thegns, Dunstan son of Æthelnoth, Gamel-Barn and Gluniairnn son of Hardwulf. Earl Tostig was far away at the time, hunting with the king in Wiltshire. The insurgents at York seized the earl's residence, probably that 'Earlsburgh' where Siward had founded his minster and been buried ten years before, and helped themselves to all the weapons and treasure they found there. On the same day they captured and executed two of Tostig's Danish housecarls, Amund and Ravenswart, presumably the leaders of his bodyguard. On the following day, in what sounds like a pitched battle, the insurgents were victorious and more than two hundred men of the earl's household troops were killed. York was theirs.

The three leaders can be identified as substantial landowners in the West Riding of Yorkshire. (Incidentally, the lynched housecarl Ravenswart held some land near their estates. One may suspect, though one cannot prove, some local rivalries between the established gentry and the intruded Danish henchman of the earl.) Because one contemporary tells us that 'all the thegns of Yorkshire and Northumberland gathered together', and another that this gathering occurred 'next', that is, after the capture of York, we should envisage several contingents of roughly comparable size to the one led by the three thegns from the West Riding. In aggregate, this must have amounted to a fairly sizeable army by the standards of the day.

The leaders of the revolt declared Earl Tostig outlawed and chose a new earl for Northumbria. The man they chose was Morcar, who belonged to the ruling dynasty of Mercia. Earl Leofric had been succeeded in the earldom of Mercia, on his death in 1057, by his son Ælfgar. He in his turn had been succeeded upon his early death in 1062 by his eldest son Edwin. Morcar was Edwin's younger brother. The speed with which Morcar joined the Northumbrian insurgents when they summoned him suggests that he was holding himself in readiness not far away. One may suspect preliminary secret negotiations during the summer of 1065 between the leaders of the prospective northern rebellion and the Mercian ruling house. For Edwin and Morcar it was an opportunity not to be missed. Here at last was a chance to hit out at the hated sons of Godwin.

Among Morcar's first acts was to entrust Bernicia to a member of the house of Bamburgh, Oswulf, the son of Earl Eadwulf who had been killed in 1041. The claims of the ancient ruling family having been thus honoured, the rebel armies moved off to the south. On their march they were joined by additional forces from Lincolnshire, Nottinghamshire and Derbyshire. They halted at Northampton, where Morcar's brother Earl Edwin joined them with further reinforcements drawn not simply from Mercia but from Wales as well.

Negotiations between the Northumbrian and north Mercian rebels and the king now ensued. Earl Harold of Wessex conducted these negotiations on Edward's behalf. The precise sequence of events is difficult to make out with confidence. What is clear is that discussions took place first at Northampton and then at Oxford. The rebels pressed their demands: dismissal and exile of Tostig, a return to the status quo in the administration of Northumbria, renewal of Canute's law. Meanwhile King Edward had assembled his leading advisers at Britford in Wiltshire. A series of stormy meetings took place. Some accused Tostig of having brought the rebellion on himself by the harshness of his rule. Tostig alleged that Harold, his own brother, had stirred up the revolt against him for devious purposes of his own. Harold, posting back from the negotiations at Northampton, cleared himself from this charge by oath. The king was all for taking the most robust measures possible: he wanted to call out troops from southern England and crush the rebellion by force. But his counsellors would not support him. It was too late in the year. The weather was against them. They did not want a civil war.

The advance of the northerners from Northampton to Oxford could have been perceived as the opening move in just such a civil strife. The government gave in. At the Oxford meeting on 28 October Earl Harold, on behalf of the king, agreed to all the rebel demands. Earl Tostig was ditched by his own brother. A few days later, accompanied by his wife, children and retainers the earl crossed the Channel to find asylum for the winter under the protection of Judith's brother Count Baldwin V. She took with her the precious gospel-book, which thus started out on the travels which would end eight centuries later on the other side of the Atlantic.

Events had moved very swiftly. From the insurgents' entry into York to the decisive Oxford meeting there had elapsed less than four weeks. The consequences of these events were, however, out of all proportion to their brevity. First, they hastened King Edward's death. Now an old man in his sixties, he was enraged by being overridden at Britford and grief-stricken at the outcome. He succumbed to what his contemporary biographer called 'a sick mind'. Perhaps he had a stroke. Eight weeks later he was dead. Second, Tostig would never forgive what he regarded as Harold's betrayal. The short remainder of his life would be consecrated to the working out of his implacable hostility. 'Alas, those brothers' hearts too hard!', as the biographer of King Edward lamented.

How right he was. If Edward had lasted longer, Duke William of Normandy would not have invaded England in 1066. If Harold and Tostig had not quarrelled, Harold would not have found himself fighting his brother in Yorkshire in the following September. If Harold had not been two hundred and fifty miles away from the south coast, William's army would not have been able to disembark in Sussex unopposed. So much stemmed directly from the turbulent events which started to unfold at York on 3 October 1065.

9

Settrington

King Edward died on 5 January 1066. On his deathbed he had designated Harold, son of Godwin and earl of Wessex, his brother-in-law,
as his successor. Harold lost no time. On the very next day, 6 January,
he was crowned king as Harold II.

Designation and haste were necessary because for a long time before
1066 uncertainty had clouded the question of the succession to the
throne of England. This uncertainty arose from the childlessness of the
king and queen. How long it had taken after Edward's marriage to
Edith in 1045 to become apparent that the royal couple were not going
to have any children we can only guess. A very few years, surely. For
at least – shall we say? – fifteen or so years before 1066, therefore, a
question mark had hung over the English succession.

There were several possible candidates. First, as to the royal house
of Wessex itself. In the wake of the Danish conquest and the death of
Edmund Ironside in 1016 his infant son Edward had been carried off
to Hungary, beyond Canute's reach, a safe haven in which to be
brought up. This Edward, known as 'the Exile', was summoned back
to England by his uncle King Edward, presumably with a view to his
succession. He arrived in 1057 but tragically died – and there is no
hint of foul play in our sources – immediately afterwards, before he
had even met the king. He left a son, Edgar, aged about five, usually
known to historians as Edgar 'the Ætheling' after the Old English term
for 'throneworthy' or 'prince of the blood'. This Edgar would have
been about thirteen or fourteen at the time of King Edward's death, or
a little older than his great-grandfather Ethelred had been at *his*
accession in 978.

There were plenty more claimants. (We should remember that in eleventh-century England the conventions governing succession to the throne were a good deal more fluid than they later became.) King Sweyn of Denmark (1047–74) was one such. He was a nephew of Canute, and put it about that Edward had promised him the English throne on more than one occasion. Harald Hardrada, king of Norway (1047–66), was another. His kinsman and predecessor Magnus (1035–47) believed, or had persuaded himself, that Canute's son Harthacanute had promised him England when the two men were allies in the carve-up of Canute's empire. King Harald regarded himself as heir to the claims of Magnus. A third foreign claimant was Duke William of Normandy. Edward had spent much of his long exile in Normandy. He was kin to the ducal family through his mother Emma. William of Poitiers, the duke's biographer and propagandist, claimed that Edward had loved William 'like a brother or a son' and that he had formally designated William as his successor.[1] Then there were the Godwinson brothers, Harold and Tostig, brothers-in-law of the king, the two most powerful noblemen in the kingdom. Tostig's fall from power and exile in 1065 ruled out his candidature and left the way open for his brother. Harold's ambitions and schemes cannot be read across nine centuries with any confidence. Yet it is unlikely that his plans were not carefully laid: you cannot improvise a great state occasion like a coronation in less than twenty-four hours.

'There will always be more questions than answers about the succession in 1066.'[2] The surviving sources – including now the pictorial evidence of the Bayeux Tapestry – are, variously, laconic, discreet, prejudiced or ambiguous. These bones have been picked over so often and so thoroughly by historians of the Norman Conquest that not a morsel of new sustenance remains. All that we need to emphasize for present purposes is that the throne of England was in contention in the aftermath of King Edward's death. Harold's 'usurpation', for in Norman eyes it was nothing less than this, made it absolutely certain that Duke William, who regarded himself as the rightful heir to the late king, would seek to displace him. Harald of Norway was determined to make a bid too; and in this he would be encouraged by Tostig, now the mortal enemy of his brother the king of England.

During the last week of April 1066 Halley's comet flashed across the night skies of England. People called it 'the long-haired star' in allusion to its prominent 'tail'. They wondered what it meant; we can see a group of them doing just this in one of the scenes of the Bayeux Tapestry. Comets were not then the innocent astronomical phenomena that they have become to the flat imaginations of today. They were messages from God, telling or warning of something to come, usually some more-or-less imminent catastrophe. So it had been in Northumbria in 1018; so it was again in 1066.

Shortly after the passage of the comet, Tostig, who had evidently supplied himself with ships and men (possibly with Norman assistance) during his winter in Flanders, appeared in English waters. He attacked the Isle of Wight, exacting tribute and supplies, and then sailed along the coasts of Sussex and Kent, landing intermittent raiding parties here and there, as far as Sandwich. There he was joined by his old crony Copsig, who had wintered in the Orkneys, with more ships. Learning that his brother was setting out from London at the head of an army to engage him, Tostig set sail northwards. He harried round the mouth of the river Burnham in north Norfolk, and then moved on to the estuary of the Humber whence he raided the northern parts of Lincolnshire. Seen off by the northern earls Edwin and Morcar, he continued further north into the coastal waters of eastern Scotland. He was received at the court of King Malcolm and remained a guest there throughout the months of summer.

Tostig seems to have spared Northumbria at this stage, presumably by design. Perhaps he nurtured hopes of reinstating himself in the earldom from which he had been so ignominiously ejected in the previous autumn. If this were so, he had failed to read the mood of the Northumbrians. Indeed, the northerners had their misgivings about his brother the king. Although it had been Harold who had negotiated the concessions of 1065; although he had been crowned by a northern prelate, Archbishop Ealdred of York; although he had prudently bound the northern earls to his interest by marrying their sister Edith; despite all this, Harold had to visit York early in his reign – apparently the first time that an English king had journeyed north of the Humber since 1031 – to secure the northerners' allegiance. They were won over by the eloquence of Harold's companion, Bishop Wulfstan of Worcester. (Well of course they were, for the information comes from the bishop's dutiful and admiring biographer, his chaplain Colman.)

At all events, Harold was back at Westminster for Easter, which in 1066 fell on 16 April, leaving an apparently loyal Northumbria behind him.

Loyal it may have been, but tense. At least two hoards of coin have come to light in Yorkshire which may plausibly be dated to the reign of Harold II. People deposit valuables for safe-keeping when times are troubled. These finds are tangible evidence of the anxieties of the summer of 1066. It was not Northumbria alone that was tense during that summer. Duke William was known to be making preparations for an invasion in support of, as he believed, his rightful claim to be Edward's heir. The busy activities of his shipwrights are vividly pictured on the Bayeux Tapestry. By mid-August his invasion fleet was ready to set sail. In England, meanwhile, King Harold had concentrated ships and troops along the south coast to repel the Norman invaders. As it so happened, the Normans were unable to set sail owing to the strong westerly winds that prevailed in the Channel for six weeks after the assembly of their fleet.

In the event, it was the king of Norway who struck first. In late August or early September Harald Hardrada's invasion fleet appeared off the mouth of the Tyne, where it was joined by Tostig. The combined forces sailed down the coast, pausing to forage in Cleveland, at Scarborough and in Holderness. Then they rounded Spurn Head and entered the Humber. They made their way up the Ouse as far as Riccall, some nine miles south of York, where they moored their ships and disembarked. Harald and Tostig then led their troops towards York along the line of what is now the A19 between Selby and York. In that featureless landscape the route barely rises above the marshy ings beside the Ouse on one side and the scrubby ill-drained heathland to the other. (It is an area still liable to flooding: during the severe floods of the autumn of 2000 the A19 became impassable for several days.) At Gate Fulford – the name means 'the road of the foul (i.e. muddy) ford' – about two miles south of York, there is a barely perceptible rise in the ground, offering a slight advantage to a defender trying to block the route of march from south to north. It was there that Edwin and Morcar, who had shut themselves up in York, chose to make their stand. The battle of Gate Fulford was fought on Wednesday 20 September 1066. The defending army of Yorkshire was routed with great slaughter and many deaths by drowning in marsh and river. The invaders went on to take possession of York.

The king of Norway and his ally dealt peaceably with the city. York evidently surrendered on terms. So much is clear from the report that hostages were not simply *taken* by the victors; they were *exchanged*. Harald and Tostig took one hundred and fifty hostages from the people of York and surrendered the same number of their own men in return. One usually reliable contemporary reported that the men of York even agreed to join forces with their conquerors to march south with them 'and subdue this country', which, if true, is an indication of the continuing strength of anti-southern feeling and reminiscent of the reception of King Sweyn of Denmark in 1013. The invaders did not subject the city to sack but withdrew from it, presumably as an earnest of their good intentions, to await elsewhere the arrival of hostages from the shire – as opposed to the city – of York as a whole. The place they chose to wait was Stamford Bridge, some eight miles to the east of York, where the line of the Roman road from York to Bridlington crossed the river Derwent. Why Stamford Bridge was chosen for the site of the temporary encampment of the Norwegian army we do not know, despite much conjecture. The most likely factor would have been the presence of well-disposed local landowners in that area and the availability of the Derwent for the transport of provisions for the army from round about. (It is easily overlooked that before the fairly recent advent of modern methods of preserving food, one of the most serious problems that commanders had to face was keeping their troops supplied with food and fuel.)

Meanwhile King Harold II of England had been alerted to the arrival of the northern invaders. He had already, as it happened, subject to the pressures just indicated, disbanded his troops and sent his ships to London in the second week of September; leaving the south coast unguarded. Quickly reassembling his army he hastened northwards, reaching Tadcaster on Sunday 24 September. Astonishingly, the news of his approach did not reach the ears of his adversaries. On Monday 25th the English army was on the move early, hurtled through York and came upon the Norwegians unawares. Battle was joined. The fight, surging round the bridge over the Derwent which had given Stamford its name, was long and hard. By the end of the day the English had won an overwhelming victory. King Harald of Norway and his ally Tostig had both met their deaths in an immense carnage. Some three hundred ships had brought the invading host; twenty-four sufficed to carry the survivors home. A chronicler writing some sixty years later claimed that the site of the battle was still easily recognizable by the great mound of dead men's bones which still lay there.

Two days after the battle of Stamford Bridge the wind in the English Channel veered to the south. After the long weeks of waiting, Duke William's invasion fleet could set sail. On the following day, Thursday 28 September, the Norman army landed, unopposed, on the coast of Sussex.

The news of the Norman landings was borne as swiftly as possible to the king. Harold was still at York, resting his men and celebrating his victory, and taking any necessary steps for the governance of the north. Oswulf seems to have continued in the rule of Bernicia with which he had been entrusted by Morcar a year beforehand. Earl Morcar himself had failed to mount a successful defence of Yorkshire against Harald Hardrada and Tostig, and had indeed – perhaps – agreed to ally with them against the English king. It seems probable that he was relieved of his office. A rather late and not always reliable source tells us that Harold appointed a man named Merleswein (properly Mærle-Sveinn) to the earldom of Deira or Yorkshire after the battle of Stamford Bridge. The report seems plausible. Merleswein was a very substantial landowner in the England of 1066, with estates scattered from Yorkshire to Cornwall. His greatest concentrations of property were in the north, in Lincolnshire and Yorkshire, and in King Harold's reign he was sheriff of the former county under Earl Edwin of Mercia. If his estates in Lindsey were among those devastated by Tostig in the spring of 1066, this could be seen as an indication of his loyalty to Harold. In the aftermath of Stamford Bridge Merleswein must have appeared as a safe pair of hands.

Harold could not tarry. Accompanied by his housecarls he covered the two hundred-odd miles between York and London in an extraordinarily short space of time, arriving at his destination probably on 6 October. On his way south he had gathered troops to his standard from the midland shires. More rallied to him while he and his men rested in London. His strategic mistake was not to wait there long enough to enable others to join him. When he impetuously marched down to Sussex (11–13 October) his forces may have been well short of the strength that they might have attained had he tarried a little longer. This did not make the outcome of the battle of Hastings on 14 October a foregone conclusion. The English army was in a strong defensive position, and fought hard and courageously. But the Norman cavalry and the Norman archers were too much for them. By the end of the day the king was dead, surrounded by the corpses of his loyal bodyguard who had fought to the death beside the body of their fallen lord; and the rank and file were scattered in flight across the darkling downland of Sussex.

In the course of the autumn of 1066 William established his authority over much of southern England. At Berkhamsted in December he received the formal submission of the kingdom's leading men: Edgar Ætheling, Archbishop Ealdred of York, the leading men of London, and others. On Christmas Day he was crowned king by Ealdred at Westminster. His artisans were already at work building a temporary castle of wood on the site which would a little later be occupied by the Tower of London. In January 1067, at Barking in Essex, he received further surrenders. These included the first submissions of lay magnates from the north: Edwin and Morcar, Copsig, and others from north Mercia.

The most intriguing name here is that of Copsig. We have already encountered him as the hated henchman of Earl Tostig in the administration of Northumbria between 1055 and 1065. Banished alongside his master in 1065, he joined him again in the spring of 1066. After joining forces with Harald Hardrada of Norway Copsig was presumably implicated in the ravaging of the east coast of Yorkshire in the late summer. He fought alongside his old master at Stamford Bridge; unlike Tostig, he survived. Survival, indeed, seems to have been Copsig's speciality. His submission to William in the early days of 1067 was an adroit new move in the same game. And it paid immediate dividends. King William, having (as he thought) pacified his new realm, wanted to return to Normandy to celebrate his triumph among his own people. He needed someone to look after the north. He appointed Copsig to the earldom of Bernicia.

It was an utterly inept appointment from a man rightly remembered for his judgement of other men and his ability to choose reliable subordinates. (It was indeed very nearly the only inept appointment that William ever made.) It suggests that at that stage William had really no idea at all about the special problems involved in trying to rule the north. In appointing Copsig he was displacing Oswulf, whose uncle Gospatric had been murdered by Tostig a couple of years earlier. Copsig had everything to fear from Oswulf and determined to strike first. Oswulf eluded him – he was among his own people – and skulked in the wilder parts of his country until he had got together enough men for the job that had to be done. On 12 March 1067 he and his band managed to corner Copsig while he was feasting in his hall at Newburn (now a suburb of Newcastle). In the confusion of the attack Copsig managed to escape to a nearby church. But his place of refuge was soon made known, and Oswulf's men set fire to the church. In trying to escape from the flames Copsig was confronted at the threshold by Oswulf himself, who struck him down and decapitated him. King William, meanwhile, had just arrived back in Normandy, accompanied by a distinguished band of hostages which included Oswulf's kinsman Waltheof, son of Earl Siward, entirely ignorant of this affront to his regal authority.

Copsig's murder was a portent of the extreme difficulties which William would have in establishing his authority in Northumbria. Another portent of the shape of things to come was a heavy levy of geld taken, or at any rate commanded, by William before his departure for Normandy: one might compare Canute in 1017–18, though we do not know the rate of the levy in 1067. Did the king respect the concessions won by the northerners in the autumn of 1065, that Northumbrian levies should remain at the level they had been before Tostig's appointment to the earldom in 1055? We do not know. Two factors, however, suggest that he might not have done. The concessions, though formally running – if very unwillingly – in the name of King Edward, had been negotiated by Earl Harold; and in Norman eyes everything that Harold had done was wrong. Second, William was notoriously a harsh man and an avaricious one; the campaign of 1066 had strained the ducal resources to the limit; and his followers expected reward. It is a plausible guess that Northumbria was taxed as heavily by William as it had been by Tostig. If this is correct, the year 1067 was one in which the Northumbrians could begin to feel the character of Norman rule. It was also one in which they could witness the sufferings of the southern English at Norman hands. During William's absence his regents, his half-brother Bishop Odo of Bayeux and his oldest and most trusted companion William fitzOsbern, 'built castles far and wide throughout this country and distressed the wretched folk'. At least some of the victims of dispossession and pillage, of random rape and violence, would have sought refuge in the north. The Northumbrians could have been left in no doubt about what was involved in being under the rule of the Normans.

In the autumn of 1067 Earl Oswulf of Bernicia was slain by a robber. King William returned from Normandy early in December, and it was probably at his Christmas court held at Westminster that a new appointment was made. This was Gospatric, the son of Maldred and Edith who was herself the daughter of Earl Uhtred by his third wife Ælfgifu, the daughter of King Ethelred II. Gospatric was therefore of the house of Bamburgh and thus acceptable to the men of his northern earldom, the same Gospatric who had accompanied Tostig on his Roman pilgrimage in 1061 and who had saved the earl from robbers by a brave impersonation. Nothing further is known of his earlier history. The choice of Gospatric was a sensible one, a huge improvement on Copsig a year previously, but it was not spontaneous. Gospatric had suggested himself to the king, offering as an inducement 'a great sum of money'. William had been unable to resist.

It was at that same Christmas court that a further levy of geld was decided upon, collection of which would have been beginning in the spring of 1068. During that same period the king was busy pacifying the south-western counties. He evidently considered his position safe enough, for he had his queen, Matilda, brought over from Normandy and crowned by Ealdred at Whitsun, 11 May 1068. In reality, he was on the brink of the greatest threat to his position as king of England that he ever had to face. It came from the north, and it began in the summer of 1068. We are well informed from at least three more-or-less contemporary sources about the disturbances that ensued; but a precise and satisfactory chronology seems unattainable. The following reconstruction seems to me the most plausible; but it is not the only one possible.

Edwin, earl of Mercia, and his brother Morcar, the former earl of Yorkshire, had been detained in honourable captivity at the Conqueror's court. They had formed part of his entourage during the visit to Normandy in 1067, to be displayed like trophies of war to his subjects. Now they somehow slipped away from the royal court, made their way to their native land of north Mercia and rose in rebellion. They were probably accompanied by Edgar the Ætheling, who could be proffered to the northern lords as a legitimate king of the house of Wessex round whom to rally. The actions of Edwin and Morcar precipitated – were indeed perhaps the prearranged signal for – a rising to the north of the Humber. Gospatric and Merleswein, the two leading figures in the government of Northumbria, put themselves at the head of the rebellion there. A general rising of numerous northern magnates, as in 1065, began to take shape. The only additional name we have is that of Arnketil (or Archill, or Arnkel), described by Orderic Vitalis as an 'extremely powerful' nobleman and shown by the testimony of Domesday Book to have been a very extensive landowner in Yorkshire. The townsmen of York were 'very fiery' in their support for the rebels, and paid no heed to Archbishop Ealdred's counsels of moderation. The rebels seem to have planned a defensive campaign: 'they prepared to defend themselves in woods, marshes, estuaries and some towns'. This presumably indicates a strategy of holding the low-lying lands which bordered the two all-important roads from south to north, the one that crossed the Humber at Barton and its westerly fellow which swung from Doncaster round by Castleford to Tadcaster. The temporary encampments of the rebels were later interpreted by the Normans as a kind of macho gung-ho gesture deserving of mockery. 'Many of them lived in tents, disdaining to sleep in houses lest they should go soft; so the Normans called them "woodies" (*silvatici*).'[3] But it was simple military necessity. Diplomatic as well as military preparations were made. Edwin and Morcar sought help from the independent princes of Wales. Gospatric put out feelers to King Malcolm of Scotland, who may have been his first cousin.[4] King Sweyn of Denmark might have been approached.

William's response to this extremely serious threat was characteristically swift and decisive. He led his army to Warwick and built a castle there. Once again we see the role of castles as instruments of pacification. Edwin and Morcar submitted to him and the north-Mercian rebellion collapsed. The king moved on to Nottingham where he built another castle. The Northumbrian rebels lost their nerve as the royal army advanced towards York. The leaders defected. Prince Edgar, accompanied by his mother and his two sisters, together with Gospatric and Merleswein, took ship for Scotland and found safety at the court of King Malcolm. As William approached York the North-umbrian rebellion, like the Mercian one, fizzled out. The city of York surrendered. The mighty Arnketil submitted and gave his own son as a hostage to the king. William built a castle at York on the peninsula between the Ouse and its tributary the Foss, on the site now occupied by Clifford's Tower. The castle was entrusted to the custody of Robert fitzRichard and the sheriffdom of York, rendered vacant by Merle-swein's flight, to William Malet. The earldom, also deemed vacated when Gospatric fled to Scotland, was for the present left unfilled. While William tarried at York Bishop Ethelwine of Durham came and submitted to him, bearing also the news that the king of Scots wished to live at peace with King William. Ethelwine was sent to Scotland with William's terms – which we do not know, but they evidently did not include the surrender of the Northumbrian refugees – to which Malcolm agreed, sending his ambassadors back to William at York to convey his acceptance. Having thus, as he supposed, pacified the north William returned to the south, commissioning castles at Lincoln, Huntingdon and Cambridge on the way.

King William's actions in the summer of 1068 amounted to the imposition of direct Norman rule upon Yorkshire for the first time. The most tangible consequence of this was the beginning of the process of transferring land from English into Norman hands. The legal fiction which underlay the transfers ran as follows. William was the rightful successor to Edward as king of England, and Harold II a usurper. Any person who had supported Harold, for example by fighting in his army at Hastings, or any person who subsequently opposed William, was a rebel and as such liable to forfeit his land as the penalty for rebellion. The estates which were forfeited in this manner came into the king's hands and could be kept by him or redistributed to whomsoever he wished to reward. The Domesday inquest conducted in 1086, its findings subsequently recorded in the two volumes of Domesday Book, was a systematic investigation of the pattern of landholding in England south of the Tees and the Ribble at the two fixed points of 1066 and 1086. What the record shows is that in the course of those twenty years very nearly all the land of the Anglo-Saxon aristocracy had been transferred into Norman hands. One ruling class had been expropriated and another had been put in its place.

Difficulties arise when we try to establish with more precision *when* grants of land were made. It would appear that in the earliest two years after the battle of Hastings Yorkshire was unaffected by this tenurial revolution. One consequence of the mortality at Fulford and Stamford Bridge, and of King Harold's precipitate departure for the south on hearing the news of Duke William's landing, was that the northern aristocracy and their retainers did not take part in the Hastings campaign. The submissions of northern magnates, at any rate of some of them, at Barking in January 1067 meant that they retained possession of their lands. It was not until the Northumbrian rebellion of 1068 that the estates of the disaffected became available for redistribution to William's followers. The earliest grants of northern estates were presumably made while William was at York in the summer of 1068. So much is suggested by the survival of a royal writ from this period addressed to the king's barons 'both French and English' in Yorkshire.[5] There is only one name about which we can be absolutely certain among the earliest beneficiaries, that of William Malet the new Norman sheriff. We know this because Domesday Book records of several Yorkshire estates that William Malet had held them 'before the castle [of York] was taken', 'until the Danes captured him' and suchlike phrases, events which, as we shall soon see, occurred in 1069.[6] The Malet lands lay in three groupings. There was a cluster of estates round York itself, his administrative capital; a block of lands in Holderness; and a big multiple estate in the far north of the county at Stokesley, strategically well placed to guard against any military threat from across the Tees. It is a fair presumption that the new Norman castellan of York, Robert fitzRichard, was also endowed with lands but we do not know where they lay.

Modern research has suggested a few other names as possible beneficiaries as early as 1068. It seems likely that another large and strategically important multiple estate, this time in the south of the county at Conisborough, was granted to William de Warenne, a prominent follower and distant kinsman of King William, at about this time. One of the Flemish adventurers who had served William with distinction, Gilbert de Gant (i.e. from Ghent), was granted a multiple estate based on Hunmanby, just inland from the Yorkshire coast between Filey and Bridlington, probably in or by 1069: another place no doubt chosen for its defensive potential, well situated as it was to repel invaders who came by sea. One last name, later to be so famous in northern history, was that of William de Percy. In 1086 he claimed that he had held Bolton Percy, near Tadcaster, when William Malet was sheriff of York.[7]

The king's final action with regard to the north in 1068, perhaps towards the end of the year, was the appointment of a new earl for Bernicia. His choice fell on Robert de Commines, another of his Flemish followers, whose task it would be to extend Norman authority into those northernmost regions of the kingdom, the present counties of Durham and Northumberland, in which King William had not yet set foot.

This is the background to the extremely violent events of the years 1069 and 1070 in Northumbria. The rule of King William turned out to be no better than the rule of Earl Tostig. In some respects it may have been a good deal worse. Heavy taxation was continuing, in the shape of the gelds of 1067 and 1068. A persistent tradition, first recorded in the early twelfth century by William of Malmesbury, a notably diligent and accurate historian, held that Archbishop Ealdred of York had first rebuked and then even cursed the king for the weight of the tax which he had laid upon Yorkshire. New officials were governing rapaciously. An 'incalculable treasure' had been hoarded by William Malet and Robert fitzRichard in the new castle at York by the spring of 1069. Prominent men who submitted to the king had to do so on harsh terms. Arnketil had to surrender his son as a hostage and almost certainly had to make a heavy cash payment to the king at the same time as the price of retaining his lands. Some were already in whole or in part dispossessed. Malet's estate at Stokesley had belonged to a king's thegn named Haward, otherwise unknown, presumably a rebel in 1068. His estate at Rise in Holderness, where Carl had killed Ealdred thirty years earlier, had been confiscated from one of Carl's

GENEALOGICAL TABLE 8
THE DESCENDANTS OF THURBRAND THE HOLD

The names in capitals are of those murdered with their unnamed sons at
Settrington in the winter of 1073/4.

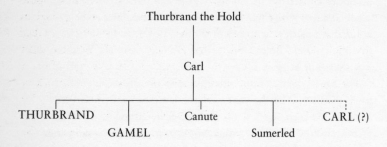

Thurbrand the Hold

Carl

THURBRAND GAMEL Canute Sumerled CARL (?)

sons. Gilbert de Gant's estate at Hunmanby had belonged to the same
powerful clan. There are hints in our sources that some lands had been
seized unlawfully. In 1086 the jurors of Holderness declared that they
'had not seen the king's writ nor seal' giving William Malet legal title
to Rise and his other estates in that region. The jurors of the wapentake
of Ainsty, just to the west of York, affirmed that Malet had held the
manors of Scagglethorpe and Poppleton 'but they do not know how
he came by them'.[8]

The trouble began at Durham. The new earl of Bernicia was making
his way northwards at the head of what was in effect an army of
occupation – variously reported as 500, 700 or 900 soldiers – randomly
pillaging the countryside as he went. Earl Robert sought to use Durham
as a staging-post on his journey. Bishop Ethelwine warned him of the
hostility of the local population but the earl insisted on staying. He
settled in the bishop's hall; his men were billeted 'in a hostile manner'
in the town. Early in the morning of 31 January the people of Durham
rose up and slaughtered all but one of the soldiers. Earl Robert himself
and his closest retainers were besieged in the bishop's hall; the building
was set on fire; the earl and his men, like Copsig two years before, all
fell victim to either fire or sword.

Shortly afterwards the revolt spread south to Yorkshire. The castellan of York, Robert fitzRichard, was killed with 'many' of his men. Presumably the encounter took place somewhere outside the city and the safety of the castle, perhaps while Robert and his soldiers were out on some local pillaging expedition. This was immediately followed by the return from Scotland of the leaders of the previous year, Edgar Ætheling, Gospatric and Merleswein, presumably alerted to the opportunity by news of the massacre at Durham. They were joined in Yorkshire by Arnketil and the four sons of Carl, together with 'other powerful men'. For the third time in four years the north rose in rebellion. But on this occasion there was a difference: they chose a rival king, 'a certain young man, nobly descended from the stock of King Edward', in other words Edgar Ætheling. The rebels seem also to have dispatched appeals for aid to King Sweyn of Denmark. The sheriff of York, William Malet, shut himself up in the castle where he was besieged by the insurgents. Before all communication was cut off he managed to send a messenger to the king with an urgent plea for help.

William gathered an 'overwhelming' army and came at once. He relieved the castle, scattered the rebels in savage street-fighting, plundered the city and in some unspecified way 'made St Peter's minster [i.e. York Minster] an object of scorn' – presumably by disregarding its right of sanctuary. Prince Edgar fled back to Scotland. William built a second castle at York on the other side of the Ouse, on the mound still known as Baile Hill after the bailey of the castle. It was probably at this time that Gilbert de Gant was appointed to assist William Malet in the custody of the castles. The king then returned to the south; he was back in Winchester to keep Easter there on 12 April. Further local disturbances followed at York, but they were put down with a heavy hand by William's subordinates.

However, this was far from being the end of the northern disturbances of 1069. King Sweyn of Denmark mounted his long-anticipated bid for the English throne. (It is not clear what, if any, connection the timing of the expedition had with the appeal of the Northumbrian rebels in the spring; nor of any manner in which the counter-claims of Sweyn and Edgar were to be resolved.) In August there appeared off the Kentish coast a Danish fleet under the command of Sweyn's sons

Canute and Harald, allegedly numbering 240 ships. If the figure is to be trusted, the invading force was not much smaller than that of Harald Hardrada of Norway three years before. After cruising northwards up the east coast of England, apparently with the aim of destroying English shipping en route, the Danish fleet reached the mouth of the Humber in late August or early September. There it was joined by more ships, bearing the by-now-familiar English dissidents – Edgar, Gospatric, Merleswein – and two of whom we have not heard before in connection with Northumbrian restiveness, Waltheof the son of Earl Siward, and another prominent figure also called Siward, known as Siward Barn. Shortly afterwards they were joined by the Yorkshire dissidents Arnketil, the four sons of Carl, and a certain *Elnocinus* or Elnoc who is not now identifiable.* The combined forces marched on York. At this critical juncture the city lost its spiritual leader. Archbishop Ealdred died on 11 September. Consistently a force for moderation in politics, and perhaps the only native Englishman north of the Humber whom King William respected, his removal from the scene may not have been without its effect on the tone of much that followed in the ensuing five months.

The Norman commanders in York, William Malet and Gilbert de Gant, had boasted that they could hold out for a year. They prepared themselves for a siege. In an attempt to prevent the enemy using the debris of houses near the castles as infill for their ditches preparatory to an assault, they ordered these buildings to be fired. The flames got out of control and fire raged throughout the city, destroying even some of the buildings of the cathedral community. As the forces of the Danes and the Northumbrian rebels advanced, like the Norwegians in 1066, along the road through Fulford they would have seen dense clouds of smoke from the thatch and wattle dwellings and warehouses of the northern capital ascending into the late summer sky. When they entered the city of hot ash and charred timbers on 21 September they were greeted as liberators. The Normans made an ill-advised sally from the castles and once again street-fighting ensued. The Normans

---

* The last name may have been transmitted corruptly. An original Æthelnoth might be conjectured, suggesting some connection with the family of Dunstan son of Æthelnoth, one of the leaders of the rising of 1065.

were completely routed, with great loss of life. Gilbert de Gant and William Malet were captured, together with the latter's wife and two children. The triumph of the insurgents was complete.

King William was hunting in the Forest of Dean, in Gloucestershire, when word was brought to him of this new northern rising. He summoned his troops and hastened northwards. The insurgents, meanwhile, were making preparations for winter. The English rebels dispersed to their homes. The Danes took to their ships and sailed down the Humber, settling at a temporary base in the Isle of Axholme between Doncaster and Scunthorpe. Perhaps they all thought that William would not undertake a winter campaign against them. If so, they seriously misjudged their man.

The king's first task was to prevent the Danes from establishing a permanent base-camp where they might overwinter. He managed to dislodge them from Axholme, and they skipped over the Humber to Holderness: for lack of ships, William could not pursue them. He then moved westward, to put down, ruthlessly, an ancillary rebellion at Stafford. While his back was turned the Danes hopped back over the Humber to Lindsey. Once more dislodged by William's lieutenants, they again retreated to the north bank of the Humber and evaded being brought to battle. It was rumoured that they planned to fall back on York, wrecked though it was, for the winter. King William, who was pausing at Nottingham on his return from Stafford, was determined to forestall this. He hurried towards York but was held up for three precious weeks at Castleford by the flooding of the river Aire, swollen by autumn rains. For the third occasion in the course of the campaign Norman mobility was hindered by the absence of shipping: the Danes had done their preliminary work of destruction methodically. A crossing-point was eventually discovered much further upstream, perhaps in the region of Leeds, and the march on York resumed. The Danes had reoccupied York but took fright as William approached and sought safety in their ships downstream. William was tactically the victor: it was too late in the year for the Danes to go home; a winter settlement at York had been prevented; and the Danes were disinclined to fight. Negotiations followed, along thoroughly traditional diplomatic lines. The Danes were bought off. They were paid a large sum of money and permitted to spend the winter 'between the Ouse and the Trent' – more or less where they had tried to settle in September – on condition that they departed for Denmark in the spring. They were allowed to keep their distinguished hostages over the winter. For William it was a costly settlement; but he had at least divided his enemies.

It remained for the king to teach the northern English rebels a lesson that they would not forget. 'King William went into the shire [Yorkshire] and ravaged it completely.' As we have already seen, the laying waste or 'harrying' of a region was a traditional response of royal government to insubordination. William's devastation of Yorkshire in the late autumn of 1069 was very thorough. It sent ripples of apprehension elsewhere: towards Christmas Bishop Ethelwine of Durham and his community of clerics withdrew with the incorrupt body of their patron saint to the safety of Lindisfarne. The Norman host was evidently capable of exciting as much fear as the 'barbarian' Scots. The harrying was interrupted over Christmas. King William had all his royal regalia sent up from Winchester and at his Christmas court in the ruined city of York he formally displayed himself in the array of a king. Or, as we should better put it, *the* king; for this was a calculated pronouncement to the Northumbrians who had come out for Edgar Ætheling that there was only one rightful king in England and that his name was William.

After this break the punishment of Yorkshire was resumed. The king learned of a band of rebels who were defying him 'in a certain corner of the shire', possibly Holderness. On his approach they fled in the only direction available to them, northwards. William pursued them up the Yorkshire coast as far as the river Tees. There the rebel leaders submitted, Waltheof in person, Gospatric with an oath sworn by proxies. The king's treatment of them was surprisingly lenient, both men being not only readmitted to the king's peace but allowed to continue in office. Edgar, Merleswein and Siward Barn had fled further north and subsequently found refuge with King Malcolm of Scotland. William returned to York, perhaps by way of the Hambleton Hills and Helmsley. After a short stay in York to supervise the restoration of the castles and probably to redistribute more northern estates to his followers the king crossed the Pennines in February of 1070 to suppress a north-west-Mercian rebellion at Chester. He was back in the south to spend Easter at Winchester on 4 April.

The 'Harrying of the North' by King William, which until recently schoolchildren in Yorkshire were taught to remember in anger and in sorrow, presents great difficulties for the modern historian. An earlier generation of historians believed that the king had reduced Yorkshire to a desert. Here is Freeman in 1871:

William's work north of the Humber was now done. The land was thoroughly conquered, but it was thoroughly conquered only because it was thoroughly wasted ... William was now lord of Northumberland; but, in being lord of Northumberland, he was lord only of a wilderness.[9]

This view of the matter could be justified by taking at face value the comments of a chronicler who was writing nearly sixty years later; and by uncritical acceptance, or misunderstanding, of the testimony of Domesday Book. We have learned to be rather more cautious than Freeman, formidable scholar though he was. The chronicler in question was Orderic Vitalis, whose comments on the English 'woodies' were quoted a few pages back. His highly coloured, not to say purple, passage about the Harrying of the North occurs in Book IV of his *Ecclesiastical History*. Here it is.

[King William] continued to comb forests and remote mountainous places, stopping at nothing to hunt out the enemy hidden there. His camps were spread out over an area of a hundred miles. He cut down many in his vengeance; destroyed the lairs of others; harried the land, and burned homes to ashes. Nowhere else had William shown such cruelty. Shamefully he succumbed to this vice, for he made no effort to restrain his fury and punished the innocent with the guilty. In his anger he commanded that all crops and herds, chattels and food of every kind should be brought together and burned to ashes with consuming fire, so that the whole region north of the Humber might be stripped of all means of sustenance. In consequence so serious a scarcity was felt in England, and so terrible a famine fell upon the humble and defenceless populace, that more than 100,000 Christian folk of both sexes, young and old alike, perished of hunger. My narrative has frequently had occasion to praise William, but for this act which condemned the innocent and guilty alike to die by slow starvation I cannot commend him.

In his account of the earlier years of William's reign Orderic was following, very slavishly, the narrative of William of Poitiers, the Conqueror's extremely loyal panegyrist. Because the quoted passage is critical of the king, there is general agreement that it must be the composition of Orderic himself. We may well believe that it represents his views: but does it represent historical reality? Orderic left England in 1085 as a child of ten, and though he revisited his native land on at least one later occasion it is unlikely that he ever in his life set foot north of the Humber. Of course, he might have listened to soldiers' tales of King William's epic winter campaign, either as a boy in Shropshire or as a monk at Saint-Evroul in Normandy. But strong indignation working on distant memories, combined with the moralizing tendency of monastic historiography, might have worked to transform much by the time he set these things down in writing in about 1125.

The real trouble is that the narrative accounts become more highly coloured the further they are removed in time from the events they describe. The earliest narratives, comprised in two versions of the *Anglo-Saxon Chronicle*, are a good deal more restrained. One, from manuscript E, has already been quoted. The other (D) simply states that the king 'utterly ravaged and laid waste that shire'. There is no talk here of the systematic reduction of Yorkshire to a depopulated wilderness – something which would in any case have been beyond the capacity of an eleventh-century army to effect, operating in the winter months betweeen November and January. I have no doubt at all that William did, as he had intended to do, a great deal of punitive damage and inflicted much human suffering; but it is impossible to believe that the damage could ever have been as extensive as the distant Orderic alleged.

One might expect that William would have singled out the estates of the ringleaders for either severe devastation or confiscation (or both). But there are surprises here. Settrington is a prime example: it was obviously still a functioning family estate when the sons of Carl gathered there for what would prove to be their last feast together four years after the Harrying. By 1086 the estate was yielding 25 per cent more annual revenue than it had in 1066. Settrington does not look like an estate that had been devastated. Yet, not only did it belong to one of the rebel leaders, it was also easily accessible from York: but it was spared. Much the same could be said of Waltheof's manors in the valley of the Derwent at Howsham and Kirkham, even closer to York.

The information regarding Settrington, Howsham and Kirkham comes to us from Domesday Book. So does a great deal more besides. Two categories of information are particularly significant in this context, the description of many estates as 'waste', and the marked, sometimes catastrophic, drop in value of many more between 1066 and 1086. For a long time it was assumed that estates registered as 'waste' were those which had suffered in the Harrying, still lying untilled sixteen years later. It was further assumed that the zones of devastation, even the king's itinerary, could be plotted from these estates on a map; and though the geographical incidence of devastation proved somewhat surprising, ingenious theories were propounded to explain anomalies away. We now know, or think we do, that the Domesday term 'waste' does not necessarily mean 'devastated'. Alternatively, it might mean 'untenanted', in the case of subordinate estates of the great territorial lordships which were still in the process of formation in Yorkshire at the time of the Domesday survey in 1086. Or again, it might mean 'information unavailable', an early example of bureaucratic jargon designed to conceal administrative shortcoming, a way of not admitting 'we couldn't find anything out'. As to the falls in value of so many estates, it is reasonable to attribute some to the effects of William's Harrying in the winter of 1069–70. But not all. Throughout the years between 1065 and 1070, and indeed at several later points during the reign of the Conqueror, the north of England was in a severely disordered state, hardly conducive to economic stability. Lands which had fallen into the king's hands were distributed to new Norman lords, but not necessarily immediately. There could be a hiatus in tenure, during which normal supervision of routines might sag or even collapse. It is demonstrable from Domesday Book that grants of land in the north were still being made right up to the end of William's reign and indeed beyond it. The enormous fief assigned to Roger of Poitou in Craven seems to have been granted to him contemporaneously with the conduct of the survey in 1086, the year before the king's death. Another was added to the record as an afterthought: 'this is the fief of Robert de Brus' – distant ancestor of King

Robert the Bruce of Scotland – 'which was given to him after the Book of Winchester [Domesday Book] was written'.[10] This addition probably belongs to the early years of the twelfth century. The point is that there were reasons altogether unconnected with the Harrying which help to account for the northern economic recession to which Domesday stands witness.

William's military subjugation of the north may be said to have been completed by the spring of 1070, three and a half years on from his victory at Hastings. His power there was gradually consolidated by the granting out of lands to his followers, so that one ruling class replaced another. This process was paralleled by the substitution of foreigners for English in the governing positions within the Church. At York, Archbishop Ealdred was succeeded by the Norman Thomas in 1070. Thomas belonged to an ecclesiastical dynasty based at Bayeux, the Norman see held by the king's half-brother Odo. Before his promotion to the archbishopric of York Thomas was described as a 'royal clerk', a term which had far more exalted connotations then than it does now; something like 'senior adviser' would be today's equivalent.[11] In short, Thomas was a man of impeccable connections and loyalty. At York the new archbishop rebuilt his burnt-out cathedral on the grandest scale and, significantly, on a slightly different architectural alignment. Thomas thus deliberately turned his back on the Anglo-Saxon ecclesiastical past and permanently altered the topography of his cathedral city. It was an architectural assertion of Norman dominance. At Durham, Bishop Ethelwine and his clergy returned from Lindisfarne with the body of their saintly patron on 25 March 1070. But the king was distrustful of Ethelwine's loyalty – one source indeed claims that he was outlawed – and later in the year the bishop decided on flight. Helping himself, as his brother before him, to some of his church's treasures, Ethelwine took ship for Germany but was blown off course to Scotland where he was forced to spend the winter of 1070–71. The Durham chronicler can tell the rest of the story.

Setting out again from there, he was captured by the king's men at Ely, and taken to Abingdon where he was held in close custody by the king's orders. He was frequently admonished to give back what he had taken from the church [of Durham], but he always affirmed on oath that he had taken nothing from it. But as one day he was washing his hands before eating, a bracelet slipped down from his arm on to his hand with everyone watching, and thus the bishop was shown to be guilty of clear perjury. So on the king's orders he was thrown into jail, where he refused to eat because of the great anguish he felt in his heart, and he died of hunger and sorrow.

His brother Ethelric had already been arrested by King William: he too died in captivity. Ethelwine's successor at Durham was a cleric named Walcher, a native not of Normandy but of Lorraine, 'chosen by the king in person', in other words another absolutely reliable loyalist like Thomas of Bayeux at York.

Another ecclesiastical initiative of these troubled years was the expansion of Benedictine monasticism into Northumbria. We have already seen that the movement of monastic revival associated with King Edgar in the tenth century had not extended north of the Humber. But now it did. The first post-Conquest foundation in the north was at Selby, the origins of whose abbey appear to belong to the years 1069–70. Although this was not a royal foundation in the sense that, say, Westminster was – it was founded by an eccentric free-lance monk from Auxerre in northern Burgundy who wanted to be a hermit – Selby was nurtured in its earliest years by successive Norman sheriffs, the king's principal officials in Yorkshire. King William himself was quickly numbered among its patrons, though the report that his youngest son, Henry, was born there seems to be a later legend. Other monastic foundations in Yorkshire would follow over the next generation, each of them associated unambiguously with the new Norman establishment.

In this manner a new lay and clerical élite of Norman birth or allegiance replaced the Anglo-Saxon ruling class. But that did not of itself render Northumbria, though cowed, less turbulent. The province was also threatened once more from Scotland. In the summer of 1070 King Malcolm led an army through Cumberland – his, it will be recalled, since 1061 – over Stainmore and down Teesdale, pillaging whatever was left to pillage as he went. After attacking Cleveland the Scots moved north of the Tees. Up in Weardale they burnt St Peter's church at Wearmouth and several other churches, some of them with refugees inside. Earl Gospatric of Bernicia led a counter-raid on

Cumberland and then shut himself up in the safety of Bamburgh. These military exchanges, of an entirely traditional kind, were succeeded in 1071 by something more menacing to King William, the marriage of Malcolm king of Scots to Margaret, the sister of Edgar Ætheling (later to be remembered as St Margaret of Scotland). This dynastic union between the Scottish royal family and the displaced Old English royal house of Wessex could not but be alarming to King William, threatening as it must have seemed a more concerted intervention in English affairs. William's response was to invade Scotland with a combined land and sea force – English shipwrights had evidently been hard at work over the previous three years – in 1072. Pressing up through Lothian, he crossed the Firth of Forth into Fife and finally came up with Malcolm at Abernethy on the Tay. The king of Scots 'made peace with King William and was his vassal and gave him hostages'. The terms probably included an undertaking not to harbour prominent English exiles, for we next hear of Prince Edgar in Flanders. The Abernethy treaty brought peace on the Anglo-Scottish border for a few years.

The accord with the king of Scots was only one part of William's attempt to settle the affairs of his northernmost province. The other was the dismissal of Gospatric and his replacement as earl of Bernicia with Waltheof. The appointment was made in the course of William's return from the Scottish campaign in the autumn of 1072.

Waltheof, as we have seen, was the son of Earl Siward, who had died in 1055, by his wife Ælfflæd, the daughter of Earl Ealdred. He was a member therefore of the dynasty which had ruled Bernicia for the last two centuries. He was probably born in about 1042 or 1043, for he was 'still young' at the time of his father's death.[12] Before the death of King Edward, and most likely after the fall of Tostig in 1065, Waltheof was given office as an earl in the south-east midlands, his authority extending over Northamptonshire and Huntingdonshire, possibly also Bedfordshire and Cambridgeshire. It is to be presumed that he was among the prominent English magnates who submitted to William either at Berkhamsted in December 1066 or at Barking in January 1067. He was certainly among those who were taken in the Conqueror's train to Normandy in 1067 as trophy-hostages. This was an honourable, precautionary captivity. Waltheof kept his office of earl, subscribing with it a diploma by which William granted Hayling Island to the Norman monastery of Jumièges in the summer of 1067. Back in England in the following year, we can trace Waltheof subscribing further royal charters at the time of Queen Matilda's coronation in May 1068.[13] Evidently he was among those Anglo-Saxon magnates – another example would be Archbishop Ealdred of York – with whom William was trying to work in harmony, was wanting to trust. In this perspective Waltheof's brief flirtation with the northern rebels, between September 1069 and his submission to the king in January 1070, was a lapse: but one which William, most uncharacteristically, was prepared to overlook. Still more surprisingly, he arranged a marriage for Waltheof which was without parallel – into his own family. The bride was Judith, William's niece, the daughter of his sister Adelaide and her husband Count Enguerrand II of Ponthieu. The marriage seems to have occurred in 1070, and in the words of Orderic Vitalis it was intended 'to make the firm friendship between them [the king and his earl] last'. No other English magnate was so highly honoured. It suggests that William was really trying hard to bind Waltheof to him; suggests too that Waltheof had personal qualities that elude the historian, such as charm and eloquence, with which to soften the stony temperament of King William. In promoting Waltheof to the earldom of Bernicia in 1072 the king was favouring a kinsman on whom he could rely, for whom perhaps he even felt affection.

Not much more than a year later, Waltheof perpetrated the massacre at Settrington in which the sons and grandsons of Carl were slaughtered. Here is the story as told by the Durham anonymous.

After some time had passed, Earl Ealdred's grandson, his daughter's son Earl Waltheof, sent a large band of young men and avenged the killing of his grandfather with the utmost slaughter. For when the sons of Carl were feasting together at the eldest brother's hall at Settrington, not far from York, the men who had been sent caught them unawares and butchered them together in bloody slaughter; except for Canute, whose life they spared because of his innate goodness. Sumerled, who was not there, survives to this day. Having massacred the sons and grandsons of Carl they returned home bringing with them much booty of various kinds.

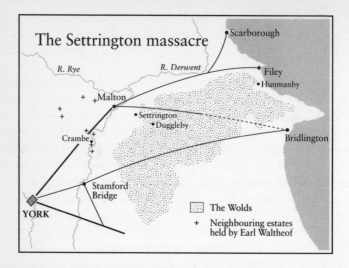

The Settrington massacre

R. Rye
R. Derwent

Scarborough

Filey
Hunmanby

+ +Malton

+
+

Settrington
Duggleby

Crambe +
+
+
+

Bridlington

Stamford
Bridge

YORK

The Wolds

+ Neighbouring estates
held by Earl Waltheof

This, the last act, or more strictly the last *recorded* act, in the feud that followed the murder of Uhtred in 1016, took place in the winter of 1073–4. It leaves us facing a problem. Why did Waltheof organize the Settrington massacre? And why just then? Customary historiographical disciplines must be suspended for a while. In the course of the next few pages there will be much resort to conjecture.

Our primary and near-contemporary sources agree that Waltheof's motive was to avenge the murder of his grandfather Earl Ealdred at the hands of Carl in Rise Wood. But that killing had taken place in 1038, at least four years before Waltheof's birth, and the feud had slumbered since then. Furthermore, in the northern rising of the autumn of 1069 Waltheof had acted in concert with the sons of Carl whom four years later he was to slay. There is something odd here, at which we can only guess. Sleeping feuds can be woken, as we saw in an earlier chapter. That is exactly what had precipitated Ealdred's death at the hands of Carl all those years before. If the family feud was somehow reawakened, reactivated, between the partnership in rebellion of 1069 and the slaughter at Settrington in 1073, we search in vain for what might have brought this about. Our sources don't offer us any clue, perhaps because the primary audience did not need to be told. Could it have been something to do with that rebellion? Not inconceivably, Carl's sons might have regarded Waltheof's submission and subsequent cosying-up to King William as a betrayal. Words could have been spoken, taunts flung, sufficient to fan the embers of the feud into hot and angry life.

We can try a different tack and ask not 'Why?' but 'How?' I think it significant that Waltheof did not lead the foray in person: our authorities agree that he 'sent' a band of men to do the killing for him. Now, there can be no doubting Waltheof's personal courage. His bravery in the fighting at York in the autumn of 1069 was celebrated by his poet, the Icelandic *skald* Thorkell Skallason. And if it be objected that a professional panegyrist in a lord's entourage is hardly an objective witness, we can point to the sober historian William of Malmesbury who also commented on Waltheof's courage. His decision to send rather than to lead has a different significance. It is most plausibly interpreted as a gesture of contempt. Waltheof sent a posse of young men to do his butcher's work for him because the sons of Carl had in some manner affronted him so seriously that he did not deign to go himself to do the job.

Massacres at feasts were not uncommon in early medieval Europe. A recent example was the slaying of Copsig in 1067. Prospective victims were conveniently (from the killers' point of view) gathered together, they were unarmed, unsuspicious, relaxed. With luck and good timing they might be bloated and fuddled with food and drink as well. We may be sure that men of the wealth and eminence of Carl's sons would not have besmirched the honour of the family by stinting themselves and their guests. Who were these sons of Carl? There were at least four of them according to Orderic Vitalis, probably here following William of Poitiers. We have to say 'at least' because the original Latin of our text is ambiguous. The Latin words *quatuor filii Karoli* can mean either 'the four sons of Carl' (i.e. all four of them) or 'four of the sons of Carl' (out of a larger number). With the invaluable assistance of Domesday Book we can make them out as follows. The eldest, in all probability, partly because he bore his grandfather's name and partly because he was the host at the feast, was Thurbrand, lord of the manor of Settrington itself. Another was almost certainly named Gamel: he can be associated with Thurbrand because they jointly held the nearby manor of Duggleby and because both Duggleby and

Settrington had passed into the hands of the same Norman lord by 1086, Berengar de Tosny. Two others are named in our anonymous source from Durham: Canute, whose life was spared, and Sumerled, who was not there. In 1066 Canute had held the estate at Rise which had belonged to his father Carl, another pointer to his identity. That makes up the tally of four. It is possible that there was a fifth. If their father Carl were dead by 1066, as seems probable, it is possible that another Yorkshire landowner named Carl was his son. But we cannot be sure of this. We know nothing of their wives or children. As to their ages, all that we can say is that they were mature landowning men in 1066 and able to take a leading part in the fighting of 1069. By 1073 their sons could easily have been teenagers or older; young men of massacre-able age.

'Sumerled, who was not there, survives to this day.' Why was Sumerled not at this big family gathering? A moment's reflection at once suggests manifold possible reasons. Perhaps he was ill, perhaps he had quarrelled with his brothers, perhaps he was reclusive by nature, perhaps he was absent visiting estates elsewhere in the country, perhaps he had gone abroad on a pilgrimage . . . We shall never know. But we can at least entertain the possibility that he was not there because he had chosen not to be there. Just supposing this to have been the case, we might care to reflect on the fact that, alone among the brothers, Sumerled owned only one rather modest estate in Yorkshire, at Crambe, on the Derwent south of Malton. His principal landholdings were in another county, Lincolnshire. Another way of putting this would be to say that Sumerled's landed interests made him Southumbrian rather than Northumbrian. That was the direction in which he faced. Was this a source of tension between him and his brothers? Domesday Book also reveals that the village of Crambe was divided between two estates. Sumerled's was one; the lord of the other estate was none other than Waltheof. Did Sumerled not like what was afoot at the Settrington feast organized by the head of the family? Could he have shared his anxieties with Earl Waltheof? Did Waltheof tip him off to steer clear of the festivities? Questions, questions, and not a hope of answering them.

When major provincial lords hold social gatherings we may reasonably suppose that there is more to them than meets the eye, that they are something more than simply occasions for a jolly family

get-together. Carl's sons had experienced defeat in rebellion, depri-
vation of property, devastation of lands, penal taxation and – most
wounding of all to high-spirited eleventh-century noblemen – humiliation. Were they planning to rise in rebellion yet again? Could that
have been the undercover agenda during the feasting at Settrington?
We shall never know. But if we suppose for a moment that this was
so, then Waltheof's action could be interpreted as doing the king's
work for him. Well in with King William after his promotion and his
very grand marriage, Waltheof could hope simultaneously to pursue
with honour a family feud and to rid Yorkshire of some of the king's
most dangerous enemies. Perhaps the king would reward him by
adding the earldom of Deira to that of Bernicia, so that like his father
Siward before him he would be lord of all Northumbria from the
Humber to the Tweed.

Whatever the covert discussions at Settrington, feasting was no
secret affair. People like the sons of Carl did not do things by halves.
Being a munificent host was an important part of aristocratic display
in the upholding of family honour and renown. We must suppose
festivities were planned which would stretch out over several days.
The preparations would have taken quite a long time and would have
attracted local notice. There would be huge quantities of fuel to be
laid in, barrels of cured fish to be brought up river, deer and boar to
be hunted, fathomless quantities of ale to be brewed. In addition to
Crambe, Earl Waltheof owned several more estates within a ten-mile
radius of Settrington – at Howsham, Kirkham, Whitwell-on-the-Hill,
Amotherby, Barton-le-Street, Terrington and Wiganthorpe. The
reeves, or stewards, of these estates would have been able to tell
Waltheof, well in advance, about the celebrations in prospect at Settrington and, in particular, exactly when they were going to take place.

If you are going to kill people at a party you must catch them
unawares. If you are going to kill people at a party at Settrington there
is one obvious quarter from which to approach in order to achieve
surprise: from the hills to the east known as the Yorkshire Wolds. The
modern village of Settrington lies about three miles due east of Malton
in the flat vale of the River Derwent, at little more than 100 feet above
sea level. The village straggles now, and probably did then, along the
course of Settrington Beck which runs into the Derwent a couple of

miles to the north. (Finding a reliable water supply has always been a problem on, and on the fringes of, the light-soiled, chalky, well-drained Wolds.) We don't know where the lord's hall stood in the eleventh century. It is a reasonable guess that it would have been not far from the church; not impossibly on roughly the same site as the present Settrington House, a handsome building of the late eighteenth century. Immediately to the east of the village the ground rises sharply to a height of about 500 feet. This is Thorpe Bassett Wold, the westernmost outcrop of the Wolds of East Yorkshire. To cover the distance from the ridge to the hall, on horseback, would take no more than two or three minutes. Surprise would be achieved.

The Wolds today are an open landscape of arable and pasture where trees are few. This was not so in the eleventh century.[14] Our modern word 'wold' is derived from the Old English *weald*, meaning 'forest'. Though most of the villages which cluster today in the folds of the Wolds (and some more that have disappeared) were in existence by the time of the Domesday survey, it is likely that these settlements were for the most part fairly recent and fairly small. The upper levels of the hills were probably still covered with light, scrubby, patchy woodland used for the summer pasturing of cows, sheep, goats and pigs. In general, the Yorkshire Wolds were sparsely settled, with perhaps no permanent population at all on the higher levels: a region which could be traversed rapidly and, during the winter months, almost unobserved.

This is to assume that Waltheof's murderous posse came across the Wolds from the east. If the young men were sent from Waltheof's earldom of Bernicia the most rapid mode of travel, and that least likely to provoke notice, would have been by sea. A landfall could have been made anywhere along the coast between Scarborough and Bridlington: the nearest point to Settrington, as the crow flies, is Filey. As it happened, nearly all the land along this coast constituted two big multiple estates which were in the hands of the king, based respectively at Falsgrave (now a suburb of Scarborough) and at Bridlington itself (which was assuming some of the features of a modest town). The only exception of any size was the estate at Hunmanby held by Gilbert de Gant, mentioned earlier in this chapter. The authority of an earl who was well in with the king and married to his niece would have been more than adequate to procure mounts and guides for his men on their arrival. After that it was just a matter of riding and waiting, until the moment for action came.

If everything went right the job would not have taken long, no longer than it had at *Wiheal* in 1016. And then there was the 'much booty of various kinds' which the young men took back to their master. That would not have taken long either: jewellery and costly raiment ripped from the dead and the still living, candlesticks and drinking-horns snatched up from the tables. And then they were off again, leaving behind them the carnage, the distraught wives and mothers, the dogs sniffing at the blood. They could have been back in their ship by the time a winter's dawn crept over the horizon of the North Sea.

IO

Haget

Earl Waltheof did not live long to enjoy his savage vindication of family honour. In 1075 he was implicated in the rebellion of two other earls, Ralph of Norfolk and Roger of Hereford, against the king. It is a tangled story, in which neither the nature nor the extent of Waltheof's involvement is wholly clear. The outcome, however, is in no doubt. William had had enough. He had trusted the earl, forgiven him for one lapse of loyalty, given him his own niece in marriage, committed wide powers to him. Waltheof had repaid him with betrayal. The full penalty for treason was to be paid. After some months' imprisonment at Winchester, Waltheof was beheaded outside the city early in the morning of 31 May 1076. In the last moments of his life the earl recited aloud the Lord's Prayer. When he had spoken the words 'And lead us not into temptation' the executioner struck. As Waltheof's severed head fell to the ground the bystanders distinctly heard his mouth utter the words, 'But deliver us from evil, Amen'.

At his widow's request Waltheof was buried at the monastery of Crowland, in the Lincolnshire Fens, of which house he had been a benefactor. Some years later the monks of Crowland sought to promote him as a kind of English martyr. In 1091 Waltheof's coffin was exhumed and opened. The corpse inside was found to be incorrupt and the head had been miraculously reunited to the body from which it had been severed. Waltheof's remains were reinterred in a place of honour, inside the monastery church next to the altar. A little later miracles of healing began to be worked at the earl's tomb. Abbot Geoffrey had a vision in which he saw the apostle St Bartholomew and Crowland's patron saint, Guthlac, standing beside Waltheof's tomb and proclaiming his sanctity. It is to the monks of Crowland that we owe the story of the speaking severed head. A Norman monk of St Albans who doubted Waltheof's holiness, alleging that he was no better than a traitor who got what he deserved, was struck with mortal illness. A cult had been born.*

Earl Waltheof left no male heir. His wife, Judith, bore him two daughters, described as 'beautiful' by the chronicler Orderic Vitalis, Adeliza and Matilda. Both were married, doubtless by their mother's agency, into the upper ranks of the Anglo-Norman aristocracy. Adeliza married Ralph de Tosny. Matilda's first marriage was to Simon de Senlis, earl of Northampton. After his death in about 1110 she made an even grander match: her second husband was David, younger son of King Malcolm and Queen Margaret of Scotland, and at the time of his marriage the holder of an English earldom, Huntingdon. He was later to rule as king of Scotland between 1124 and 1153, with Matilda as his queen.

We hear no more of the great Yorkshire feud after the massacre at Settrington. Canute and Sumerled survived as potential prosecutors of it. Since the Durham anonymous, writing perhaps *c.* 1090, makes no allusion to episodes of violence subsequent to Settrington, we may fairly assume that no moves had been made by the time he wrote. Canute and Sumerled were still alive in 1086: how much longer they lived we do not know. Their obvious potential victims would have been Earl Waltheof's grandsons, not one of whom could have been born before about 1090 and could not therefore have been of fighting age before the first decade of the twelfth century. By that time Canute and Sumerled, if still alive, would have been old men. Whether or not the brothers left any descendants we do not know. After Settrington our story just fades out.

If we return to the place where it all began, Wighill in the wapentake of Ainsty – supposing *Wiheal* to have been Wighill – but a century and

---

* There is a whiff of family piety here. Abbot Geoffrey's successor at Crowland was a monk named Waltheof. This Abbot Waltheof (*c.* 1126–38) was a son of Gospatric, earl of Bernicia between 1067 and 1072, the man deposed from his earldom by King William I, who after exile in Flanders made his way to Scotland where he was rewarded by King Malcolm with the earldom of Dunbar. Gospatric was a nephew of Earl Ealdred, the victim of Rise Wood and grandfather of Earl Waltheof. Thus the two Waltheofs were, albeit remotely, kinsmen.

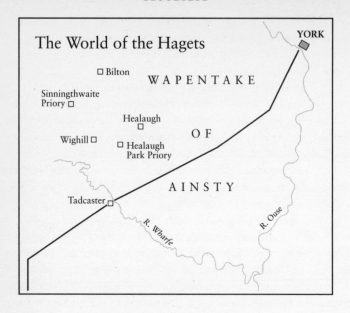

The World of the Hagets

YORK

☐ Bilton

WAPENTAKE

Sinningthwaite
Priory ☐

Healaugh
☐

OF

Wighill ☐   ☐ Healaugh
              Park Priory

AINSTY

Tadcaster ☐

R. Wharfe

R. Ouse

a half after the slaughter of Uhtred and his retainers in 1016, we find
that we have moved into a different cultural atmosphere. In the middle
years of the twelfth century the village and manor of Wighill were in
the possession of a family named Haget (or Hackett). The origins of
the family are not known for certain, though there are some clues
which point towards western Normandy or even Brittany. By about
1140, when we first catch sight of them in our records, the Hagets
were settled in Yorkshire as tenants of the great Anglo-Norman magnate family of Mowbray. The earliest member of the family whom we
can trace is a certain Bertram Haget whose name appears in records
between 1138 and the early 1160s. Bertram's enduring monument was
the nunnery at Sinningthwaite, about a mile from Wighill, founded by
him at some date before 1155, in which year the foundation was
confirmed by King Henry II. (Access to the royal chancery for the
purpose of obtaining this royal charter was perhaps owed to the
patronage of Bertram's lord, Roger de Mowbray.) Bertram's daughter
Gundreda – tactfully named after his lord's mother, Gundreda de
Gournay, mother of Roger de Mowbray – became a nun at Sinning-

GENEALOGICAL TABLE 9
THE HAGET FAMILY

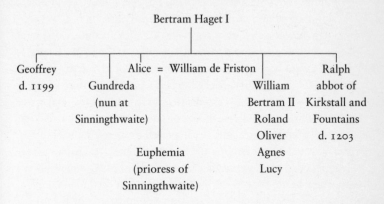

Bertram Haget I

Geoffrey	Alice = William de Friston		Ralph
d. 1199	Gundreda	William	abbot of
	(nun at	Bertram II	Kirkstall and
	Sinningthwaite)	Roland	Fountains
		Oliver	d. 1203
	Euphemia	Agnes	
	(prioress of	Lucy	
	Sinningthwaite)		

thwaite. It is indeed possible that the house had been founded expressly for the purpose of providing for the vocations of Gundreda and other female relatives. Sinningthwaite was very characteristic of its time and place. Large numbers of nunneries were founded in Yorkshire in the middle years of the twelfth century and they tended to exhibit shared features. They were small, modestly endowed communities, typically established by founders who were below the ranks of the higher aristocracy, houses which could be seen from one perspective as an expression of family identity and solidarity, through the prayers of whose inmates family salvation in the hereafter might be ensured.

Bertram Haget's wife, of whom not even the name is known, bore no fewer than ten children, six boys and four girls. Two of the boys seem to have predeceased their father: their names were Oliver and Roland, perhaps offering a hint of their parents' poetic tastes and chivalric ambitions. The three girls who remained in secular life (unlike their sister Gundreda), Agnes, Lucy and Alice, made respectable marriages to local men of similar rank and wealth to their father and brothers. One of Alice's daughters, Euphemia, became a nun at Sinningthwaite and rose to be its prioress in the early thirteenth century. Euphemia's brother (or possibly cousin), Reiner, became parish priest of Healaugh, the village next door to Wighill: it would perhaps not be inappropriate to think of him as an early example of a squarson. Of the four surviving boys, William and Bertram II seem to have lived the uneventful lives of knightly landowners. The remaining two, Geoffrey and Ralph, turned into men of more than local note.

Geoffrey Haget acted as a royal justice in Yorkshire on several occasions between 1183 and his death in 1199. The role of a justice at this period went beyond the administration of the law in any narrow sense. Under the Angevin kings Henry II (1154–89), Richard I (1189–99) and John (1199–1216), such men were multi-functional royal officials in the expanding machinery of government, who carried out a variety of administrative and fiscal as well as strictly judicial duties. Geoffrey would have been literate, and would have needed an up-to-date knowledge of the changing law: we should very much like to know where he got his education. A reference in a deed to his *camera*, his 'chamber' or 'treasury', suggests an administrator of his estates consciously adopting the language and perhaps the style of royal financial management. In addition to his country estates Geoffrey owned property in York, prime urban real estate in the city's main thoroughfare, Coney Street, which would have furnished a residence for him on those frequent occasions when the king's business required him to be in York. Geoffrey was a generous benefactor to several religious communities: the family nunnery at Sinningthwaite, of course; St Clement's nunnery in York; St Mary's Abbey in York, the premier Benedictine house in Yorkshire; and Fountains Abbey, the leading monastery in northern England of the relatively new and very fashionable order of the 'White Monks' or Cistercians. (There was a family connection with Fountains as well, as we shall see in a moment.) He was also the patron of a hermit named Gilbert who settled at Healaugh Park (now Healaugh Manor Farm between the villages of Healaugh and Wighill), an establishment which became a small priory of Augustinian canons with the assistance of his sister Alice and his sister Lucy's son early in the thirteenth century. The piety and patronage of Geoffrey and his siblings may also be glimpsed in the superlative sculpture which decorates the south doorway of Wighill church, datable to about 1160–80. The same sculptors seem also to have worked at nearby Bilton and Healaugh churches, and may have been responsible for the carving of a serpent which decorates the surviving doorway into what was the nuns' refectory at Sinningthwaite.

The other brother who made a mark was the youngest, Ralph. Brought up to a knightly career, Ralph gradually became dissatisfied with a life in the lay world. It was his custom to visit Fountains Abbey where he formed a friendship with a lay brother named Sunnulf, a man renowned for holiness of life, who became his spiritual counsellor. Under Sunnulf's instruction Ralph prayed for guidance in his predicament. It came in the form of an intense vocational experience when he was about thirty years of age. As he later told the story, at a moment of spiritual crisis early one morning he went into a chapel where, standing before a crucifix, he earnestly besought God's help. To his astonishment the figure of the crucified Christ addressed him: 'Why do you not come? Why do you delay so long?' And Ralph knew that he must become a monk forthwith, so he took the habit of a Cistercian monk at Fountains. This was in about 1170. Some of his later spiritual experiences were recorded by one of his fellow monks. They have been likened by the late Dom David Knowles to the transcendental experiences of St Teresa of Ávila.[1] But Ralph – again like Teresa – was evidently a capable ruler as well as a mystic. In 1179 he was appointed abbot of Kirkstall, a daughter-house of Fountains, which he governed for some eleven years. Then, in 1190 or 1191, he was elected to the abbacy of his former house. He remained abbot of Fountains until his death in 1203.

The records of the Hagets in the second half of the twelfth century reveal a family of provincial gentry, busy, careful, respectable, pious, of a kind which, *mutatis mutandis*, could be found in Yorkshire in any succeeding century down to and including the twentieth. Their world seems orderly, peaceful, prosperous, predictable; a long way distant from the remorselessly violent and unstable world of the families of Earl Uhtred and Thurbrand the Hold. It must at once be admitted that there is an element of sleight-of-hand in this contrast. Deeds which shed light on the everyday transactions of family life among the northern squirearchy survive in abundance from the mid twelfth century onwards. As readers who have got this far will know, we simply haven't got them from the eleventh. Change in the quantity and nature of our original sources enables historians to probe new areas of enquiry, ask more searching questions, shed light on different groups and networks, attain a deeper understanding of society and culture. There were, of course there were, continuities as well as changes between the ages of Earl Uhtred and Geoffrey Haget, Bishop Ealdhun and Abbot Ralph of Fountains. There was still much violence and bloodshed among the ruling classes of northern England in the late twelfth century; there would continue to be violence and bloodshed for centuries to come. So much, and more, may be conceded, yet one is still left with a strong sense that the Northumbria of the Hagets was markedly different from the Northumbria of Uhtred and Thurbrand.

There had been economic development to underpin all manner of other changes. Aristocratic and monastic landlords had encouraged the colonization of hitherto unexploited or under-exploited land. When William the Conqueror's son William Rufus repossessed Cumbria for the English crown in 1092 he imported settlers from Wessex, even from Flanders, and they brought with them southern agrarian expectations and routines. Although we cannot quantify this, it is almost certain that arable cultivation was on the increase in the north in the course of the twelfth century. We saw in an earlier chapter that York was the only town worth the name in northern England about the year 1000. A century and a half later it had been joined by others such as Carlisle, Durham and the 'New Castle' on the Tyne. All three possessed royal mints before the death of Henry I in 1135. There were plentiful much smaller market towns too, such as Beverley, Richmond, Appleby, Penrith. There was more money around, more use of it in trafficking. By Abbot Ralph's day the Cistercians were making embarrassingly large fortunes out of wool as a cash crop. The customs or by-laws of Newcastle, committed to writing in the middle years of the twelfth century, speak to us revealingly of merchants and shipping, of trade in salt and wool and hides, of migration from the countryside to the town, of the legal privileges of the townsfolk. Jewish businessmen thought it worth their while to settle in York. The building, or enlargement, or embellishment of hundreds of village churches, like Wighill, testify to wealth as well as to piety and pride.

Institutionally, the remote Northumbrian principality of the lords of Bamburgh such as Oslac and Uhtred had been redrafted into the counties of Durham, Northumberland, Cumberland, Westmorland

and Lancashire, administered on behalf of the king (or, in the case of Durham, the bishop) by busy officials of the stamp of Geoffrey Haget. Royal justices were conducting regular 'eyres', or circuits, to hear pleas and discipline malefactors. Sheriffs were rendering annual accounts of their stewardship at the king's exchequer. There was vastly more reading, writing and counting in the conduct of the king's government. When the Anglo-Scottish border was fixed by the treaty of York in 1237, along a line from which it has hardly deviated since then, all the elaborate details were recorded in writing.

Horizons and identities had subtly shifted. Back in the days of Bishop Ealdhun or Archbishop Wulfstan the Church in Northumbria had managed its affairs to all intents and purposes without interference from outside. By the latter part of the twelfth century prelates were bombarded by a stream of papal letters delegating judicial business, asking favours, passing on complaints. The traffic went both ways: even so modest an establishment as the Haget nunnery of Sinning-thwaite sent off to the papal chancery for a privilege confirming its possessions in 1172. A *Northumbrian Priests' Law* would have been inconceivable in the twelfth century. The western Church was now regulated by the norms of a canon law codified by dons in Bologna. Abbot Ralph was a member of an international order: like all other Cistercian abbots he had to journey every year to the order's mother house, Cîteaux, to attend the general chapter, or annual conference, of the order. There was a new insistence on regulation and uniformity; old and anomalous institutions were tidied into new clothes. At Hexham a community of hereditary priests had existed time out of mind; in the twelfth century they were reformed into celibate canons following the Augustinian Rule.

For the laity too Christendom had got bigger. Uhtred and Thurbrand were northern magnates to whom the world beyond the Humber mattered little but for the occasional dutiful and wary visit to the West Saxon royal court. Bertram Haget's lord, Roger de Mowbray, possessed extensive estates in Normandy as well as in England. He went crusading in the Holy Land on at least two occasions. In 1187, by then an old man of about sixty-seven, he fought against Saladin at the disastrous battle of Hattin, was captured by the victorious Muslims and subsequently ransomed by the Knights Templar. He died in Palestine in the following year. Bertram Haget named two of his sons after heroes of Old French epic whose adventures had taken them to fight the Saracens in Spain. Robert de Ros, lord of Helmsley in the late twelfth and early thirteenth centuries, had campaigned in Ireland, was married into the Scottish royal family, planned to go on crusade (but probably never did) and ended his life as a Templar.

From one point of view we are witnessing in all these changes a phase of what has been called, perhaps a little mischievously, 'the Europeanization of Europe', the process by which the fringes of Christendom took on the culture deriving from the Carolingian 'core' zones of northern Italy, western Germany and eastern France.[2] From another, we can see under the Norman and Angevin kings a continuance of that integration of peripheral regions into the single institutional framework of an English monarchy which had begun under the West Saxon rulers who followed Alfred on the throne. From this angle, what was happening to Northumbria in the century and a half after 1066 was roughly comparable to what had happened to Mercia in the tenth century: aggregation to a West Saxon or southern English system of authority. Of course, the process of aggregation had its ebbs and flows. Kings and their servants could push too hard and cause opposition. Earl Tostig had done just this, and provoked the Northumbrian rebellion of 1065. William II and Henry I had stepped up the pressure, but it had been loosened during the troubled reign of King Stephen. After 1154 under the Angevins, and especially after the 1170s, the pressure of royal authority upon the north, exercised through agents such as Geoffrey Haget, became ever more assertive, burdensome and chafing. It would eventually provoke one of the most acute constitutional crises of English history, the northern baronial rebellion of 1212 that led to King John's issue of Magna Carta in 1215. The king had to make concessions to the rebels in 1215, concessions of a far-reaching constitutional nature whose beneficial consequences we still enjoy. But there was no retreat from the administrative, fiscal and judicial initiatives which had provoked the crisis. By the thirteenth century the north was more effectively integrated into the English kingdom than ever before. In such a kingdom there was no room for a semi-independent Northumbria managed by the princely dynasts of Bamburgh. In any case, they were no longer there. They had destroyed themselves in the course of the bloodfeud chronicled in this book. The tale of the feud between the families of Uhtred and Thurbrand is not just one of bloody strife in a distant epoch which we can at best only half-understand. It is also a modest episode in a far grander story about the fashioning of an enduring national community.

APPENDIX

Chronological Tables

CHRONOLOGICAL TABLE I
THE EARLS OF NORTHUMBRIA 952–1075

There are many uncertainties about the succession of the Northumbrian earls and this list should be regarded as an approximation only. For much of our period there were distinct earls in the two halves of Northumbria, Bernicia and Deira. At certain times the more senior of two earls seems to have enjoyed a primacy of honour and office over his colleague as earl of all Northumbria; at other times there was a single earl for the whole province of Northumbria: these senior and single earls have been indicated by capitals. In the turbulent years after 1068 the leading official in Deira appears to have been the sheriff of York, the earldom of Deira being left vacant.

Bernicia	Senior/Single ('*All Northumbria*')	Deira
	OSWULF 952/4?–966?	
	OSLAC 966?–975	
Eadwulf 'Evil-child' traceable 973		
Waltheof 975/8?–1006?		Thored 975/9–92

Bernicia	Senior/Single ('All Northumbria')	Deira
		Ælfhelm 993–1006
	UHTRED 1006–16	
Eadwulf Cudel 1016–1020/25?		Eric of Hlathir 1016–23/33
Ealdred 1020/25?–38		Siward 1023/33–41
Eadwulf 1038–41		
	SIWARD 1041–55	
	TOSTIG 1055–65	
	MORCAR 1065–6	
Oswulf 1065–7		Merleswein? 1066?–8?
Copsig 1067		
Gospatric 1067–8		
Robert de Commines 1068–9		

Bernicia	Senior/Single ('All Northumbria')	Deira
Gospatric 1070–72		
Waltheof 1072–5		

CHRONOLOGICAL TABLE 2
THE ARCHBISHOPS OF YORK 931–1100

WULFSTAN I	931	removed from office 952/4? died 26 December 956
OSKETEL	954?	died 1 November 970 or 971
EDWALD	970/71	resigned at once, 970/71
OSWALD	971	died 29 February 992

The see was vacant between 992 and 995.

EALDWULF	995	died 6 May 1002
WULFSTAN II	1002	died 28 May 1023
ÆLFRIC PUTTOC	1023	died 22 January 1051
CYNESIGE	1051	died 22 December 1060
EALDRED	1061	died 11 September 1069
THOMAS OF BAYEUX	1070	died 18 November 1100

CHRONOLOGICAL TABLE 3
THE BISHOPS OF CHESTER-LE-STREET AND DURHAM 990–1096

EALDHUN	990	died 1018

The seat of the bishopric was transferred to Durham in 995.

The see was vacant between 1018 and 1021.

EDMUND	1021	died 1040?
EADRED	1040?	died 1041?
ETHELRIC	1042	resigned 1056
ETHELWINE	1056	deposed 1071
WALCHER	1071	murdered 1080
WILLIAM OF ST CALAIS	1080	died 2 January 1096

Bibliography

1. Wiheal

I have found the following recent discussions of medieval feuding useful. They are listed in chronological order of publication. Their notes and/or bibliographies contain ample references to earlier publications.

Peter Sawyer, 'The bloodfeud in fact and fiction', *Acta Jutlandica* 63 (1987), pp. 27–38.

Geoffrey Koziol, 'Monks, feuds and the making of peace in eleventh-century Flanders' in T. Head and R. Landes (eds.), *The peace of God. Social violence and religious response in France around the year 1000* (Ithaca, 1992), pp. 239–58.

Guy Halsall (ed.), *Violence and society in the early medieval west* (Woodbridge, 1998), the remarks in the editor's introduction, pp. 19–29, and the contribution by M. Bennett, 'Violence in eleventh-century Normandy: feud, warfare and politics', at pp. 126–40.

Stephen D. White, 'The politics of anger' in Barbara H. Rosenwein (ed.), *Anger's past. The social uses of an emotion in the early middle ages* (Ithaca, 1998), pp. 127–52.

Paul Hyams, 'Feud and the state in late Anglo-Saxon England' is an important paper which the author very generously allowed me to see in advance of its publication.

2. England

The best introduction to the history of England before 1066 is James Campbell (ed.), *The Anglo-Saxons* (Oxford, 1982), a work which unites beautiful and apposite illustrations to a scintillating text contributed by three leading scholars. For more detail Pauline Stafford's *Unification and conquest. A political and social history of England in the tenth and eleventh centuries* (London, 1989) is warmly recommended. Alfred Smyth, *Scandinavian York and Dublin* (2 volumes: Dublin, 1975, 1979) offers a detailed treatment of Northumbria between 876 and 954. Dorothy Whitelock's *English Historical Documents* volume I – hereafter abbreviated *EHD* I (2nd edition, London, 1979) provides a generous if somewhat conservative selection of original written sources in translation with commentary. David Hill's *Atlas of Anglo-Saxon England* (Oxford, 1981), which is a great deal more than just an atlas, is an invaluable mine of information.

3. Northumbria

A trail-blazing study was Dorothy Whitelock's article 'The Dealings of the Kings of England with Northumbria in the Tenth and Eleventh Centuries' in Peter Clemoes (ed.), *The Anglo-Saxons. Studies in some aspects of their history and culture presented to Bruce Dickins* (London, 1959), pp. 70–88. William E. Kapelle, *The Norman Conquest of the North. The region and its transformation 1000–1135* (London, 1979) is the only recent comprehensive treatment of Northumbrian history in the later Anglo-Saxon and early Norman periods. Two invaluable works on the city of York are Richard Hall, *The excavations at York. The Viking dig* (London, 1984), and David Rollason with Derek Gore and Gillian Fellows-Jensen, *Sources for York history to A.D. 1100* (York, 1998). The best introduction to multiple estates is the study by G. W. S. Barrow, 'Pre-feudal Scotland: shires and thanes' in his volume of collected essays *The kingdom of the Scots* (London, 1973), pp. 7–68, which despite its title is almost as much concerned with northern England as with lowland Scotland. A. A. M. Duncan, *Scotland. The making of the kingdom* (Edinburgh, 1975) is a masterly introduction to its subject, while A. O. Anderson, *Early sources of Scottish history* (2 volumes: Edinburgh, 1922) remains the indispensable collection of written sources in translation with commentary.

4. Ethelred the Ill-advised

Simon Keynes, *The diplomas of King Æthelred 'the Unready' 978–1016. A study in their use as historical evidence* (Cambridge, 1980) is for the most part a tough and technical study of the documents issued in Ethelred II's name, not a book for beginners; but its long final chapter, 'A framework for the reign of King Æthelred', at pp. 154–231 contains the most up-to-the-minute narrative of the reign. It may be supplemented by a collection of specialist papers edited by David Hill, *Ethelred the Unready. Papers from the Millenary Conference* (British Archaeological Reports, British Series, 59: Oxford, 1978). Else Roesdahl, *Viking age Denmark* (London, 1982) and Peter Sawyer, *Kings and Vikings. Scandinavia and Europe AD 700–1100* (London, 1982) are good introductions to the Scandinavian world from which King Ethelred's enemies came. Several outstanding papers by James Campbell investigate the England of *c.* 1000: they are to be found in the two volumes of his collected writings, *Essays in Anglo-Saxon history* (London, 1986) and *The Anglo-Saxon state* (London, 2000). Charles Insley very kindly allowed me to read his paper entitled 'Politics, Conflict and Kinship in early eleventh-century Mercia' in advance of its publication in the journal *Midland History*: it casts much light on the complex web of aristocratic networks and rivalries in the latter part of Ethelred's reign.

5. Millennium

The most comprehensive study of Canute's reign is M. K. Lawson's *Cnut. The Danes in England in the early eleventh century* (London, 1993). Archbishop Wulfstan is now best approached by way of Patrick Wormald's essay 'Archbishop Wulfstan and the holiness of society', most easily accessible in his collected essays *Legal culture in the early medieval West. Law as text, image and experience* (London, 1999) pp. 225–51; and of the passages devoted to Wulfstan in Wormald's *The making of English law. King Alfred to the twelfth century. Volume I, Legislation and its limits* (Oxford, 1999), especially pp. 449–65. On millennial ideas, see most recently Richard Landes, 'The fear of an apocalyptic year 1000: Augustinian Historiography, Medieval and Modern' in *Speculum* 75 (2000), pp. 97–145, with full bibliography. Different theatres of the Peace movement are illuminatingly investigated in the collection of essays edited by Thomas Head and Richard Landes, *The peace of God. Social violence and religious response in France around the year 1000* (Ithaca, 1992). There is a clear introduction to Anglo-Saxon taxation in H. R. Loyn, *The governance of Anglo-Saxon England 500–1087* (London, 1984) at pp. 118–26. The theory of the three orders of society is discussed in a wide context by Alexander Murray, *Reason and society in the Middle Ages* (Oxford, 1978), chapters 2–4.

6. Rise Wood

I should like to acknowledge again my indebtedness to Paul Hyams's paper 'Feud and the state' listed in the Bibliography to chapter 1. On late Anglo-Saxon law in general, Patrick Wormald's *The making of English law. King Alfred to the twelfth century. Volume I, Legislation and its limits* (Oxford, 1999) is the first instalment of what in its entirety will be a very important work, though it makes no concessions to the uninitiated. Susan Reynolds, *Kingdoms and communities in Western Europe 900–1300* (Oxford, 1984) has a good chapter, no. 3, on guilds. Richard Morris, *Churches in the landscape* (London, 1989) is an attractive and wide-ranging introduction to its subject. In chapter 4, 'Pilgrimage and pilgrims', of my book *Saint James's catapult. The life and times of Diego Gelmírez of Santiago de Compostela* (Oxford, 1984) I have attempted a summary of recent thinking about the phenomenon of pilgrimage with special reference to the tenth and eleventh centuries.

7. Ecgfrida's Dowry

On women in late Anglo-Saxon England there is a good introduction in Pauline Stafford's *Unification and conquest* (see Bibliography for chapter 2), chapter 10; and see also her *Queen Emma and Queen Edith* referred to in note 3 to this chapter. For the north in general Kapelle (see Bibliography for chapter 3) remains indispensable. For the church of Durham in particular the early parts of William M. Aird, *St Cuthbert and the Normans. The church of Durham 1071–1153* (Woodbridge, 1998) are useful. On Scotland Duncan (see Bibliography for chapter 3) continues to be an excellent guide and may be supplemented with G. W. S. Barrow, *Kingship and unity: Scotland 1000–1306* (London, 1981).

8. Siward and Tostig

Edward A. Freeman's monumental work *The history of the Norman Conquest of England, its causes and its results* (Oxford, 1867–79) is still of very great value: open to criticism, indeed to mockery, on several grounds, it yet remains a mine of detailed information on English history in the eleventh century; volume II deals with the reign of Edward the Confessor. It is instructive to compare Freeman's approach with that of Edward's most successful modern biographer, Frank Barlow in his *Edward the Confessor* (London, 1970). Works already cited more than once retain their use: Kapelle on the North, Barrow and Duncan on Scotland, Aird on the church of Durham. Robin Fleming, *Kings and lords in conquest England* (Cambridge, 1991) is illuminating (in chapter 3) on the colossal wealth and power of Godwin and his family.

9. Settrington

Freeman's *Norman Conquest*, volumes III and IV, continues to be invaluable. Among modern works, to Kapelle's *Norman Conquest of the North* should now be added Ann Williams, *The English and the Norman Conquest* (Woodbridge, 1995), especially chapters 2 and 3. On the land settlement, Robin Fleming's *Kings and lords* continues useful, and specifically on the Normans in Yorkshire there is a persuasive study by Paul Dalton, *Conquest, anarchy and lordship. Yorkshire 1066–1154* (Cambridge, 1994). Janet Burton, *The monastic order in Yorkshire 1069–1215* (Cambridge, 1999) is a very able treatment of its subject: the curious tale of the foundation of Selby occurs in chapter 1. For the history and topography of York, David Rollason with Derek Gore and Gillian Fellows-Jensen, *Sources for York history to A.D. 1100* (York, 1998) is essential.

10. Haget

Hugh M. Thomas, *Vassals, heiresses, crusaders and thugs. The gentry of Angevin Yorkshire 1154–1216* (Philadelphia, 1993) is a cheerful introduction to its subject. Materials on the Haget family are to be found scattered in the magnificent collection of *Early Yorkshire charters*, volumes I–III edited by William Farrer (Edinburgh, 1914–16), volumes IV–XII edited by Sir Charles Clay for the Yorkshire Archaeological Society, Record Series (Leeds, 1935–65); and in *Charters of the honour of Mowbray*, ed. D. E. Greenway (British Academy: London, 1972). On the Romanesque sculpture at Wighill and other places in the wapentake of Ainsty I received invaluable assistance, many years ago, from Sir George Zarnecki and Dr Kit Galbraith. The narrative of Ralph Haget's conversion to the monastic life occurs in Hugh of Kirkstall's *Narratio de Fundatione Fontanis Monasterii*, edited by J. R. Walbran, *Memorials of the Abbey of St Mary of Fountains* (Surtees Society, vol. 42: Durham, 1863). Janet Burton, *The monastic order in Yorkshire 1069–1215* (Cambridge, 1999) continues indispensable. There is a succinct examination by Paul Dalton of 'The Governmental Integration of the Far North, 1066–1199' in *Government, religion and society in Northern England 1000–1700*, edited by John C. Appleby and Paul Dalton (Stroud, 1997), pp. 14–26. For this later period, no more than glanced at in my closing pages, Sir James Holt's *The Northerners. A study in the reign of King John* (Oxford, 1961) is a classic; and R. R. Davies's *The first English Empire. Power and identities in the British Isles 1093–1343* (Oxford, 2000) deserves to become one.

Notes

1. Wiheal

1. We do not know the precise date of Uhtred's murder. A reliable contemporary reporter (*ASC*/D for 1016) tells us that after the killing Canute appointed his own brother-in-law, the Norwegian Eric of Hlathir, to succeed Uhtred as earl of Northumbria. It is a fair guess that this appointment would have been confirmed publicly at York. The same source informs us that Canute was back in southern England by Easter, which in 1016 fell on 1 April. In the light of these movements and of what we know about rates of travel in the eleventh century, the murder of Uhtred can hardly have occurred later than the middle of March.

2. The anonymous pamphlet is the work known as *De Obsessione Dunelmi* ('The Siege of Durham'), of which the Latin text is to be found in *Symeonis Monachi Opera Omnia*, volume I, ed. T. Arnold (Rolls Series: London, 1882) pp. 215–20. There is an English translation in Christopher J. Morris, *Marriage and murder in eleventh-century Northumbria: a study of the 'De Obsessione Dunelmi'* (Borthwick Paper no. 82: York, 1992) at pp. 1–5.

3. The papal letter alluding to the ghastly events at Medina del Campo survives as an original in the cathedral archive of Salamanca and is printed in *Documentos de los Archivos Catedralicio y Diocesano de Salamanca (siglos XII–XIII)*, ed. José Luis Martín Martín and others (Salamanca, 1977), no. 51, pp. 136–7 (where incorrectly dated: *recte* 29 June 1166).

4. Sukey Christiansen drove me from her home in North Carolina across the state boundary to Galax, Virginia, on a cold and squally day in April 2000 and Eric Christiansen introduced me there to Harmon's Museum of Virginia where I bought a copy of Ronald W. Hall, *The Carroll County courthouse Tragedy* (Carroll County Historical Society: Hillsville, Virginia, 1998): a remarkable account of an extraordinary story.

5. J. M. Wallace-Hadrill, 'The Bloodfeud of the Franks' in his collection of

essays *The Long-haired kings and other studies in Frankish history* (London, 1962) at p. 143.

6. Otto Brunner, *Land and lordship. Structures of governance in medieval Austria* (English translation, Philadelphia, 1992), pp. 23–4.

7. Jacob Black-Michaud, *Cohesive force. Feud in the Mediterranean and the Middle East* (Oxford, 1975), p. 17.

8. Patrick Wormald, *The Making of English law. King Alfred to the twelfth century. Volume I, Legislation and its limits* (Oxford, 1999), p. 39.

9. Marc Bloch, *Feudal society* (English translation, London, 1961), p. 102.

3. Northumbria

1. M. K. Lawson, *Cnut. The Danes in England in the early eleventh century* (London, 1993), p. 22.

2. *EHD* I, p. 257.

3. For a reconstruction of what Bamburgh might have looked like at this era see the sketch in R. H. Hodgkin, *A history of the Anglo-Saxons*, volume I (Oxford, 1935), figure 34 at p. 198.

4. *ASC*/C for 975, in *EHD* I, p. 209.

5. William E. Kapelle, *The Norman Conquest of the North. The region and its transformation 1000–1135* (London, 1979), p. 19, and see also pp. 20 and 24 and the implicit contradiction on p. 245 (note 9). See too the similar objections of Bennett, 'Violence in eleventh-century Normandy' in Halsall (ed.), *Violence and society* (see Bibliography for chapter 1), 'expressions of politics and warfare, not feud' (p. 136). Judgements such as these rest in the last resort on questions of definition, perhaps in this case employing unrealistically strict criteria. The debate gives signs of becoming sterile.

6. Kapelle, *Norman Conquest of the North*, p. 90.

4. Ethelred the Ill-advised

1. S 877, translated in *EHD* I, no. 120, pp. 531–4. This and comparable cases have been illuminatingly discussed by Patrick Wormald, 'Giving God and King their due: conflict and its regulation in the early English state' in his volume of collected essays *Legal culture in the early medieval West. Law as text, image and experience* (London, 1999), pp. 332–54.

2. F. M. Stenton, *Anglo-Saxon England* (3rd ed., Oxford, 1971), p. 379.

3. See the documents catalogued in S 716, 1453, 1660: for the 'enigmatical'

see D. M. Stenton (ed.), *Preparatory to Anglo-Saxon England, being the collected papers of Frank Merry Stenton* (Oxford, 1970), p. 218.

4. E. A. Freeman, *The history of the Norman Conquest of England, its causes and its results*, volume I (2nd ed., Oxford, 1870), Appendix, Note SS, p. 673.

5. Pauline Stafford, *Unification and conquest* (London, 1989), pp. 57–8.

6. A. O. Anderson, *Early sources of Scottish history* (Edinburgh, 1922), volume I, p. 512.

7. Symeon of Durham, *Libellus de Exordio atque Procursu istius hoc est Dunhelmensis Ecclesie*, ed. and trans. D. W. Rollason (Oxford Medieval Texts: Oxford, 2000), pp. 148–9.

8. Anderson, *Early sources of Scottish history*, I, p. 525.

9. Simon Keynes, *The diplomas of King Æthelred 'the Unready'* (Cambridge, 1980), p. 211.

10. E. W. Robertson, *Historical essays* (Edinburgh, 1872), p. 172.

11. C. R. Hart, *The early charters of Northern England and the North Midlands* (Leicester, 1975), no. 130, pp. 126–7.

5. Millennium

1. A generous selection from Wulfstan's writings is translated in *EHD* I: the passage quoted here occurs on p. 855.

2. *EHD* I, pp. 409–11.

3. See Gertrud Schiller, *The iconography of Christian art* (English translation, London, 1972), volume II, pp. 117–21.

4. *EHD* I, pp. 405–9. Ken Lawson (*Cnut*, p. 59) was the first to spot the significance of the place-name Enham in this context.

5. *The chronicle of John of Worcester*, ed. and trans. R. R. Darlington, J. Bray and P. McGurk (Oxford Medieval Texts: Oxford, 1995–) for 1041.

6. Lawson, *Cnut*, p. 173.

7. *EHD* I, p. 424.

8. Ibid., pp. 416–18.

9. J. Campbell, 'Norwich' in M. D. Lobel (ed.), *The atlas of historic towns*, volume II (London, 1975), p. 1.

6. Rise Wood

1. The date of the battle of Carham is disputed, some historians preferring the date 1016. For the comet of 1018 see Symeon of Durham, *Libellus de Exordio atque Procursu istius hoc est Dunhelmensis Ecclesie*, ed. and trans. David Rollason (Oxford, 2000), iii.5, p. 154.

2. For Edmund's election see Symeon, *Libellus*, iii.6, pp. 156–60. There are some chronological problems which I here pass over.

3. J. M. Kemble, *The Saxons in England* (London, 1849), volume I, p. 268.

4. *EHD* I, p. 795.

5. Ibid., nos. 33 and 38.

6. K. J. Leyser, *Rule and conflict in an early medieval society: Ottonian Saxony* (London, 1979), p. 33.

7. *Historia Silense*, chapter 86, translated in Simon Barton and Richard Fletcher, *The world of El Cid. Chronicles of the Spanish reconquest* (Manchester, 2000), p. 48.

8. *EHD* I, no. 136.

9. Ibid., no. 117. One may suspect that there was more to the background of this dispute than we are told.

10. Ibid., nos. 130 and 150.

7. Ecgfrida's Dowry

1. Black-Michaud, *Cohesive force* (see chapter 1, note 7), p. 78.

2. M. E. Durham, *High Albania* (London, 1909), p. 164.

3. These two women have been the subject of a recent and very able study by Pauline Stafford, *Queen Emma and Queen Edith. Queenship and women's power in eleventh-century England* (Oxford, 1997), a model of disciplined and sensitive scholarship.

4. *EHD* I, no. 51.

5. II Canute *c*. 74, in *EHD* I, p. 429.

6. *EHD* I, no. 128.

7. Ibid., no. 53. On its authorship see Wormald, *Making of English law* (see Bibliography for chapter 6), pp. 396–7. For the 'tactical' use of consanguinity to secure a divorce see Peter Biller, *The measure of multitude. Population in medieval thought* (Oxford, 2000), p. 31.

8. Arnold, in *Symeonis Opera* (see chapter 1, note 2) I, p. 215, note a.

9. Sir Frank Stenton, *Anglo-Saxon England* (3rd ed., Oxford, 1971), p. 417.

For nickname and legends see respectively *Vita Ædwardi Regis*, ed. and trans. Frank Barlow (Nelson's Medieval Texts: Edinburgh, 1962), p. 21 and Saxo Grammaticus, *Danorum Regum Heroumque Historia*, trans. Eric Christiansen, volume I (British Archaeological Reports, International Series vol. 84: Oxford, 1980), p. 190.

10. Rodulfus Glaber, *Historiarum Libri Quinque*, ed. and trans. John France (Oxford Medieval Texts: Oxford, 1989), II.ii.3, pp. 54–7; Lawson, *Cnut* (see chapter 3, note 1), p. 104.

11. *EHD* I, pp. 231, 311.

12. *Symeonis Opera* (see chapter 1, note 2) II, p. 198.

13. Symeon, *Libellus de Exordio*, ed. Rollason (see chapter 6, note 1), iii.9, p. 168.

14. On Moray a good introduction is provided by D. P. Kirby, 'Moray prior to *c.* 1100', being Text 13, pp. 20–21, in Peter McNeill and Ranald Nicholson (eds.), *An historical atlas of Scotland* (St Andrews, 1975).

15. Symeon, *Libellus de Exordio*, ed. Rollason, iii.9, p. 170. Janet Cooper has attempted to sort out 'The Dates of the Bishops of Durham in the first half of the eleventh century', *Durham University Journal* 60 (1968), pp. 131–7.

16. *Symeonis Opera* II, p. 198.

17. James Campbell, *The Anglo-Saxon state* (London, 2000), p. 95.

8. Siward and Tostig

1. *The chronicle of John of Worcester*, ed. and trans. R. R. Darlington, J. Bray and P. McGurk (Oxford Medieval Texts: Oxford, 1995–) for 1042, pp. 532–5.

2. Gospatric's writ is edited, translated and discussed at length in F. E. Harmer, *Anglo-Saxon writs* (Manchester, 1952), pp. 419–24, 531–6.

3. Hugh the Chanter, *The history of the church of York 1066–1127*, ed. and trans. Charles Johnson, revised by M. Brett, C. N. L. Brooke and M. Winterbottom (Oxford Medieval Texts: Oxford, 1990), pp. 52–3.

4. A. O. Anderson, *Early sources of Scottish history* (Edinburgh, 1922) I, p. 588.

5. *Vita Ædwardi Regis*, ed. and trans. Frank Barlow (Nelson's Medieval Texts: Edinburgh, 1962), pp. 31–2.

6. Ibid., p. 43.

7. Kapelle, *Norman Conquest of the North*, pp. 91–3, convincingly sorts out the chronological problems.

8. Symeon, *Libellus de Exordio*, ed. Rollason (see chapter 6, note 1), iii. 11, p. 174.

9. *Capitula de Miraculis et Translationibus Sancti Cuthberti* in *Symeonis Opera*, ed. Arnold (see chapter 1, note 2) I, pp. 243–5.

10. By Frank Barlow, in his edition of the *Vita Ædwardi*, p. 34, note 4.

11. Ibid., p. 50, note 4.

12. *Chronicle of John of Worcester* (see note 1 above) for 1065, p. 598.

13. *The making of English law*, I, p. 133.

9. Settrington

1. William of Poitiers, *Gesta Guillelmi*, ed. and trans. R. H. C. Davis and M. Chibnall (Oxford Medieval Texts: Oxford, 1998), p. 68.

2. Pauline Stafford, *Unification and conquest* (London, 1989), p. 97.

3. *The ecclesiastical history of Orderic Vitalis*, ed. and trans. M. Chibnall (Oxford Medieval Texts: Oxford, 1969–80), volume II, pp. 216–18. Although Orderic was writing much later (*c.* 1120), there is general agreement that in his account of the years 1068–70 he was drawing upon (now lost sections of) the *Gesta Guillelmi* of William of Poitiers composed in 1073–4.

4. But see the cautions of Ann Williams, *The English and the Norman Conquest* (Woodbridge, 1995), p. 29, note 34.

5. *Regesta Regum Anglo-Normannorum. The Acta of William I (1066–1087)*, ed. David Bates (Oxford, 1998), no. 32.

6. *Domesday Book* (henceforward *DB*) volume I, folios 373a1, 374a2. I have worked from *The Yorkshire Domesday*, editor-in-chief Ann Williams, county editors D. M. Palliser and F. R. Thorn (Alecto Historical Editions: London, 1987–92), three superlative volumes of facsimile, translation and studies. Mention should also be made of the pioneering translation by R. H. Scaife, originally published in the *Yorkshire Archaeological Journal*, then in book form as *Domesday Book for Yorkshire* (London, 1896), which is still of value in the identification of place-names.

7. Ibid., 321a2, 326a2, 374a1.

8. Ibid., 374a1, 374a2.

9. *Norman Conquest*, IV, pp. 307–8.

10. *DB* I, 332b1.

11. Bates, *Acta of William I*, no. 162.

12. Henry of Huntingdon, *Historia Anglorum*, ed. Diana Greenway (Oxford Medieval Texts: Oxford, 1996), p. 380.

13. Bates, *Acta of William I*, nos. 159, 181, 286.

14. On the landscape of the Wolds see Joan Thirsk (ed.), *The English rural landscape* (Oxford, 2000), chapter 2.

10. Haget

1. David Knowles, *The monastic order in England 940–1216* (2nd ed., Cambridge, 1966), p. 358.
2. See Robert Bartlett's fine book *The making of Europe. Conquest, colonization and cultural change 950–1350* (London, 1993), especially chapter 11.

Index

The following abbreviations are used in the index:
Abp – Archbishop; Abpric – Archbishopric; Bp – Bishop; Bpric – Bishopric;
d – daughter; E – Ealdorman *or* Earl; K – King; Q – Queen; R – River; s – son;
St – Saint